The French Who Fought for Hitler

Thousands of Frenchmen volunteered to provide military help to the Nazis during World War II, fighting in such places as Belorussia, Galicia, Pomerania, and Berlin. Utilizing these soldiers' memoirs, *The French Who Fought for Hitler* examines how these volunteers describe their exploits on the battlefield, their relations to civilian populations in occupied territories, and their sexual prowess. It also discusses how the volunteers account for their controversial decisions to enlist, to fight to the end, and finally to testify. Coining the concepts of "outcast memory" and "unlikeable vanquished," Philippe Carrard characterizes the type of bitter, unrepentant memory at work in the volunteers' recollections and situates it on the map of France's collective memory. In the process, he contributes to the ongoing conversation about memory, asking whether all testimonies are fit to be given and preserved, and how we should deal with life narratives that uphold positions now viewed as unacceptable.

Educated in Switzerland, Philippe Carrard has taught at the University of Pennsylvania, the University of California at Santa Barbara, the University of California at Irvine, and the University of Vermont, and is currently a Visiting Scholar in the Comparative Literature Program at Dartmouth College. Over the past twenty years, his research has mainly concerned factual discourse – the discourse that claims to represent actual events and situations. In this area, he has published *Poetics of the New History: French Historical Discourse from Braudel to Chartier* (1992), as well as numerous articles and book chapters that analyze conventions of writing in nonfiction.

The French Who Fought for Hitler

Memories from the Outcasts

PHILIPPE CARRARD

CAMBRIDGE
UNIVERSITY PRESS

CAMBRIDGE UNIVERSITY PRESS
Cambridge, New York, Melbourne, Madrid, Cape Town, Singapore,
São Paulo, Delhi, Dubai, Tokyo, Mexico City

Cambridge University Press
32 Avenue of the Americas, New York, NY 10013-2473, USA

www.cambridge.org
Information on this title: www.cambridge.org/9780521198226

First published 2010

Printed in the United States of America

A catalog record for this publication is available from the British Library.

Library of Congress Cataloging in Publication data
Carrard, Philippe.
The French who fought for Hitler : memories from the outcasts / Philippe Carrard.
p. cm.
Includes bibliographical references and index.
ISBN 978-0-521-19822-6 (hardback)
1. Légion des volontaires français contre le bolchevisme – Biography.   2. Waffen-SS.
Französische SS-Freiwilligen-Sturmbrigade – Biography.   3. Waffen-SS. Waffen-
Grenadier-Division "Charlemagne," 33 – Biography.   4. World War, 1939–1945 –
Personal narratives, French.   5. World War, 1939–1945 – Participation,
French.   6. Soldiers – France – Biography.   7. Soldiers – Germany –
Biography.   8. Outcasts – France – Biography.   9. Collective memory –
France.   10. World War, 1939–1945 – Regimental histories – Germany.   I. Title.
D757.32.C36 2010
940.54′0944–dc22   2010024616

ISBN 978-0-521-19822-6 Hardback

FOR IRENE

Contents

Acknowledgments

First of all, I must thank Dartmouth College and the University of Lausanne (Switzerland), whose libraries were prime resources for my research. At Dartmouth, I am particularly thankful to the Comparative Literature Program, which provided me with a home; to librarian Miguel Vallarades, who guided me through the maze of information available on the Internet; and to the Humanities Resource Center staff members Susan Bibeau and Thomas Garbelotti, who facilitated my endeavor by solving several computer problems.

On this side of the Atlantic, I am grateful to Mary Jean Green, Lynn Higgins, and Thomas Trezise, for rewarding conversations about the period of the Occupation in France; to Konrad Kenkel, for sharing his knowledge of World War II and its aftermath in Germany; to Atina Grossmann, for communicating valuable information about the condition of women in Germany toward the end of World War II; to Marion Kaplan, for offering generous feedback on a paper I had given on the subject of the volunteers' memoirs; to Ronald Smelser and Edward Davies, for answering my questions about the popularity of some World War II literature in the United States; and to Dominick LaCapra, for encouraging a project that first appeared difficult to carry out.

Overseas, I want to express my appreciation to Siegfried Heimann, who taught me a lot about Berlin and its history; to Peter Schöttler, who passed on several unpublished documents about Hitler's plans for Europe and the role of the French volunteers in the defense of Berlin; to Eric Lefèvre, who liberally shared his historian's expertise on the subject of the French volunteers; to my Swiss friends Jean-Pierre Allamand, Alain Campiotti, Marc Comina, Valérie Cossy, Catherine Dubuis, Mondher

Kilani, Myriam Meuwly, Bertrand Müller, Jacques Pilet, Agnès Rochat, Marianne Schoch-Kilani, Jean-Jacques Tschumi, Monique Tschumi, and the late Jean-Luc Seylaz, who never failed to inquire about the state of my writing activities and put up with my not-so-flexible schedules; and last but not least, to my family, who did not question the choice of a topic they could only find worrisome, and especially to my mother, Mireille Carrard, who insisted on reading some of the strange books she had seen on my desk.

Cambridge University Press has nurtured the project from the start. I am particularly indebted to the three anonymous readers for their useful suggestions and comments, and to my editors, Eric Crahan and Jason Przybylski, for their accessibility and the quality of their professional advice.

This book could not have been written without the complicity and support of my first and demanding reader, Irene Kacandes. Many passages in my text bear the trace of her familiarity with the subject of memory, and most pages, the imprint of her editorial assistance. The book is thus dedicated to her.

Brief portions of the text were published in *French Historical Studies* 31:3 (2008). I thank Duke University Press for permission to reprint.

A Note about Documentation and Translations

The system of documentation I am using is Parenthetical Documentation by Date of Publication and List of Works Cited. When an author is represented on that List by a single book, the documentation provided in parenthesis does not include the date of publication, only the page number(s). Most of the memoirs in my corpus and several of the scholarly studies to which I refer are in French and have not been translated into English. I have included, in brackets, a translation with the first mention of every title, when it did not involve obvious English cognates. When English translations exist, I have supplied in parenthesis the information "published in English as…." I am using the same conventions when I cite the titles of German memoirs and scholarly studies. All translations of excerpts from the memoirs in my corpus, as well as from French and German scholarly studies, are mine, unless otherwise indicated.

Introduction

One of the most striking moments in Marcel Ophuls's celebrated documentary *Le Chagrin et la pitié* [*The Sorrow and the Pity*] (1971) is certainly André Harris's interview with Christian de La Mazière, the former French SS volunteer. Filmed at the castle of Sigmaringen, in remembrance of a "pitiful expedition" he had undertaken there in the hope of meeting Marshall Pétain (La Mazière 2003, 203), La Mazière recounts how he enlisted in the SS in the summer of 1944, then went on to fight the Russians in Pomerania in February–March 1945. This interview, as Henry Rousso (1987a, 119) points out in his analysis of Ophuls's movie, brought to light an aspect of the Occupation that had been "unrecognized and forgotten": Thousands of Frenchmen had volunteered to fight on the German side during World War II. Moreover, according to Rousso, these men had not acted out of "venality" or "moral or intellectual turpitude," as some stereotype of the collaborationist has it; they had become involved out of "political and ideological conviction" – to defend on the battlefield the cause that for them was the correct one.

While La Mazière's appearance in *Le Chagrin et la pitié* reminded viewers of the military side of the collaboration, it also signaled the existence of a specific type of memory: Several of the French who had fought with the Nazis were ready to testify, more precisely, to tell why they had enlisted, what they had experienced during the war, and how they had (or had not) adjusted after the end of the conflict. In fact, La Mazière's testimony was not the first one to be offered. A few among the former volunteers had already published memoirs, some as early as 1948. But the texts they had written had largely gone unnoticed, a fate shared by many other testimonies about the war brought out at a time when the French – to use the names

I

of the initial stages in what Rousso (1987a) calls the "Vichy syndrome" – first seemed unable to complete their "work of mourning," and then "repressed" most critical subjects related to the period of the Occupation. According to the statistics that Annette Wieviorka supplies in her study of the genocide, French deportees had produced over 100 books and pamphlets about the camps between 1944 and 1947; but these reports had been ignored at the time, as most people in France were anxious to resume life as usual after four years of hardship, and historians presumed that the deportees did not want to speak about an ordeal that was "unspeakable" to begin with (Wieviorka 1992, 163). The "repression" that Rousso describes was not specific to one country, however. As several scholars (e.g., Zelizer 1998, 166) have noticed, works about the dark aspects of World War II that later became bestsellers, such as Elie Wiesel's *Night*, Anne Frank's *Diary*, and Primo Levi's *Survival in Auschwitz*, were first turned down by publishers in the United States, Holland, and Italy; audiences, it was assumed, were not ready for this kind of woeful material.

Professional historians have investigated the military sides of the collaboration, and I occasionally draw on their works to provide a context for the narratives that the volunteers are reciting. My objective, however, is not to add to this type of research by producing a new, more accurate account of the events in which the volunteers were involved in such places as Belorussia, Galicia, Pomerania, and Berlin. It is to investigate the texts that those volunteers have written and, in so doing, to investigate a particular type of memory. Indeed, among the many studies that explore the subject "memory of Vichy," few take up the topic "memory of France's military collaboration with the Germans." In fact, the only significant references to the volunteers' testimonies I found are included in *Les Echos de la mémoire: Tabous et enseignements de la Seconde Guerre Mondiale* [Echoes of Memory: Taboos and Lessons of World War II] (1991), the proceeding of a colloquium edited by Georges Kantin and Gilles Manceron. In their contributions to this volume, Pascal Ory, Marie-José Chombart de Lauwe, and Christophe Champclaux consider issues raised by memoirs written by collaborationists, including those by some of the former volunteers. They ask, among other things, whether those memoirs are dangerous because they offer a certain fascination for the evil, celebrate war as the site of heroic adventures, and present a complacent view of the Nazi military units that the French volunteers had elected to join. I will, of course, return later to these controversial issues, as they pertain to discursive and ethical matters that are central to the texts I am considering.

Several reasons account for the lack of research on the memory of France's military collaboration. The main one arguably pertains to focus of interest. Since the renewed concern for the Vichy period in the 1970s, work on memory has generally centered on the "good," "worthwhile" testimonies of camp survivors (e.g., Wieviorka 1998, Coquio 1999) and to a lesser extent on those of members of the Resistance (e.g., Guillou and Laborie 1995, Boursier 1997). The reminiscences of other categories of war participants, however, have not been granted the same attention. While scholars (e.g., Durand 1994, Harbulot 2003, Vittori 2007) have investigated the ordeal of the French prisoners of war and of the men forced to go work in Germany on the program Service du Travail Obligatoire (STO), they have hardly concerned themselves with studying the way members of these ill-fated groups remember the war in their testimonies. There still seems to be some discomfort about what POWs and draftees of the STO have to say, possibly because they do not qualify as victims as obviously as do the political and the racial deportees. As Richard Vinen puts it in the chapters of *The Unfree French* (2007) he devotes to these groups, POWs are felt to be "inadequate in some way," especially if they did not manage to "escape or be rapatriated" before 1945 (212); and forced laborers of the STO, "blamed for going," are also upon their return "encouraged to keep quiet" about their experience because it no longer fits into "France's vision of herself" (278). That discomfort, of course, is compounded in the instance of the volunteers: It is difficult to summon much sympathy for people who chose to fight for the Nazis, and whose cause, to begin with, never really agreed with France's "vision of herself." Likewise, it is legitimate to ask whether devoting a whole book to the memory of the military collaboration is wise, as it may, indirectly at least, imply the rehabilitation of individuals and standpoints that were rightly denounced after the war.

My assumption is that no subject should be taboo for scholarly research, and that examining the writings left by a certain group does not mean endorsing the values represented by that group. In this instance, studying the texts that the former volunteers have produced involves neither sanctioning National Socialism, nor issuing a blanket condemnation to the individuals who, for reasons I review later, elected to fight with the Germans on the Eastern Front. I aim to assume the position that the sociologists Michel Pinçon and Monique Pinçon-Charlot describe in their self-reflexive comments about the work they have conducted on social classes (e.g., the French haute-bourgeoisie), places (e.g., castles), and activities (e.g., hunting) with which they clearly have few affinities.

Specifically, adopting the "empathy" that Pinçon and Pinçon-Charlot (71) deem to be necessary for the understanding of a group, whatever one might think of its members' behavior, I abstain from making judgments on the choices and the actions of my memoirists. Indeed, the latter have already been sentenced in several ways: They were defeated on the battlefield, where they became part of the German collapse; in the courts, where they were found guilty of treason; and in the judgment of History, where they are now linked with a side that is regarded as criminal. Adding my own condemnation would thus be pointless and smack of self-righteousness; as Tzvetan Todorov has submitted in his essay on the abuses of memory, "to give lessons of morality has never been evidence of virtue" (43). The methodological empathy that I model after the sociologists', however, is not without limits. I do not shy away from taking up the political and ethical issues that the volunteers' memoirs are raising, for instance, when the authors describe the way they treated civilian populations in Belorussia, claim that they were unaware of the existence of extermination camps, and express no regret about their involvement during the war.

My corpus is restricted to published works. Unlike the body of texts used by Paul Fussell in *The Great War and Modern Memory*, it does not include material that is only available in the archives of war museums and specialized libraries. It consists of thirty memoirs, twenty-four of which were written by French volunteers. For the sake of comparing experiences and attitudes, and because their authors are French-speaking, I have admitted six additional testimonies provided by volunteers coming from Alsace, Belgium, and Switzerland. This list makes no claim at exhaustiveness. Not counting the memoirs that have remained in the manuscript stage, more texts may be out there, brought out at the author's expense or by small, quickly vanished presses. Scholars, in this area, like in many others, would be imprudent to submit that they have read "everything," as long out of print, nowhere to be found texts can at some point turn up on internet sites like Abebooks or be reissued by publishing houses that specialize in "alternative" materials about World War II, such as Arctic, Dualpha, L'Homme Libre, and Lore. Thus, I had completed a first draft of this study when Lore brought out (in 2008) Bayle's *De Marseille à Novossibirsk*, a book that the author had first self-published in 1994, and that I had been able to obtain only in its German translation. Those same publishing houses have also unveiled new texts (no less than six in 2007 and 2008 alone), though without always explicating when those texts had been written or how they had found their way to the desk of a publisher at this point in time. According to the head of one of these firms, who spoke under the condition of anonymity, the sudden arrival of so many volunteers' memoirs is due to the fact that their authors have recently died; the veterans had written their reminiscences and were eager to see them in print, but they did not want to cause any trouble in their old age and had left to their families the responsibility for contacting publishers after their death.

The fact that we know when the veterans' memoirs were published but, in most cases, not when they were written is certainly a liability with respect to their status as historical documents. It makes it difficult to determine what prompted an author to come out of his silence when he did, obliging us to take at face value the explanations that he himself is supplying. More importantly, it keeps us from placing the memoir in a precise context, that is, from ascertaining which contemporary groups, political or other, its author might have been addressing or seeking approval from. The more general historical framework in which the volunteers' recollections can be situated is of course the Cold War. From the early 1950s on, as Ronald Smelser and Edward Davies argue in their study of the "myth" of the Eastern Front, it became acceptable to conceive of the Wehrmacht's operations in the USSR as "a prelude to our own struggle against Soviet Communism" (3). Though made about the United States, Smelser and Davies's diagnosis is certainly valid for France. In fact, part of French public opinion had probably turned earlier against the USSR, as the imposition of communist regimes upon several countries in Central Europe, as well as the presence in France of a strong, then Stalinist Communist party, made people both wary of the USSR and liable to buy into "alternative" views of the Second World War.

While the texts in my corpus pose problems of dating, they also raise issues of representativeness similar – though not identical – to those identified by Raul Hilberg (2001, 48) in his discussion of the testimonies of Holocaust survivors. Submitted to the standards of the social sciences, the surviving volunteers as a whole do not form in Hilberg's terminology a "random sample" of the volunteer community. That is, those who testified do not form a "random sample" of the surviving volunteers, and their testimonies do not form a "random sample" of their experiences. True, such considerations of method do not invalidate the volunteers' memoirs, as they do not invalidate the testimonies of Holocaust survivors and of their families. But they must be taken into account, as one might ask under what conditions individuals can represent the group to which they belong; in this instance, to what extent about thirty memoirists can be viewed as speaking "for" the thousands of French, Belgian, and Swiss men who elected to bear arms for the Germans during World War II. I take up these issues in Chapter 6, though obviously not from the statistical perspective that Hilberg had in mind. Doing a close reading of the works under consideration, I assess their authors' claim to "represent" their comrades, in the different meanings that much-glossed verb may have in a particular type of discourse, namely, the memoir.

As a genre, the memoir belongs to the more comprehensive category that Sidonie Smith and Julia Watson (2001) call "life narratives": A category that includes autobiographies, letters, and diaries – texts in which individuals recount what they themselves have experienced at a certain time and place. While autobiography has been the subject of numerous studies, the memoir has attracted less attention. The theorists who have sought to differentiate between these two types of life narrative have generally done so in terms of subject matter. Martin Löschnigg, for example, writes in his entry "Autobiography" in the *Routledge Encyclopedia of Narrative* that autobiographies emphasize "inner life," whereas memoirs foreground "the author's public role among well-known contemporaries" (35). Similarly, the *Merriam Webster's Encyclopedia of Literature* states that while writers of autobiographies are concerned "primarily with themselves," memoirists are usually "persons who have played roles in, or have been close observers of, historical events, and whose purpose is to describe or interpret those events" (749). Löschnigg's and *Merriam Webster's* definitions certainly apply to the classical model of the memoir, such as Saint-Simon's *Mémoires* and Chateaubriand's *Mémoires d'outre-tombe* [Memoirs from Beyond the Grave]), as well as to modern texts written by politicians and high-ranking soldiers, such as Winston Churchill's *The Second World War* and Charles de Gaulle's *Mémoires de guerre* [published in English as *War Memoirs*]. In current usage, though, "memoir" often refers to the recollections of ordinary people, people who, in some cases, lived through historical events but played no "public roles among well-known contemporaries." Furthermore, the term today seems to imply a restriction in time rather than a choice of subject matter. "Autobiography" suggests temporal comprehensiveness: The author recounts her/his life from childhood up to the moment of writing. "Memoir," on the other hand, refers to a limited time span. As Marcus Billson submits in his essay on the genre, the author "relates a segment of his own life that was important to his identity as a social being," such as "an exile, an imprisonment, the course of a career, participation in war, in politics, in an artistic coterie" (267). As far as number is concerned, the singular "memoir" is used in current practice to denote a genre, and the plural "memoirs," a certain type of contents synonymous with "memories" or "recollections." In this respect, Anglo-American usage differs from French usage; in French, the plural "mémoires" means both "a memoir" and "recollections," whereas the singular "mémoire" signifies "memory" (in the sense of "capacity for remembering") if the gender is feminine, "report" or "study" if it is masculine.

The texts in my corpus certainly fit this present-day Anglo-American sense of "memoir," even though they may be labeled "mémoires" in French. Most of them were written by low-ranking soldiers, soldiers who were involved in "historical events" but did not lead what Jean-Louis Jeannelle (10) calls the "vies majuscules [lives writ large]" of such people as Churchill and de Gaulle. The volunteers, moreover, devote little space, if any, to their activities before and after the war; they usually center on the war itself, that is, on the period in their lives that they regard as tellable – as worthy of being recounted and preserved. In this respect, their memoirs are structurally similar to numerous life narratives produced in the late twentieth and early twenty-first centuries, beginning with texts written by camp survivors, which, for that matter, often have "memoir" in their subtitle: Vivette Samuel, *Rescuing the Children: A Holocaust Memoir*; Alexander Donat, *The Holocaust Kingdom: A Memoir*; Jana Renée Friesova, *Fortress of My Youth: Memoir of a Terezin Survivor*, and the like. To be sure, the deportees did not leave their homes of their free will, and the experiences that they report are radically different from those of the veterans in my corpus. Still, like the volunteers', most of their memoirs have authors who are little-known, ordinary people; and like the volunteers', they recount not a whole life, but the particular moment – however painful – that made that life extraordinary and therefore worth being told and remembered. I will return at times to this parallel between the volunteers' and the deportees' memoirs, as the latter have come to serve as a paradigm for memoirs in general and traumatic war memoirs in particular.

My approach to the volunteers' reminiscences is both thematic and textual. When I take up, say, the topic "combat on the Eastern Front," I do not just ask where the volunteers fought and what they did or did not accomplish; I also consider the rhetorical strategies and conventions of representation on which they draw, examining, among other things, the point of view from which they describe the fighting, the terms that they employ to designate the enemy, and the reference systems on which they rely to account for their experiences. Such an approach may seem inappropriate in the case of historical testimonies, where "content" usually receives priority. However, as Carole Dornier and Renaud Dulong (2005) have argued in their introduction to a series of essays devoted to the testimony as genre, "memory" does not spontaneously metamorphose into "a memoir." It must at some point undergo a process of textualization, and I intend to investigate that process when I examine the volunteers' accounts of their experiences.

My purpose is thus twofold, as it fits an interdisciplinary endeavor that partakes both of historiography and of a literary reading of texts that do not belong to "literature," at least not if defined as "works of imagination." By exploring a set of reminiscences that, for understandable reasons, have been largely suppressed, I want to contribute to the knowledge of the memory of World War II in France. By probing the ways in which those reminiscences are inscribed in memoirs, however, I also want to add to the poetics of that genre – to the study of the rules, codes, and conventions that shape the textualization of personal experiences. The attention I lend to procedures of writing, however, is not imperialistic. In contrast to Hayden White (1987) and others, I do not believe that all texts eventually have the same status, and that the distinction that Dorrit Cohn (1999) establishes between "fictional" and "referential" discourses should therefore be collapsed. For one thing, my memoirists claim to make true statements about the past, and that claim, although it should not remain unexamined, must be taken seriously. Indeed, it has important textual implications: it shapes several aspects of the writing, aspects whose function is to tell readers, or to confirm for them, that the book they hold in their hands describes events that the author actually lived through.

The questions I ask of the memoirs in my corpus unfold in seven stages. Chapter 1 provides the kind of background information that is necessary for the understanding of the veterans' recollections. I describe the organizations that the volunteers could join and then review the studies that historians have devoted to France's military collaboration. Chapter 2 takes up an issue that is crucial for the memoir as genre: authenticity. I examine the strategies that the memoirists employ to establish that they were "really there," and then describe the debates that have been taking place about some of the books they have written, for example, about Guy Sajer's *Le Soldat oublié*. I also consider problems of authorship, as some of the texts in my corpus were avowedly written with the collaboration of ghostwriters, whereas others probably received an assistance that remained unacknowledged. Chapter 3 raises the related but distinct question of veracity: If the memoirists were "really there," are they reliable? I look at a test case – diverging testimonies about the battle of Berlin – and then discuss passages in which the volunteers seem to over- or underreport the events in which they were involved, such as the atrocities that they witnessed on the Eastern Front. Passages of this type, I argue, pose an important question about the memoir as a genre, namely how the veracity of a testimony can be assessed when the version of an event that it offers can be confronted neither with other versions nor with documentary evidence. Chapter 4 explores some specifics of the volunteers' writing related to modes of remembering and types of focalization. The veterans display total recall, which means that they account in detail for events in which they participated several years or even decades earlier. They also report those events "from below," that is, from the limited perspective of the foot soldier often stuck in mud and snow. I show how this way of describing the fighting illustrates what Omer Bartov calls the "demodernization" of warfare on the Eastern Front, and Jonathan Littell, the demise of the ideal of the "hard," "vertical" fascist soldier. Chapter 5 investigates the ideological facets of the volunteers' testimonies. Buying unconditionally into Nazi propaganda, the veterans demonize the Soviets and disparage the western Allies for such "war crimes" as the bombing of the German cities. But they also describe their experiences at the front by drawing on French poetry, British drama, and American film, that is, by turning to a reference system that almost entirely ignores Germany's contribution to literature and the arts. I discuss that contradiction, submitting that it exposes the volunteers' ambivalence toward Germany – their endorsement of German political and military goals, as well as their parallel indifference to things German in the cultural domain. Chapter 6 examines how the volunteers justify themselves – how they account for decisions that will certainly trouble today's readers. Specifically, I ask how the veterans explain why they enlisted on the side that is now universally viewed as the "wrong" side; how they vindicate their resolution to fight to the end, when the war was obviously lost; and why they elected to testify afterward, at the risk of losing their jobs and alienating their friends when their tainted past would resurface. Chapter 7 examines how the veterans describe their postwar status, that is, how they portray themselves as people who did not commit any offense and were unfairly sentenced in their own countries, both by the justice system and in public opinion. I ask whether this self-assessment is warranted and show how the volunteers themselves have contributed to their exclusion. Pointing out that the veterans' unbending attitudes raise ethical issues, I ask in my Conclusion whether we should regard their testimonies as danger-ous. I present the arguments of critics who hold texts of this type to be harmful, because their authors are blind to the truth, cannot accept con-tradiction, and reject any kind of guilt. Looking at the memory boom of the past twenty years, however, I also surmise that the volunteers' reminiscences enable us to pose several fundamental questions about life writing, specifically to ask whether all testimonies are fit to be preserved, and how we should treat the ones that uphold positions now regarded as unacceptable.

The scholarly apparatus on which I draw to conduct my analyses is most diverse. It includes works on World War II, especially on the Eastern Front (e.g., Bartov 1986 and 1991, Grenkevich 1999, Slepyan 2006, Müller and Ueberschär 2009); on the contribution of foreign volunteers to the German war effort (e.g., Gordon 1980, Conway 1993, Estes 2003, Giolitto 1999, Müller 2007); on the representation of World War II in literary and nonliterary texts (e.g., Higgins 1987, Smelser and Davies 2008); on memory and testimony as sources for our knowledge of the past (e.g., Cru 1929, Loftus 2000, Dulong 1998, Ricoeur 2000); and on the poetics of personal texts, as opposed to fictional ones (e.g., Lejeune 1975, Smith and Watson 2001, Suleiman 2006). Because I wish to avoid circularity, however, I will also question that apparatus. More precisely, I will ask to what extent the corpus I am considering obliges us to revisit the current views about the military collaboration; the idea that testimo-nies provide us with a window into the past; and the status of the mem-oir as a "factual," "referential" text (Genette 1991, Cohn 1999), whose conventions must be distinguished from those of fiction. My analyses, therefore, participate in the ongoing debates on the nature and function of memory and on the appropriateness of a textual reading to the com-prehension of nonliterary works. "Participating," however, does not mean "closing." I want the issues that I raise throughout the book to remain open, all the more so since those issues concern a body of texts that so far has remained relatively unexplored. Ultimately, I hope that my study will prompt further research on the subject of the memory not just of the "French who fought for Hitler," but of other groups who were involved in World War II and whose testimonies – for some reason – have not been investigated as they could have been.

I

Backgrounds

When Susan Suleiman, in her *Crises of Memory and the Second World War*, discusses such texts as Lucie Aubrac's *Ils partiront dans l'ivresse* (published in English as *Outwitting the Gestapo*), André Malraux's *Antimémoires* (published in English as *Anti-Memoirs*), and Georges Perec's *W ou le souvenir d'enfance* (published in English as *W, Or, the Memory of Childhood*), she can assume that the learned readers to whom her study is addressed are somewhat familiar with these texts, their authors, and with the political and cultural context to which they refer. She does not need to introduce Malraux, nor to explain that France was occupied during World War II, that part of the country's Jewish population was deported, and that there was a resistance movement. Dealing with the memoirs of the French volunteers who fought for Germany allows no such assumption. Specialists of the Occupation may be acquainted with the names of the writer Saint-Loup, the miliciens Pierre Bassompierre and Léon Gaultier, and the Belgian politician leader Léon Degrelle; they may be aware that La Mazière, after starring in *Le Chagrin et la Pitié*, wrote two books of reminiscences; and they may recall that Rousso's first study, *Pétain à Sigmaringen*, includes an imaginary dialog with one of my memoirists, Eric Labat. However, unless they have done the same research as I have, it is unlikely that they recognize such people as Jacques Auvray, Gilbert Gilles, Serge Mit, Christian Malbosse, Henri Philippet, and Pierre Rostaing. Furthermore, although La Mazière's *Le Rêveur cas-qué* (published in English as *The Captive Dreamer*) and Sajer's *Le Soldat oublié* (published in English as *The Forgotten Soldier*) were commercial successes, none of the titles in my corpus has been a bestseller comparable to, say, Pierre Clostermann's *Le grand cirque* (published in English as *The*

Big Show) and Roger Sauvage's *Un du Normandie-Niemen* [One Member of the Normandie-Niemen Squadron], the memoirs of two French pilots who volunteered to fight on the side of the Allies, respectively in England and in the USSR. Most of the books I am discussing are now out of print and obtainable only through bookstores specializing in militaria or through Internet sellers such as Ebay, Amazon, and Abebooks. Finally, the events in which the volunteers were involved on the Eastern Front are not as famed as, say, the battle of Stalingrad. The Swiss volunteer Lobsiger was in Kharkov, and the Alsatian Sajer, in Kursk; but the French "from France" did not take part in any major military operation until they faced the Russians in Galicia, Pomerania, and Berlin during the last months of the war. Since I cannot take for granted that readers are familiar with the authors whose works I investigate, nor more generally with the specifics of French military collaboration, I begin by providing some background information about the French units that were deployed on the Eastern Front and the events in which they were involved. Then, I survey the works of the historians who have studied France's military collaboration and whose research offers overviews that contrast with the necessarily limited accounts provided in the volunteers' reminiscences. Short biographies of the memoirists and a few data about the texts they have authored are provided in an Appendix at the end of the book.

FROM THE LVF TO THE CHARLEMAGNE

Three main organizations grouped the French who were intent on helping the Germans on the battlefield:

1. The Légion des Volontaires Français contre le Bolchevisme, or LVF. The LVF was formed in July 1941 at the initiative of collaborationist leaders in Paris, who had received with enthusiasm the news of Germany's attack on the USSR on June 22, 1941. Half-heartedly supported by the German and Vichy governments, the LVF remained a private organization. The volunteers who enlisted trained in Poland and then participated in the Moscow offensive in November–December 1941 as the 638th Infantry Regiment of the 7th Division of the Wehrmacht. Stopped at Djukovo, a village located about 40 miles from the capital, they were ruled unfit for the frontline by the German command and pulled out. Assigned to the 186th Security Division that was fighting the partisans in Belorussia, they remained in this area from early 1942 to June

1944, when they were swept into the hectic retreat of Army Group Center. After fighting one "real" battle against the Red Army at Bobr, near the Berezina River, they regrouped in Greifenberg, in Pomerania. Disbanded in November 1944, the LVF became part of the newly created Division Charlemagne.

2. The 8. Französische SS-Freiwilligen Sturmbrigade, abbreviated the Brigade Frankreich, or even more briefly the Frankreich. The Sturmbrigade was formed in July 1943, after both Hitler and Laval agreed that Frenchmen could join the Waffen-SS. The Brigade trained at Sennheim (Alsace) and at the Neweklau Training Camp of the Waffen-SS at Beschenau (south of Prague), the officers being sent to specialized schools in Bad Tölz (Bavaria) and Posen-Treskau (near Danzig). In August 1944, the Brigade became part of the SS Division Horst Wessel, which was seeking to contain the Russian advance in Galicia. Immediately engaged in brutal battle in the area of Sanok and the Wisloka River, the Frankreich lost many of its members in less than two weeks. The survivors retreated to Pomerania, where – together with the men left from the LVF – they became part of the Division Charlemagne.

3. The 33. Waffen-Grenadier Division der SS Charlemagne, abbreviated the Division Charlemagne, or even more briefly the Charlemagne. The Charlemagne is the most famous of the French units that fought on the German side, but in fact it was only in existence for a few months. Formed in September 1944, the Charlemagne gathered men coming from the LVF and the Frankreich; it added volunteers from other organizations, including a strong contingent of miliciens (members of the Milice, the militia formed in 1943 by Vichy to fight the Resistance), who had fled France upon the Allies' rapid progress and the constitution of the Liberation government. Formed of two Regiments (numbers 57 and 58, each comprising three Companies), the Charlemagne trained in Wildflecken, about 60 miles northeast of Frankfurt-am-Main. Sent to Pomerania in mid-February 1945 but poorly equipped, it was bowled over by the advanced echelon of the Red Army's Second White Russian Front in such places as Hammerstein, Körlin, Belgard, and Kolberg. In late April–early May, a few of its members also participated in the battle of Berlin.

I have focused on the LVF, the Brigade Frankreich, and the Division Charlemagne, but the French who were eager (or at least willing) to help

Germany could join other organizations. Pierre Lambert and Gérard Le Marec, in their study of the subject, list no less than 24 such groups, including the Nationalsozialistische Kraftfahrkorps, or NSKK (which employed drivers, mechanics, and motorcyclists); the construction Organisation Todt (which built the "Wall" on the Atlantic that was supposed to prevent any landing); the Kriegsmarine (which enlisted seamen); the Technische Nothilfe, or Teno (which was responsible for maintaining and repairing roads and railroad tracks); the Phalange Africaine (which briefly fought the Allies in Tunisia in 1943); and the Bezen Perrot (a group of autonomists from Britanny that tracked the Resistance in western France). Exact numbers are difficult to determine, but Lambert and Le Marec (240) estimate that 40,000 Frenchmen joined German organizations, while 46,000 integrated into the "Free French Forces" that were active on the side of the Allies.

The constitution of such units as the LVF, the Brigade Frankreich, and the Division Charlemagne must also be placed in the context of a more general, "European" military collaboration of several countries with the Third Reich. As early as April 1940, SS divisions had been formed with volunteers from Denmark, Norway, Holland, and Belgium (Stein 94). The movement accelerated upon Germany's attack on the USSR in June 1941, the SS leadership, from then on, admitting more and more foreigners who were mostly grouped into divisions whose names denoted the origin of their members. The Scandinavians became part of the "Wiking" and the "Nordland"; the Dutch, of the "Nederland"; the Belgians, of the "Wallonie" and the "Langermark"; the Estonians, of the "Estland"; the Russians and Belorussians, of the "Weissruthenien"; the Bosnians, of the "Handschar"; and the Hungarians, of the "Hunyadi," the "Gombos," and the "Maria-Theresa." In 1944, these divisions comprised more than 400,000 men; forming about 50 percent of the Waffen-SS, they included 40,000 Dutch, 25,000 Flemish, 8,000 Walloons, 700 Swiss, 25,000 Latvians, 18,000 Russians, 30,000 Ukrainians, 30,000 Cossacks, 20,000 Bosnians, and 40,000 Hungarians (*Historia* 1973, 15). Measured against these figures, the statistics that Lambert and Le Marec provide must be qualified. While 40,000 Frenchmen served in the German army, the number of volunteers engaged in military operations never exceeded 3,000 for the LVF, 2,500 for the Brigade Frankreich, and 8,000 for the Charlemagne (Rousso 1987, 64). Such figures obviously are weak, especially if compared to those of the Belgian units; in fact, they are among the lowest for occupied Europe, both in "absolute and relative numbers" (Rousso 2007, 110). They confirm that in spite of what some historians (e.g., Paxton

2000) call the "State collaboration" between Vichy and Berlin, neither government ever really warmed up to the idea of France contributing significant military help to Germany; Vichy was mainly concerned with keeping France out of the conflict, and Berlin was worried about anything that might resemble the reconstitution of the French army.[1] These statistics also show that although most Frenchmen, as Burrin puts it, "accommodated themselves" fairly well to the Occupation (1995, 183), few of them were ready to go one step further and join the Germans on the battlefield; the volunteers were never popular and became pariahs after the war – a subject to which I will return in Chapter 7. France's feeble military involvement on the side of the Axis, however, does not make the testimonies I want to examine less worthy of consideration. To the contrary, it raises issues of motivation and representativeness: If the volunteers were not encouraged to enlist, why did they nevertheless do so? If they were so few, what cause did they intend to help while fighting the Russians? And when they elected to jot down their recollections, what group did they mean to speak for?

ITINERARIES

The memoirs written by the French and French-speaking volunteers obviously do not offer comprehensive accounts of the operations that took place on the Eastern Front during World War II. They generally foreground the events in which their authors were directly implicated, conveying experiences that were very different in duration and intensity. La Mazière, for example, owes his fame more to his appearance in *Le Chagrin et la pitié* than to his exploits on the battlefield. He arrived in Hammerstein (Pomerania) with the Division Charlemagne on February 27, 1945, fought around Körlin from March 1 to March 5, then retreated with a small group and was taken prisoner by the Poles on March 27 (La Mazière 1972, 111, 119, 130, 153). Gaultier's, Mit's, and Costabrava's days in Galicia with the Brigade Frankreich were even fewer. The three volunteers left the training camp in Beschenau in late

---

[1] In April 1942, on the initiative of its germanophile minister Jacques Benoist-Méchin, the Laval government formed the Légion Tricolore, a free corps that was to include the LVF and go fight in the USSR bearing a French uniform. The project was torpedoed by the Germans in September 1942, Benoist-Méchin being by the same token evicted from the government. For a detailed narrative of this episode, see Giolitto (155–98). Benoist-Méchin himself recounts this failed attempt to radicalize the collaboration in his memoir (1985 II, 134–210).

July 1944, and started fighting on August 9; Gaultier was wounded on that same day, and Mit on August 20; the two men were then evacuated to military hospitals, while Costabrava was taken prisoner on August 21 (Mit 92, 103, 133; Gaultier 221; Costabrava 147). In contrast, Dupont, Rostaing, Rusco, and Leverrier spent more than two years chasing partisans in Belorussia, then went on to Pomerania and even (Rostaing) to Berlin. Though not as long, Bayle's, Bassompierre's, and Gilles's times at the front were particularly challenging. All three men, after fighting in Belorussia (Bassompierre) or Galicia (Bayle), were engaged in Pomerania; taken prisoner, they spent several months in Russian camps before being returned to France, where they were prosecuted and tried.

The Swiss and Alsatian volunteers had generally much longer stays at the frontline than the French; unlike the LVF soldiers busy fighting partisans, they also were involved in some well known, consequential battles against the Red Army. As a member of one of the most prestigious SS Divisions, the Leibstandarte Adolf Hitler, the Swiss Lobsiger took part in the campaign in the Ukraine, then went to France and Italy. Sajer, allowed to enroll directly in the Wehrmacht because he was from Alsace and regarded as German, also joined a famed Division, the Grossdeutschland, with which he fought in Poland, the Ukraine, and Pomerania. Following the Grossdeutschland to East Prussia in the fall of 1944, he participated in his unit's retreat along the Baltic Sea in early 1945, surrendering in April to the British. Among the French-speaking volunteers, the Belgians probably had the longest and toughest time. As members, successively, of the Légion Wallonie, the SS-Sturmbrigade Wallonien, and the SS-Grenadier Division Wallonien, they were engaged at some of the most exposed places on the Eastern Front, namely the Caucasus, the Ukraine, Estonia, and Pomerania. The end of the war found Philippet at an officers' school in Bavaria and Gruber and Terlin in military hospitals. The three men eventually returned to Belgium, where they were tried and sentenced for treason. Their commandant, Léon Degrelle, was luckier. Managing to move from Pomerania to Copenhagen to Oslo, he boarded a plane that flew him to Spain, where he lived until his death.

Although the French, Swiss, Belgian, and Alsatian volunteers had different experiences at the front, they nevertheless can be viewed as constituting a relatively homogeneous group. They enlisted for the same reason: to bring down Bolshevism. They fought a common enemy: the Red Army. They met comparable fates when they returned home after the war: Regarded as traitors, they had to face the justice system of their countries. Last but not least, they exhibit similar attitudes in their memoirs: Unrepentant, they insist that they fought for a just cause and express no regret about their involvement on the side of the Nazis.

While historians have not investigated France's military collaboration with Germany as thoroughly as the Resistance or the deportations, they still have taken up the subject. Their contributions, by and large, fall under two main categories:

1. Scholarly studies grounded in archival research. Academic historians, as I indicated in my Introduction, have shown little interest in France's military collaboration with Germany and even less concern for Belgium's and Switzerland's contributions to Germany's war efforts. The only scholarly books entirely devoted to this subject are Pierre Giolitto's *Volontaires français sous l'uniforme allemand* [French Volunteers in German Uniforms], Eddy de Bruyne and Marc Rikmenspoel's *For Rex and Belgium*, and Vincenz Oertle's *"Sollte Ich aus Russland nicht zurückkehren": Schweizer Freiwillige an deutscher Seite* ["If I should not return from Russia": Swiss Volunteers on the German Side]. Next to these studies, sections about the volunteers can be found in books that treat the collaboration in general, such as Martin Conway's *Collaboration in Belgium*; Michelle Cotta's *La Collaboration*; Jacques Delarue's *Trafics et crimes sous l'Occupation* [Deals and Crimes during the Occupation]; J. Delpierre de Bayac's *Histoire de la Milice*; Bertram Gordon's *Collaborationism in France during the Second World War*; Ory's *Les Collaborateurs*; Werner Röhr's *Okkupation und Kollaboration*; Rousso's *Pétain et la fin de la collaboration*; Franz Seidler's *Die Kollaboration: 1939–1945*; and Dominique Venner's *Histoire de la collaboration*. Chapters about the LVF, the Brigade Frankreich, and the Division Charlemagne also figure in studies that examine the role of foreigners in the German army during World War II, such as Chris Bishop's *Hitler's Foreign Divisions*; Kenneth Estes's *A European Anabasis*; David Littlejohn's *Foreign Legions of the Third Reich*; Rolf-Dieter Müller's *An der Seite der Wehrmacht* [On the Side of the Wehrmacht]; Hans Werner Neulen's *An deutscher Seite: Internationale Freiwillige von Wehrmacht und SS* [On the German Side: International Volunteers of the Wehrmacht and the SS]; and J. Lee Ready's *The Forgotten Axis: Germany's*

Partners and Foreign Volunteers in WW II. Finally, a few scholarly articles focus on the French volunteers, such as Owen Anthony Davey's "The Origins of the Légion des Volontaires Français contre le Bolchevisme"; Albert Merglen's "Soldats français sous l'uniforme allemand 1941–1945"; and James G. Shields's "Charlemagne's Crusaders: French Collaboration in Arms 1941–1945." The above studies mostly follow the rules of academic writing. Their authors provide evidence for what they assert, they indicate in foot- or endnotes where that evidence can be found, and they include a bibliography. Readers, as a result, can thus return to the sources that the historians have furnished, check them, and possibly argue that they find them incomplete or susceptible to being interpreted differently.

2. Popularizations based largely on interviews and correspondence with surviving participants. Works that fall under this category are more numerous than scholarly studies. In France, they are mainly due to three authors: Pierre Mabire, Eric Lefèvre, and Saint-Loup. Mabire wrote four books about the French SS: *La Brigade Frankreich, La Division Charlemagne, Mourir à Berlin* [To Die in Berlin], *Mourir pour Dantzig* [To Die for Danzig]; and two books about the Belgian volunteers: *Légion Wallonie: Au Front de l'Est* and *Brigade d'assaut Wallonie: La Percée de Tcherkassy* [Assault Brigade Wallonie: The Breakout from Cherkassy]. In collaboration with Lefèvre, he added a trilogy about the LVF: *La LVF 1941: Par -40 devant Moscou, La Légion perdue: Face aux partisans 1942* [The Lost Legion: Facing the Partisans 1942], and *Sur les pistes de la Russie centrale: Les Français de la LVF 1943* [On the Trails of Central Russia: The French of the LVF 1943]. Saint-Loup, besides his memoirs *Les Partisans* and *Götterdämmerung*, wrote a book about the LVF: *Les Volontaires*; two books about the French SS: *Les Hérétiques* and *Les Nostalgiques*; and a book about the Division Wallonie: *Les SS de la Toison d'Or* [The SS of the Golden Fleece]. Unlike the scholarly studies mentioned above, these works are not consistently documented. Mabire indicates in forewords that his accounts are based on "reminiscences" and "documents" supplied by the former volunteers (1973, 7; 1975, 15). He singles out as particularly useful the manuscript written by Robert Soulat, the former secretary of the Division Charlemagne, a manuscript that academic historians such as Gordon and Rousso have also been able to consult, although it has so far remained unpublished.

Similarly, Saint-Loup explains in "Warnings" that he has relied on survivors' "testimonies" (1965, 9), as well as on "newly uncovered French and German archives" (1963, 9). Yet the only such archives he mentions are those included in *Hitlerslagebesprechungen*, the published transcripts of conversations held at Hitler's headquarters during the war. Neither Mabire nor Saint-Loup, moreover, refer their information to the source in which it is supposedly grounded; their texts may include short bibliographies, but they admit neither notes, nor indications of the type "according to X" or "as Z told me." Unlike Giolitto's *Volontaires français sous l'uniforme allemand* and Gordon's *Collaborationism in France*, such works as *La Brigade Frankreich* and *Les Hérétiques* are thus difficult to discuss in a scholarly manner. Readers are not provided with documents against which they can measure the veracity of what Mabire and Saint-Loup are asserting. They are invited to trust the data that these authors furnish, as well as to show indulgence toward some aspects of the writing. Mabire, for instance, states that his goal in *La Brigade Frankreich* was to combine "historical rigor" and "novelistic color" (1973, 5); and Saint-Loup, that *Les Hérétiques* belongs to "history, period," as the purpose of the book's "novelistic tone" is only "to make reading more pleasant" (1965, 5).

Richard Landwehr's *French Volunteers of the Waffen-SS* and Robert Forbes's *Pour l'Europe: The French Volunteers of the Waffen-SS* constitute particular cases. They are the works of specialists on the German Army that Smelser and Davies call "gurus," that is, authors who combine a "painfully accurate knowledge of details" in such areas as medals, uniforms, and vehicles, with a "romantic heroicization" of the Wehrmacht and the Waffen-SS (5). Thus, Landwehr includes in his book a whole documentary apparatus, comprised of photographs and statistics concerning the number of foreigners in the Waffen-SS. He does not, however, refer to sources in the body of his text, which contains neither footnotes nor intratextual references to other historians' works or participants' testimonies. In contrast, Forbes documents his account of the feats of the Frankreich and the Charlemagne in most zealous manner. Many of the 348 pages of his book have the look of an old-fashioned scholarly study, as the footnotes often overtake the text, the author explaining how he has obtained his information and discussing it. Page 182 – to take just one example – admits seven lines of text and 53 lines of footnotes. Typical of the author's obsession with specifics, the problem is to establish whether the 2nd Battalion of the Charlemagne reached the Pomeranian town of Bärenhutte on February 25 or 26, 1945. Forbes's footnotes, however, never refer to French, German, or Russian archives; his documentation is based mostly on interviews and correspondence with surviving witnesses, as well as on published studies of World War II. While Landwehr's and Forbes's works do not qualify as scholarly histories, they cannot be viewed as popularizations either, because their distribution remains too private. Mabire, Lefèvre, and Saint-Loup have been published by major French houses, such as Fayard and Les Presses de la Cité. But *French Volunteers of the Waffen-SS* was issued by Landwehr's own press, Siegrunen Publications, a small company based in Oregon that specializes in the history of the Waffen-SS. As for Forbes's *Pour l'Europe*, it was probably published at the author's expense. According to the editorial information furnished on page 4, the book was "printed and bound" by Redwood Books, in Trowbridge, England. But that same page contains no reference to a publisher, only the phrase "This edition is limited to 500 copies." Such a small run, together with the book's A4 size, hardback format, and quality paper, suggest an audience of enthusiastic amateurs of militaria, one ready to pay a large amount of money for this kind of work: In late 2009, Forbes's book was priced at $99.95 on Amazon and $125.00 on Abebooks.[2]

While scholarly studies and books based on witnesses' testimonies differ in the way data are collected and displayed, they also offer antithetical views about the exact worth of France's military collaboration. Academic historians have generally stressed that the French volunteers came from warring political organizations, never received much support, and in any case were too few to play a meaningful role on the battlefield. Shields, for example, argues that the LVF and the French SS divisions accomplished very little because they were mined by deep conflicts between "Christian 'crusaders' and neo-pagan 'Nazis', narrow nationalists and Europeanists, reactionaries and nationalists, between those owing their paramount allegiance to the Pope and those happy to swear it to the Führer" (102). Merglen, both a general and a military historian, is even more severe. Acknowledging that the volunteers fought "with courage and loyalty" (83), he nevertheless maintains that these "lost soldiers" were "duped and exploited," and that their military role appears "insignificant," especially

---

[2] A new, less private edition of *Pour l'Europe* was published in February 2010 by Stackpole Books in their series "Stackpole Military History." The list price of $21.95 was discounted by Amazon to $14.93, making the book more affordable.

if compared to that of the 15,400 French volunteers who participated in the Spanish Civil War on the side of the Republicans after joining the International Brigades (84). Making a more balanced judgment, Estes distinguishes between the performances of the Sturmbrigade Frankreich, the LVF, and the Charlemagne. For him, the Frankreich showed that volunteer units "could fight as first-rate troops when provided with proper weapons and comprehensive training." The LVF, on the other hand, "failed miserably," and the "unlucky" Charlemagne, sent to Pomerania without artillery and supply columns, could not even do what it was supposed to do – maintain "the continuity of the front" (Chapter 6, 11).

Conversely, nonacademic historians such as Mabire, Lefèvre, Landwehr, and Forbes have steadily maintained that if the French volunteers were few, their military contribution must be viewed as most valuable. According to them, the French were not just courageous, as Merglen has it; they were also efficient, particularly in slowing down the Russians in Pomerania and delaying the taking of Berlin. This position is best exemplified by Landwehr who, passing a general judgment on the battle of Berlin, affirms in hyperbolic fashion: "Whatever their number, the French SS soldiers in Berlin left an unsurpassable legacy in heroism and combat effectiveness" (73). In this respect, the mere length of the books that historians such as Mabire and Forbes have devoted to the Charlemagne is already revealing. It inscribes the importance that their authors lend to the enterprises of the volunteers, as Mabire's two studies are respectively 198,000 and 200,000 words long, whereas Forbes's reaches 287,000.

The German generals of the Waffen-SS who were in charge of the foreign volunteers have also assessed the performance of the French units, and their evaluations have generally been favorable. Gustav Krukenberg, the "General Inspector" of the Charlemagne, writes in his reports that the French behaved in Pomerania with "extreme bravery," enabling "thousands of civilians to escape" (1980, 3). He also emphasizes that in Berlin, the French were "involved in combat up to the end," singling out the soldiers "Vaulot, Fenet, and Apollot" for their "exceptional actions" as members of antitank units (1964, 26, 29).[3] Likewise, Felix Steiner hails

---

[3] I want to thank Peter Schöttler for sharing copies of "Probleme um die Division Charlemagne [Problems about the Charlemagne Division]" and "Kampftage in Berlin [Days of Fighting in Berlin]," two unpublished manuscripts in which Krukenberg accounts for his activities as head of the Division Charlemagne in Pomerania and Berlin. According to Schöttler, "Probleme um die Division Charlemagne" was written in 1980, in response to questions asked by an unnamed French historian or journalist. As for "Kampftage in

in his book about the Waffen-SS the "fighting spirit" of the Frankreich in Galicia (1958, 291), as well as the "bravery" of the Charlemagne in the operations it conducted around Kolberg (1958, 314). But he saves his highest praise for the Légion Wallonie, which was part of the German army that in the Ukraine was encircled in the "pocket" at Cherkassy and had to break out through Soviet lines. There, according to Steiner, the Belgians did not just "keep the enemy in check"; they showed an admirable "spirit of initiative" (1958, 232) under the inspired leadership of the "passionate, proud, bold, goodhearted" Léon Degrelle (1958, 118).

These disagreements about the exact role and accomplishments of the French volunteers do not only denote different ways of collecting, ordering, and interpreting data; they also point to deeply divergent ideological standpoints. Abiding by their professional standards, the academic historians who have investigated France's military collaboration have usually striven to remain neutral and objective. However, they have not always been able (or willing) to conceal where they stood with respect to the cause that the volunteers had defended from Belorussia to Berlin. Giolitto concludes his study by deploring that "the most upright" among the volunteers did not place their "enthusiasm and taste for action" at the service of "an ideal aimed at freeing their country," choosing instead to help the "torturers" whose goal was to "enslave" France (443). Likewise, after rating the role of the volunteers as "insignificant," Merglen ends his article by calling for more research on the young people from Alsace and Lorraine, who were forcibly incorporated into the German army. According to Merglen, this subject has been overlooked, although it is of "national interest"; scholars should thus take it up instead of investigating the "poor French soldiers of the LVF and the Waffen-SS," whom "misery or ideology" led into the "voluntary servitude imposed by the victor and exploiter of their country" (84).[4]

At the other end of the political spectrum, Mabire, Saint-Loup, Landwehr, and Forbes have insisted that the volunteers were, if not on the "good" side, at least on a side that deserves rehabilitation in the face of continuing slander. As a scholar of all things military and a supporter of right-wing causes such "Algérie française" and "Autonomy for Normandy," Mabire displays throughout his books on the Frankreich

---

Berlin," it was written in 1964 at the request of Cornelius Ryan who was doing research for his book *The Last Battle*. Schöttler himself is preparing a biography of Krukenberg.

[4] Merglen's article was published in 1977, and the historian's wish that more research on the "malgré nous" be undertaken has since then been fulfilled. On this subject, see Jeanclos (2003), Riedweg (1995), and Rigoulot (1990).

and the Charlemagne the utmost admiration for the discipline and battle-field efficiency of the Waffen-SS; it is no accident that he had written several studies on the different units of this organization, for instance, on the Divisions Nordland, Hitlerjugend, and Götz von Berlichingen. Saint-Loup, politically, is even more of an extremist than Mabire. An avowed fascist and racist, he sees the French who enlisted in the German army, and especially in the Waffen-SS, as belonging to an elite: to the handful of men who "blow open the moral and spiritual frameworks of their time," who represent the "dynamic element of the evolution curiously named 'movement of history'," and who "carry along with them, in the long or the short run, the vegetative masses" (1963, 10). Landwehr is as explicit as Saint-Loup when it comes to proclaiming the elite status of the Waffen-SS, as well as the rightness of the cause that they and the French volunteers defended on the battlefield. According to him, the conflict was not just between Germany and the USSR; it was between Europe and Asiatic Russia, the foreign Waffen-SS being in this regard at the vanguard of the "European Army" that was battling "for Western Civilization" and whose story must be "forever remembered as a triumph of the human spirit engaged in noble endeavor" (8).

Viewed from an ideological standpoint, the judgments that the German generals pass on their foreign troops are no less biased. Steiner spent most of his postwar life seeking to restore the reputation of the Waffen-SS – a corps that according to him had been unfairly attacked by people unfamiliar with its history and its exact role during the conflict. In this respect, the titles of Steiner's books, *Die Freiwilligen der Waffen-SS: Idee und Opfergang* [The Volunteers of the Waffen-SS: Idea and Sacrifice] and *Die Armee der Geächteten* [The Army of the Ostracized], are already revealing for they point to their author's wish to rehabilitate the orga-nization of which he was a zealous member. What Steiner writes about the French and Belgian troops must be understood in this polemical context. Both units, according to him, fought basically for an "idea"; they "sacrificed" themselves for just causes, such as the defense of the West; and their surviving members were inequitably "outlawed" after the war, victims of a justice system that was looking for scapegoats (1958, 9). Krukenberg's reports have a different slant. While praising the Charlemagne, Krukenberg is also concerned with establishing that he did his best to reorganize the Division and then to carry out the hopeless task of defending Berlin against the Russians. His target, therefore, is not the people who wrongly charge the Waffen-SS for having been involved in criminal activities. It is the Nazi political and military leadership that failed to plan for an efficient defense of the capital, thus "deceiving" and "sacrificing" both the civilian population that had remained there and the foreign troops that had come to help (1964, 37). More self-servingly, Krukenberg also insists that it would have been easy for him to leave the city, head west, and become a prisoner-of-war of the Americans (1964, 42). Instead, "out of respect for the volunteers," he elected to stay in Berlin (1964, 43). His only option was then to surrender to the Russians, who sentenced him to 25 years in jail for "causing a prejudice to the Red Army through military resistance in Pomerania and Berlin" (1964, 43). Krukenberg eventually was freed after 11 years in East German prisons, and he settled in the Bonn area.

My purpose, as I stated earlier, is not to judge the actions of the French volunteers. I have provided this overview in order to situate, with respect to the available historiography, the memoirs I am about to discuss. Therefore, I won't seek to establish whether the LVF, the Frankreich, and the Charlemagne were efficient or not on the battlefield. Nor will I try to decide whether the volunteers in fact defended a just cause, or at least a cause that in some regard deserves reconsideration. My goal is to probe how the volunteers account for their actions and to take up some of the key issues that their narratives are raising. I attend next to a problem that is central for all life narratives, namely authenticity.

2

Authenticity

Like all testimonies, the texts written by the French volunteers first pose problems of authenticity. According to Paul Ricoeur, the witness makes the basic statement "I was there," to which he/she adds the two *clausulas* "Believe me" and (as a kind of challenge) "If you do not believe me, ask someone else" (2000, 206). In other words, as Renaud Dulong submits in extending Ricoeur, to witness an event does not really mean "to be a spectator of that event"; it means "to state that one has seen that event" and to commit oneself to recounting it "as one has seen it" (1998, 12). What Ricoeur and Dulong say about witnessing of course applies to life writing. Authors of memoirs, too, pledge to tell the truth, establishing between themselves and their audience what Philippe Lejeune (1975, 26–7) calls an "autobiographical contract": They promise that the author, the narrator, and the main character of their narrative is the same "person" who reports "with sincerity," "to the best of his/her recollection," what he/she experienced at a certain time and place.

VERIFICATIONS AND GUARANTEES

Given this initial promise, historians, journalists, or merely inquisitive readers are of course entitled to check whether the witness was "really there," either by "asking someone else" (i.e., other witnesses) or by confronting the content of the testimony with archival research. In short, as Laurent Douzou puts it, they are entitled to "call" the witness (269); for by accepting to testify, the witness has given up the "propriety rights" he/she has over his/her past, transferring them to different categories of inquirers who can use them as they see fit. In turn exercising these rights, historians and journalists have conducted investigations that at times have led to incriminating discoveries, revealing that the witness was not "really" where he/she claims that he/she was. In the late twentieth–early twenty-first centuries, the most publicized of these exposures has probably concerned Binjamin Wilkomirski's book *Fragments: Memories of a Childhood* (1996), which the author offered as a testimony on his experiences as an infant in Warsaw, Maidanek, and Auschwitz-Birkenau. Yet, as the journalist Daniel Ganzfried and the historian Stefan Maechler determined after investigating the case, Wilkomirski did not spend the war in Poland, but rather in Switzerland; his real name was Bruno Dössekker – the name of the family that had adopted him after his mother had given him up for adoption when he was two years old (his name was then Bruno Grosjean). Wilkomirski/Dössekker/Grosjean, therefore, had not lived through the events that he recounts in *Fragments*; he had forged them using testimonies and historical studies about the Holocaust, of which his library contained a large amount.

Fragments, of course, is not the only text in which the author invented for him/herself an interesting biography. Ben Yagoda, in his history of the memoir, affirms that "the past four decades will probably be remembered as the golden age of autobiographical fraud" (247), as writers installed in the comfort of their homes have pretended to be, or to have been, prostitutes, drug dealers, victims of abusive parents, or Holocaust survivors. Another well-known example of the latter type of false testimony is Misha Defonseca's *Misha: A Memoir of the Holocaust Years* (1998), the story of a six-year-old Jewish girl who, protected by wolves, searches around Europe for her deported parents. The actual author turned out to be Monique de Wael, a Catholic Belgian woman living in Boston. Confronted with such evidence as her baptismal certificate, de Wael confessed to the deception. In her defense, she alleged that, as the daughter of a man who worked for the Gestapo during Belgium's occupation by the Germans, she had always wanted to fashion her own identity.

Whether Dösseker and de Wael are deluded or deliberately fabricated their testimonies is irrelevant to my discussion of a memoirist's contractual obligations. What their cases show or confirm is that authors who present their texts as personal reminiscences do take a chance; opening those texts to procedures of verification, they run the risk of being charged with distorting the events that they recount, or even with forging them altogether. Such charges, of course, would be meaningless to press against a novelist who writes a life story that he/she explicitly offers as fictional; the facts that he/she reports cannot be confirmed or disproved, whether by consulting documents or by interviewing people who knew the author. Debates that followed the Defonseca and especially the Wilkomirski affairs, therefore, demonstrate that the boundary between "referential" and "fictional" discourses (Cohn 1999), in this instance, between historical and fictional memoirs, is still well marked in our culture. Granted, as postcolonial critics have argued, regional differences must be taken into account. Sending "cautionary notes" to narrative theorists, Sidonie Smith and Julia Watson (2006) have contended that such genres as the Latin-American "testimonio" should not be judged by the standards of the western "testimony," more generally, that the poor and the disenfranchised, when they tell their lives, should be empowered to negotiate their own conditions for truth and verifiability. The question of knowing whether there should be one or several truth conditions for life narratives has been widely discussed, and I won't ask here whether such texts as *I, Rigoberta Menchù: An Indian Woman in Guatemala* help the marginalized or, as some critics maintain, "deligitimate their lived experience," leading to a "corrosive skepticism" (Lauritzen 31). Indeed, the problematic life narratives I used as examples of hoax were brought out in Europe and North America, and the verdict in those cases was one-sided; the authors were immediately censured by critics, by the publishing business, and in public opinion. Such univocal response shows that Lejeune's autobiographical contract is still in place, at least in the West, and that breaking it has ethical implications. Readers of *Fragments* and *Misha*, at any rate, felt betrayed when these testimonies were exposed as hoaxes; they were all the more indignant in the case of *Fragments* since Wilkomirski had confirmed his story in numerous interviews, accepted literary prizes from several Jewish organizations, and even guided discussion groups with "other" child survivors.

Investigating the authenticity of the volunteers' memoirs is particularly difficult. Jean Norton Cru, in his groundbreaking study of soldiers' testimonies written during and after World War I, introduces every text by supplying a series of data concerning the author's biography, his membership in a specific military unit, and the reliability of his report. Because several among my memoirists are unknown and no information about them is available, I must begin the presentation of the authors in my corpus at a lower level. More precisely, I must first ask: Do we have proof of these people's existence? And do we have proof that they actually fought alongside the Germans – that their reminiscences are not, like Wilkomirski's and Defonseca's, fictional rather than factual? Depending on their notoriety and accomplishments besides writing one book of

memoirs, the authors whose testimonies I am considering can be distributed into three main categories:

1. Known figures whose both existence and enlistment in the LVF
   and/or the French SS is well established, such as Bassompierre,
   Gaultier, Laurier, Saint-Loup, and Degrelle. These names may be
   familiar to specialists of the 1930s and the Occupation, as they
   are found in studies of the period in general and the collaboration
   in particular. Bassompierre had functions in the Milice; Gaultier,
   in the Milice and the Vichy government; Laurier and Saint-Loup,
   under their birth names Pierre Vigouroux and Marc Augier, had
   activities as journalists; and Degrelle was a well-known politician
   who headed the proto-fascist Rexist Party in Belgium.

2. Lesser-known figures whose existence nevertheless is attested
   because they worked with other people, gave interviews, or published texts in addition to their memoirs, such as Rusco, Rostaing,
   Costabrava, Bayle, Terlin, Gilles, Sajer, and La Mazière. Rusco,
   Rostaing, and Costamagna wrote their books in collaboration;
   Bayle (1984) and Terlin (1973) contributed pieces to the magazines
   Historama and *Historia*; Gilles (1973) was interviewed in *Historia*,
   and Sajer (1993), in *39/45 Magazine*; La Mazière, as mentioned
   earlier, was one the main interviewees in *Le Chagrin et la pitié*. Of
   course, the fact that these authors' existence is confirmed does not
   guarantee the authenticity of their testimonies. I will consider later
   the two most contested cases, those of Sajer and Gilles.

3. Unknown people whose only trace is the book that they left
   about their (supposed) experiences, like Auvray, Cisay, Dupont,
   Emmanuelli, Gruber, Malbosse, Mit, Philippet, and the anonymous
   author of *Vae Victis* [Woe to the Vanquished]. To my knowledge,
   these authors have never given magazine interviews, and they have
   not written any text beyond their memoirs. The only information available about them is that supplied in their books, as even
   extended Internet databases like Google do not offer additional
   data, merely signaling the mail-order business from which their
   works can be obtained. The books published by these memoirists
   obviously are the most problematic. They raise the possibility that
   they were written by someone who then disappeared from public
   view, as several returning volunteers understandably did; that they
   describe authentic experiences but were written under a pseudonym for the purpose of avoiding legal trouble; or that they are

works of imagination, whose authors, unlike Wilkomirski, have not been exposed.

Aware of the issues of authenticity that memoirs may raise, publishers often seek to establish from the start that the texts they are bringing out under this label constitute genuine testimonies. The need to provide guarantees is especially obvious when the authors are little known or even unknown. Warrants that the memoirist was "really there," in these instances, are often supplied at once in the paratext, specifically, in what Genette calls the "publisher's peritext" (1987, 20): information located "around" the text but within the confines of the bound volume, whether on the book's cover, on the title page, or in the preface. Emmanuelli's *Et j'ai cassé mon fusil* [And I Broke my Gun], for example, was published by Laffont in the series "Vécu" (literally: "Experienced"), a label that immediately situates the text in the category "testimony." The blurbs on the back cover confirm this status, asserting: "A man speaks and his colored language, his loud voice draw us in. His name is Jean-Baptiste Emmanuelli …" Together with the information about the series, these two sentences immediately trigger Lejeune's "autobiographical contract": They affirm that the author, the narrator, and the main character here are the same "person" who recounts episodes in his own life. Similarly, the blurbs on the back cover of Labat's *Les Places étaient chères* [The Seats Were Expensive] reproduce excerpts from a reader's report, in this instance the novelist Roger Nimier's, who writes: "We find here the reasons Eric Labat had, or rather did not have, to enlist in the LVF … Then we are in Russia, where the French, responsible for ensuring the security of the rear, play a 'wargame' against the partisans that demonstrates all their skills." The publishing house La Table Ronde, which brought out *Les Places étaient chères*, attests here to the genuineness of the book it is releasing through the judgment of one famed member of its editorial board, who apparently never doubted (did he have proof?) that Labat really had fought in Belorussia.[1] Another publishing house, La Jeune Parque, relies on an even wilier strategy when it entrusts the preface of the anonymous *Vae Victis* to Colonel Remy, a prestigious member of the Resistance (though one with right-wing sympathies) who was in the process of writing his own recollections. To be sure, Remy states clearly that he disapproves of the choices that the volunteers had

---

[1] La Table Ronde regrettably supplies no further information about Labat. For more biographical data about him, see the appendix "Biographical Notices."

made. By prefacing the book, however, he substantiates the presentation of *Vae Victis* as a valid testimony, sanctioning La Jeune Parque's decision to bring out this anonymous work. The Belgian publisher Bibliothèque Royale Albert 1er resorts to a similar scheme when it includes a preface by a Resistance member and holder of the "Croix de guerre avec palmes" (a prestigious decoration) Louis De Lentdecker in Gruber's *Nous n'irons pas à Touapse* [We Won't Go to Tuapse], and the Editions Arctic, when they a add to Marotel's *La longue marche* a preface in which the historian Eric Lefèvre affirms that it was for him an "honor" to "introduce" and "annotate" the book (7). By including this type of paratextual information, authors and publishers obviously aim to program the reception of the text; they supply specific instructions of reading, tell us how to "take" the text as a whole. One must emphasize: as a whole. If *Vae Victis* and *Nous n'irons pas à Touapse* had come with the generic subtitle "a novel," our expectations and subsequent reading would have been quite different. For one thing, we would not have asked whether guarantees of the memoir's authenticity were provided, and in what forms.

The information about genre provided by the paratext of the volunteers' narratives, however, is not always as categorical as in the examples I have just examined. Dupont's *Au temps des choix héroïques* [At the Time of Heroic Choices] provides a case in point. The copy I obtained from an internet bookstore is inscribed not by Dupont himself but by his son, who writes: "For François, in memory of my father, Pierre Henri Dupont, and of his comrades of the Division Charlemagne, who sacrificed themselves in order to save Europe from Bolshevism. Let their memory live. March 2007. B. Dupont." Through this inscription, "B. Dupont" certifies that his father was indeed a member of the Charlemagne. But he does not affirm explicitly that *Au temps des choix héroïques* is his father's memoir, and the peritext includes neither a subtitle nor blurbs on the back cover, which would clarify the odd narrative situation: Using a heterodiegetic narrator, Dupont tells the story of "Henri Duval," a young Frenchman who participates successively in the campaigns of the LVF, the Brigade Frankreich, and the Division Charlemagne. Is "Henri Duval" actually "Pierre Henri Dupont," and *Au temps des choix héroïques* what Lejeune calls an "autobiography in the third person": A text in which the author "speaks about himself as though someone else were speaking about him, or as though he were speaking about someone else" (1980, 184)? Life narratives consistently written in the third person are extremely rare. Lejeune only refers to *The Education of Henry Adams* and to Norman Mailer's *The Armies of the Night*, his other examples being of sophisticated literary texts that move occasionally from the first to the third person, such as *Roland Barthes/par Roland Barthes* [published in English as *Roland Barthes*]. Furthermore, *Au temps des choix héroïques* is not an autobiography in the third person strictly speaking; author and main character do not have the same name, a dissymmetry that cancels the autobiographical contract, or at least calls it into question. The epitext, that is, the information about the text provided outside the bound volume, does nothing in this instance to solve the discursive and epistemological problem posed by the text itself. The 2009 catalog of L'Homme Libre, the publishing house that brought out *Au temps des choix héroïques*, offers Dupont's book as an "historical novel" but adds that the author, "when he was 18 years old, enlisted in the LVF and then in the Charlemagne." Dupont's narrative would thus be a novel, though one that is based (to what extent?) on the author's own experience on the Eastern Front. France's Bibliothèque Nationale, however, classifies the same edition of *Au temps des choix héroïques* under the "Subject(s): World War (1939–1945) – Campaigns and battles – USSR – French personal narratives – Légion des volontaires français contre le bolchevisme – Biographies." That is, the BN regards Dupont's text as referential, not fictional, a decision that is confirmed by the call number assigned to the book: "Indice(s) Dewey: 940.541 343." (Viewing the book as "literature" would have entailed an 800 call number.) The fact that the epitext should give conflicting information about the genre of *Au temps des choix héroïques* is not insignificant. If the text is indeed the narrative of Dupont's actual journey, this would be the only testimony of a volunteer who went from the LVF to the Frankreich to the Charlemagne – a journey that none of the other memoirs in my corpus so far has documented.

In addition to the paratextual assertion that the authors were "really there," several of the volunteers' memoirs back up their claim to authenticity by providing documentary evidence. The front cover of Rusco's *Stoï!* displays the photograph of the four men who are identified in the blurbs (one of them is Rusco), and the book contains other photographs confirming that the author actually fought in Belorussia. Similar pictures are found in other books, such as Saint-Loup's *Les Partisans*, Bayle's *De Marseille à Novossibirsk*, Gilles's *Un ancien Waffen SS français raconte* [A Former French Member of the Waffen-SS Reports], and especially Lobsiger's *Un Suisse au service d'Hitler* [A Swiss in Hitler's Service], Gruber's *Nous n'Irons pas à Touapse*, and Philippet's *Et mets ta robe de bal* [And Put Your Party Gown on]. Lobsiger proudly displays his portrait in SS uniform on the front cover and then attaches seven photographs of himself in the Soviet Union, in Germany with his fiancée, and at the German-Swiss border with his father (n.p.). Philippet's book contains as many as fifteen pictures of the author, either in German uniform (e.g., II, 21, 89), in prisoner's clothes when he was in a Belgian jail (e.g., II, 270), or in an elegant suit after his liberation and marriage (II, 323). Philippet is also careful to tell (to the extent that it is possible) where and when the pictures that he includes were taken, and to provide the names of the people who appear in them. Thus, he indicates in a caption (I, 123) that two of the men in the photograph are Léon Degrelle and the Wallonie's commandant Lucien Lippert, and that the picture was taken on October 9, 1942, on the occasion of a medals presentation; more impressively, he also identifies (I, 22) thirteen out of the sixteen lesser-known Belgian volunteers who pose in front of a railroad wagon, the preceding and opposite pages stating that the setting is the Ukraine, and the date is October 1941.

In addition to photographs of people and landscapes, my memoirists frequently supply reproductions of written evidence that confirm their participation in the war. Bayle, eager to prove that he spent time in a Russian POW camp, includes the photograph of a bizarre document: the "Attestation," dated February 10, 1987, in which the vice-consul of the USSR in Paris states that "Mr André (Michel, Edouard) Bayle, born on 20 May 1926 in Marseille ... was a prisoner of war in the USSR from 8 March 1945 to 8 November 1945" (203). Similarly, Lobsiger exhibits the certificate given to him on May 20, 1945 by the secret service of the Waffen-SS, showing that "Herr Brandenberger," a "Swiss civilian" employed in Germany, "has been let go at his own request." He attaches the "safe-conduct" given to him by the Italian partisans in Tyrol upon presentation of the fake German certificate (n.p.), and explains that these two IDs allowed him to travel in northern Italy for several weeks after the end of the war (224). Philippet, again, is the memoirist who supplies the most abundant documentation. Anxious to demonstrate that his services at the front were deemed valuable, he displays the forms acknowledging that he received decorations, namely the *Ostmedaille* (I, 123), the *Eiserne Kreuz 2.Klasse* (II, 75), and the *Eiserne Kreuz 1.Klasse* (II, 112). Likewise, to attest that he was hounded and finally sentenced for his involvement on the side of the Nazis, he includes two photographs: one of an extract from the Belgian "Index of investigations for crime against the security of the State," which lists "Philippet, Henri-Guillaume-Jean-Joseph" among the people being wanted for treason (II, 237); and the "last paycheck" that he received before his release, "on 7 August 1948," for his work in a coal mine as a convict (II, 277).

The photographs and documents included in such books as *Stoï*! and *Un Suisse au service d'Hitler* have a strong rhetorical function. They do not merely "illustrate" the text, in the sense that they enhance it with pictures and provide suitable examples. They also, as Roland Barthes has argued about photographs, create a powerful reality effect: The object that appears in a photograph is "*necessarily* real," since "there would be no photograph without it" (1980, 120). In short, photographs make it impossible to deny that "the thing was there," and their being mechanically recorded imposes both the idea that the past exists and that its existence is independent from a cognitive subject. But photographs in general, and war-related photographs in particular, also raise several issues of correctness and reliability. Studies about the iconography of World War II have demonstrated that pictures can easily be falsified or touched up, and that the data about characters, places, and time offered in the captions must be treated with prudence. Janina Struk, in her study of Holocaust photographs, has shown that the infamous "death pit" picture representing five naked men (including a child) about to be shot poses many problems to the scholar concerned about accuracy. Depending on the print of that photograph, Struk explains, a German soldier can or cannot be seen pointing his finger at the naked men on the right-hand side of the frame (6); and the accompanying information locates the scene in many different places and times, such as Poland, Lithuania, and Latvia, and 1939, 1941, 1943, and 1944 (12). Likewise, Barbie Zelizer has pointed out that the photographs of the liberation of Dachau, Buchenwald, and Bergen-Belsen that appeared in the British and American press came with imprecise captions. Whereas the narratives of reporters provided "minute details" of the camps' topography, the "visual representations" of those camps often left them "unnamed," illustrating less the reality of Dachau or Bergen-Belsen than a broad, generalized "atrocity story" (93).

The photographs that figure in the texts I am considering cause readers to pose similar questions. For instance, were the pictures of Flemish and French volunteers, which Philippet (II, 87) and Saint-Loup (1986a, n.p.) affirm were taken near Leningrad and at Djukovo, really taken there? In both cases, the setting is nondescript; it could be anywhere at the front, and we are invited to believe that the references to Leningrad and Djukovo are indeed accurate. Conversely, one could ask what locations are represented on the photographs of soldiers walking in the snow that come in Bayle's memoirs with generic captions, such as "Icy snow storms must be surmounted" and "Moving forward is painful" (n.p.). Since Bayle was a member of the Charlemagne, should we assume that these pictures were taken in Pomerania in February-March 1945? And could a specialist in World War II, identifying places, weapons, and uniforms, tell whether Philippet's and Saint-Loup's information is correct and complete Bayle's captions by disclosing which army is fighting, where, and when? In none of the volunteers' memoirs, moreover, does the author (or the editor) answer a question that specialists in iconography now regard as basic: Who took the picture? Whether a photograph originates with a war correspondent, an employee of a propaganda service, a soldier who owned a camera, or a local in the vicinity, is not immaterial. The identity and qualifications of the photographer, as well as his membership in a specific group, can determine whether the picture will be saved or not, how it will be used, and what its caption will tell or pass over in silence. The photos that the texts in my corpus include obviously have been saved; but they remain uncredited, as the accompanying captions never specify whether they were taken by the German Propaganda Service, members of news agencies, or the volunteers themselves.[2]

Similar issues can be raised about the written documents that the volunteers' memoirs occasionally include. Auvray opens *Les derniers grognards* [The Last Grumblers – name given to Napoléon's soldiers] with a reproduction of his SS *Soldbuch* (soldier's ID and paybook), comprising a portrait of Hitler and three pages of personal information. Yet the name "Auvray" is nowhere to be found, a lack that makes readers ask why this document figures in the first place. The evidence offered in Lobsiger's memoirs may provoke similar suspicions. Italian partisans, as Lobsinger explains, gave him a pass on the basis of a false ID fabricated by the SS. However, that ID is dated May 20, 1945, whereas the Italian safe conduct is dated May 13. Was the SS ID intentionally antedated? Did the Italians overlook the date? Or did they decide not to investigate any further and attend to more important business? However that may be, the discrepancy poses a problem that Lobsiger does not address in the caption that comes with the photograph nor in the body of the text. As is the case with Auvray's *Soldbuch*, the document here produces a boomerang effect; appended to augment the memoir's authenticity, they

---

[2] The French publishing house Grancher has recently brought out a photo album titled *Les Archives Keystone de la LVF*. Most of the photographs in that album were taken in France; they represent such events as parades, meetings, and reviews of troops. Only nine were taken in the East (in Poland and near the Berezina River), though not at the front properly speaking. None of the photos that come with the texts in my corpus are credited to the news agency Keystone.

in fact undermine it, at least for readers who search for this kind of inconsistency or merely are attentive to it.

One might ask, finally, whether the use of a memoir in a scholar's documentary apparatus is itself a warranty of that memoir's authenticity. The question can be raised about several of the volunteers' testimonies, which professional historians employ as valid sources without always interrogating their epistemological status. Serge Mit's *Carcasse à vendre* [Carcass for Sale] – to take just one example – figures in the footnotes of such major studies of the collaboration as Gordon's (e.g., 273, 275) and Giolitto's (e.g., 334, 344, 345, 349); the two historians also list Mit's memoir in the bibliographies that they affix to their works, on the same plane as academic works and testimonies whose authenticity is well established. Yet neither Gordon nor Giolitto comment on the fact that Mit is among the volunteers who have never been interviewed, of whom we have no photograph, and who apparently have disappeared after the publication of their only piece of writing. Readers, in this instance, are asked to trust the authority of the scholar; specifically, they are asked to assume that trade historians such as Gordon and Giolitto have played the game by the rules – that they have checked, before drawing on them, the validity of the testimonies that they have elected to use.

THE SAJER CASE

Issues of authenticity have been raised about a few of the memoirs in my corpus. The most debated case has been Sajer's, whose *Le Soldat oublié* has provoked lively discussions among servicemen, specialists in military history, and more casual readers. The basic problem here is a simple one. It is to determine whether Sajer truly was on the Eastern Front with the Grossdeutschland Division, as he claims that he was, or invented the story using novels, histories, and other peoples' life narratives for his documentation. In other words, it is to determine whether *Le Soldat oublié* is a genuine testimony or a hoax, similar to Wilkomirski's *Fragments*, Misha Defonseca's *Misha*, and other fake memoirs about World War II.

The first edition of *Le Soldat oublié*, brought out in 1967 by the mainstream publishing house Laffont, comes with the generic subtitle *Récit*, that is, "Narrative." The term *récit* is ambiguous in French, as it is found as a subtitle to both referential texts, such as Robert Antelme's Buchenwald memoir *L'Espèce humaine* (published in English as *The Human Race*), and to fictional ones, such as André Gide's *L'Immoraliste*. Extensive blurbs of that same edition of Sajer's memoir are more explicit.

Starting on the back cover and continuing on the flap of the front cover, they state that the book "surpasses in truth, horror, and greatness all the texts written on the subject," because the author "has really experienced all that he reports" and knows "how to see things and make them visible in detail with an extraordinary power." "Readers," the blurbs conclude, "cannot doubt that everything in this book is true"; they know that they are not dealing with "literature," with "purple passages [morceaux de bravoure]", but with a faithful representation of what it was like to live in "fear," misery," and "horror." Other components of the paratext confirm the status of *Le Soldat oublié* as an authentic testimony. Documenting Sajer's travels, a map on the back of the front cover shows his journeys with the Grossdeutschland Division from Poland to Belorussia to the Ukraine to East Prussia, as well as the routes of his leaves and his repatriation as a POW from Kiel to the French border. In addition, a "Note from the publisher" describes Sajer's manuscript and traces its history: Sajer began to write his story in school notebooks in 1952; some of his friends published excerpts in a Belgian magazine; and the whole work, made of seventeen notebooks, "at some point, reached us" (8). Laffont published subsequent editions of *Le Soldat oublié* in the series *Vécu*, together with other texts offered as genuine testimonies, such as Emmanuelli's *Et j'ai cassé mon fusil* and La Mazière's *Le Rêveur casqué*.

Le Soldat oublié was successful in France. In 1968, it received the Prix des Deux Magots, a literary prize that is awarded to young, promising talents in the areas of fiction, autobiography, and literary criticism. Members of the Deux Magots jury apparently had no concern about the authenticity of Sajer's testimony; although they often give the prize to novelists, they doubtless would not have rewarded a memoir that they knew was in fact a piece of fiction. The reviewers of the 1971, first English-language edition of *Le Soldat oublié* did not question the status of Sajer's story, either. J. Glenn Gray, for example, a philosophy professor and World War II veteran, wrote in the *New York Times Book Review*: "Sajer... succeeded uncommonly well in describing the details of action and feeling, of suffering and terror, that fell to his lot as a private... Those who have never known war first hand will be unable to grasp more than a fraction of the reality he describes. Even veterans of combat will conclude that what they experienced was child's play in comparison" (4). Similarly, the literary critic Walter Clemons wrapped up his *New York Times* review by stating: "We are reading the memoir of a man whose freshest, deepest feelings were aroused by the ordeal of war, who came out physically whole but never cared so much about anything again" (37).

The *New York Times* reviewers' enthusiasm was shared by career soldiers. Writing in the "From My Bookshelf" section of the *Military Review*, Colonel Harold W. Nelson ("Chief of Military History, Department of the Army, Washington, DC") had no hesitation to declare about *Le Soldat oublié*: "My real list would begin with this book. I believe all of us must keep the trials and contributions of the front-line soldier uppermost in our minds as we do our work, and I know of no more powerful firsthand account than Sajer's book" (90). Listing texts for the same "From My Bookshelf" section, General Michael F. Spigelmire ("US Army") did not have more qualms than his colleague when he explained: "Sajer presents fascinating memoirs of a very young man who fought on the Eastern Front from 1942 to 1945. His book offers an intimate eyewitness account of the savage combat with the Red Army and Soviet partisans, as well as conditions in wartime Germany and the gradual disintegration of the Wehrmacht" (90). In the particular context of a military journal, such expressions as "firsthand account," "fascinating memoirs," and "intimate eyewitness account" are most revealing. They show that professional soldiers had no doubt about the authenticity of Sajer's book – a book that they present as required reading for officers who need to keep in mind the role of the ordinary troopers who bear the brunt of battles. The fact that two high-ranking American soldiers should have selected the memoir of a German private for their "Bookshelf," next to such works as *The Maneuver Warfare Handbook* and James M. McPherson's Pulitzer prize-winning study *Battle Cry of Freedom*, is also noteworthy. That choice is most likely traceable to the Cold War, specifically to the rapprochement between the United States and Germany. Starting in the 1950s, as Smelser and Davies have demonstrated, American defense strategists turned more and more to former Wehrmacht generals for advice, on the assumption that the battles the Germans had fought on the Eastern Front provided scenarios for the battles that western armies could possibly fight against Russian invaders. The references to Sajer's book in the *Military Review* indicate that high-ranking officers in the American army also valued the experiences of frontline German soldiers. Indeed, unlike their American counterparts, German privates knew firsthand what it meant to face the Russians, and the stories they told about their struggles in the USSR could prove helpful to the United States command.

Not all specialists, however, were as convinced of the authenticity and usefulness of Sajer's work as Nelson and Spigelmire. One of the most skeptical was Lieutenant Colonel Edward L. Kennedy Jr. ("Combat Studies Institute, Fort Leavenworth, Kansas"), who argued in another military

journal, *Army History*, that *Le Soldat oublié* was in fact "a carefully written novel that cleverly disguises as a factual account ... a hoax with no
attempt to present it as such" (1992, 23). To support his thesis, Kennedy
listed a series of "errors" that for him disqualify the text as a valid testimony: Sajer claims that in July 1942, he trained with Hans-Ulrich Rudel's
famed Stuka Luftwaffe unit in Chemnitz, whereas that unit was based in
Graz at the time; he states that his Grossdeutschland insignia was placed
on the right sleeve of his uniform, whereas in fact it was placed on the
left sleeve; he affirms that he was a member of the 17th Battalion of the
Grossdeutschland, whereas that battalion did not exist; he introduces his
commander's name as "Wesreidau," whereas no "Wesreidau" ever led a
company in the Grossdeutschland; and his claim that he was part of that
same division cannot be substantiated, as no record of the presence of a
"Guy Sajer" can be found on its muster rolls. *Le Soldat oublié*, Kennedy
concluded, is thus an "interesting example of a fictional work taken at
face value by well-read soldiers, and even cited for purposes of professional study"; but it remains a piece of fiction, making it necessary for
military personnel "not to place too much stock in its lessons, without
due consideration of the source of these lessons" (1992, 23–24).

Kennedy's charges did not remain unanswered. In a long reply, Douglas
E. Nash ("US Southern Command, MacDill Air Force Base, Florida")
sought to account for Sajer's "errors," which for him concerned mostly
details that did not jeopardize the authenticity of *Le Soldat oublié* taken
as a whole. For instance, while Rudel's Stuka squadron was based in
Graz in 1942, a "training and evaluation element" might have been stationed in Chemnitz (1997, 13); whereas there was no 17th Battalion in
the Grossdeutschland, there was a 17th *Abteilung*, and Sajer might have
used the word "*bataillon*" because there is no real equivalent in French
for *Abteilung* (13–14); while the names "Sajer" and "Wesreidau" cannot
be found on the available personnel rolls of the Grossdeutschland, this
fact is irrelevant, since many wartime divisional records have been "lost,"
"destroyed," or "seized in Berlin by the Russians" (14–15, 19); and if
Sajer misplaces his uniform's insignia, this inaccuracy means little: Sajer
is often "careless" about details, the location of the unit cuff title on his
uniform being one of them (15).

The controversy, which started in *Army History*, continued in letters to
the *Military Review*, but neither of the two specialists brought new arguments that would definitively solve the case. Kennedy, in his last contribution to the debate, still deemed *Le Soldat oublié* to be a piece of fiction,
one that "professional soldiers" should not use as a "legitimate historical

reference" providing useful information about the Eastern Front (1997, 3). Nash, on the other hand, remained persuaded not just of the genuineness of the book, but of its pedagogical value for members of the armed forces. If readers want to know, he wrote, "what it was like to be a Russian Front soldier, to be afraid, to fight alongside a band of brothers," then Sajer's is still "one of the finest accounts," and one that "deserves to remain on professional military reading lists" (1998, 3). Nash also mentioned that a book published during his debate with Kennedy by the military historian Stephan G. Fritz: *Frontsoldaten: The German Soldier in World War II* (1995) does not just quote Sajer, but uses *Le Soldat oublié* as one of its main sources and never raises issues of authenticity about this text. Nash did not bring up that Sajer's book is also quoted in another, celebrated study about World War II, Omer Bartov's *Hitler's Army*. Specifically, Bartov (1991, 117) quotes from the passage in which Sajer reproduces a speech by Wesreidau, his company commander – a speech that Bartov regards as representative of the way junior officers, indoctrinated by National Socialism, sought in turn to instil National Socialist values in their men. Yet Bartov, no more than Fritz, seems to be aware of the problems surrounding *Le Soldat oublié* in general, the existence of a Grossdeutschland officer by the name of "Wesreidau" in particular. Unlike the career soldiers I quoted earlier, who implicitly rehabilitate the German army when they pick Sajer's memoir for their "Bookshelf," Bartov cites that same text to bolster his thesis about the Wehrmacht; that is, to debunk the myth of an apolitical, "clean" Wehrmacht that had nothing to do with the crimes committed by such corps as the Waffen-SS and the Einsatzgruppen.[3]

Sajer himself has hardly commented on the controversies surrounding his book in the United States. Asked by Nash to provide his standpoint, he was difficult to locate (he lived in a rural village east of Paris) and slow to respond. In a letter to the German historian Klaus Schulz, whom Nash had used as a middleman, he acknowledged his "mistakes" but also expressed his irritation toward the "historians and archivists" who asked

---

[3] The latest American edition of *Le Soldat oublié* (Potomac Books, 2000) adds a new twist to the debate. Although it does not include an introduction that would discuss the problems related to the authenticity of the book, it admits 49 photographs, of which 25 have excerpts from Sajer's text as captions. The caption of a house burning, for example, reads "Toward noon the next day ... the place was filled with smoke'" (n.p.), making it difficult not to infer (1) that the photograph illustrates what Sajer states happened "toward noon the next day," and (2) that the book is authentic, since it contains photographs illustrating the text. None of the photos in the Potomac edition is credited, and only seven make a specific reference to time and/or place.

him "questions of chronology, situations, dates, and unimportant details" (Nash 1997, 17). Indeed, his intention was never to produce a "historical reference book" that could be used in military academies; rather, it was to write about his "innermost emotional experiences, as they related to the events that happened to [him] in the context of the Second World War" (17). Sajer made similar comments in a letter that he finally sent to Nash himself. Accounting for his inaccuracies, he also implicitly asserted his presence on the Eastern Front when he made such statements as "we didn't know exactly where we were ... in the black Russia of winter, I would not have been surprised if someone had told me that we were in China" (Nash 1997, 18). Likewise, his responses in a long interview about the movie *Stalingrad*, published in *39/45 Magazine*, were those of someone who positions himself as an actual witness. By answering a question about the way German soldiers' attitudes are depicted in the movie with the affirmation "Yes, that's how it was" (1993, 5), Sajer again implicitly affirmed that he fought in the Soviet Union. The editors of *39/45 Magazine*, for that matter, apparently had no hesitation consulting Sajer as an expert on the subject "Eastern Front." As for Sajer himself, he seemed to be less reluctant to answer their questions than he was to respond to the "archivists and historians" he angrily mentions in his letter to Schulz.

Lacking qualifications to intervene in this debate, I will only append a few data that my investigation of Sajer's biography has produced. First, as Kennedy himself recognizes (1997, 2), Sajer is a "real guy"; he has a physical existence, even though pictures of him are most rare. "Sajer" is his mother's maiden name, while his original last name is "Mouminoux." He enlisted in the Wehrmacht under "Sajer" because it sounded more German, and also to avoid possible ridicule: "Mouminoux" is the homonym of *mou minou* (soft kitten), and one imagines the jokes that army men familiar with the French language could have made about this surname.[4] Sajer kept using his mother's maiden name after the war, and he wrote *Le Soldat oublié* under it; the correspondence and interviews I quoted were also conducted with "Guy Sajer." Yet Sajer has still a third identity. Under the pen name "Dimitri," he is a well-known and prolific author of comic strips and graphic novels, which have been serialized in

---

[4] In *Le Soldat oublié*, Sajer writes that mistaken at the end of the war for a *malgré nous* (an Alsatian forcibly enrolled in the Wehrmacht), he signed the form for enlisting in the French army with his French surname "in order to avoid further trouble" (1967, 539). Sajer does not spell out this "French surname," but one can guess that he enrolled under "Mouminoux."

French magazines specializing in that genre, such as *Spirou, Tintin, Pilote,* and *L'Echo des savanes.* As *Le Soldat oublié* does, some of these texts, for instance, *Kursk* (about the battle in the Ukraine), *Kaleunt* (about German submarines), and *Kamikazes* (about Japanese pilots), stage World War II episodes recounted from the perspective of the Axis. Sajer has told about his career as a graphic artist in a memoir: *La BD: Un merveilleux métier de chien* [Comic Strip Artist: A Marvelous Dog's Trade], which gives an image of him that markedly differs from the picture of a bitter, misanthropic recluse that he offers in his letters to Nash and Schulz. Indeed, as he portrays himself in *La BD*, Sajer is not, or not only, a "dark, pessimistic personality," who prefers "to live with the memories of his wartime service, while holding the current world in contempt" (Nash 1997, 17). As a graphic artist at least, he is also an engaging character who frequently travels from his house in the country to Paris in order to discuss business with publishers and get together with fellow artists and writers. Thus, *La BD* includes several accounts (137–49) of meeting with the boisterous editors of the satirical magazines *Charlie-Hebdo, Hara-Kiri,* and *Charlie Mensuel* – meetings that according to Sajer would inevitably end in lengthy meals and heavy drinking. As if to separate his activities as a memoirist and an author of comic strips, Sajer does not refer to *Le Soldat oublié* by name in *La BD*. He merely mentions that for some time, "at night, [he] plunged body and soul into a narrative he had started about a painful period in [his] youth" (114), and only returns to this subject to bring up that the "long, very long autobiography [he] had written about a certain journey of [his]," had received the Deux-Magots prize (134). Whether Sajer's choice not to mix his former and present lives can be traced to modesty, to the difficult position of a former collaborationist, or to the discretion of the author of a hoax, is of course open to question. Such a reserve, however, is not unusual among victims or witnesses of traumatic events – a point to which I will return when examining the postwar attitudes of the volunteers, as displayed in their memoirs.

INTERNET DEBATES

Since the popularization of the Internet, discussions about World War II in general and the foreign volunteers who fought for Germany in particular have often been conducted on sites dedicated to these topics, such as feldgrau.com, axishistory.com, and division-charlemagne.com. Like most Internet debates, these discussions usually have little value from a scholarly standpoint; the contributors generally use pseudonyms, and the opinions that they express remain, in most instances, unsubstantiated. I will nevertheless give a few examples of these exchanges, as the places where they are conducted constitute, after all, what Pierre Nora (15) calls "sites of memory": places where memory is inscribed, as it is in manuals, dictionaries, and museums. Such sites, moreover, are often the only venues where the works I am studying are considered, and it might be useful to take a close look at some of the comments that can be found there.

Sajer – to return briefly to his case – has been the subject not just of articles in military journals, but of countless posts on sites devoted to World War II. The forum of ww2incolor.com, for example, contains numerous assessments of *Le Soldat oublié*, coming from fellow soldiers who sometimes provide their rank and a portrait of themselves with helmet or cap that add authority to their evaluations. Thus, Sergeant Major "Hosenfield" writes that Sajer's book is still "one of the best written war memoirs ever with deep personal analysis"; and Corporal "Trooper," that his "instinct" tells him the book is "authentic," as "only a soldier would be able to describe the horrors, hardships and comradship with such intensity." Private First Class "Rockatansky," on the other hand, believes that Sajer "added to his own personal experience in the war to create the book ... as Remarque did in *All Quiet on the Western Front*"; and Staff Sergeant "FluffyBunnyGB," that *Le Soldat oublié* is "a bit of a cross-over, somewhere with Sven Hassel's *Legion of the Damned*."[5] Apart from these mere opinions, the only real argument I found in the admittedly small sample I consulted on ww2incolor.com, originates with "arhob1," a sergeant based in Blighty, Gloucestershire, England. Apparently aware of the controversies about the nonexistent 17th Battalion of the Grossdeutschland, "arhob1" writes: "I have heard of many young soldiers in the British Army who don't know what Division they are in, so as the author was only 16–20 years old at the time it wouldn't be too surprising if he got a few things wrong." To be sure, it might be imprudent to compare young soldiers of the twenty-first century with motivated volunteers fighting in World War II. But "arhol1," unlike his fellow panelists (who just assert), seeks here to argue by using analogy, and the move is too rare on this type of site to remain unnoticed. (All quotations on http://www2incolor.com/forum. 4/22/2007).[6]

---

[5] A Dane naturalized German, Hassel wrote several books supposedly based on his experience as a soldier during World War II. Like Sajer's, his claim to report what he himself had lived through has been questioned.

[6] I have taken these posts at face value, but I am not unaware that some of them could be fakes: "arhob1" could be anybody eager to play a British sergeant and deride the current

Opinions, however, can be expressed on the Internet with much more harshness than they have on the posts I have just quoted. Discussing books about the French Waffen-SS on the site division-charlemagne.com, the page's webmaster (frank.lesseire@division-charlemagne.com) thus issues a strong "warning" about Mit's *Carcasse à vendre*, which he dismisses as "a hoax in all its glory," whose author "is completely delirious." Mit, as mentioned earlier, is one of the problematic figures among the volunteers-turned-memoirists, since he has never been interviewed nor photographed, and *Carcasse à vendre* is the only text published under his name. Yet Lesseire does not elaborate upon his "warning." He does not ask, for instance, why scholars like Gordon and Giolitto refer to Mit without apparent reservation. More basically, he does not explain where the problem exactly resides: If Mit was not on the Eastern Front, where did he spend the war? And if he was there but did not experience what he claims that he did, where are the discrepancies? In short, Lesseire cautions in his post that *Carcasse à vendre* raises serious issues. But he does not even begin to take them up, thus posing acutely the problem of Internet sites and the definitive judgments that often are made through them. (Quotes on http://division-charlemagne.com.1/25/2008.)

Apart from Sajer's, the most debated case about my memoirists on the Internet has probably been Gilles's. A member of the Division Charlemagne, Gilles kept serving extremist causes after the war, joining the Organisation Armée Secrète (OAS) during the Algerian conflict and then Le Pen's Front National in the 1970s. In 1989, he published *Un ancien SS français raconte*, the story of his exploits in Pomerania with the Charlemagne. The book came with warranties: pictures of Gilles in SS uniform, detailed maps of the locations where Gilles and his comrades had fought, and a preface by Colonel Argoud, a noted supporter of *Algérie française* whom Gilles had met in jail after the two men had been sentenced for their OAS activities. However, Gilles had already recounted his adventures to some people earlier. He certainly had talked to Saint-Loup, who in *Les Hérétiques* (Saint-Loup's "history" of the French SS) stages a

---

state of the British Army. I do not know what kind of control the webmasters of the site "ww2incolor.com" actually exercise, specifically what kind of identification the panelists are supposed to provide before being allowed to contribute. I have also restricted my sample to posts written by soldiers, or people claiming to be soldiers, on sites devoted to things military. But Amazon.com, in November 2009, had 214 customer reviews of the English-language version of Sajer's memoir, running the gamut from enthusiastic endorsements to indictments of the book either for being a hoax or for presenting the standpoint of someone who took part in a war of extermination. Amazon's French site (Amazon.fr) had only 14 reviews of *Le Soldat oublié*, none of which holding the book to be a hoax.

"Gillet" whose journey from Heinrichswalde to Belgard to Dievenow is exactly the narrator's in *Un ancien SS français raconte* (Saint-Loup 1965, e.g., 183, 185, 199, 268, 295–96, 325, 334, 341–42). He also had been interviewed by Jean Piverd for the special issue of the magazine *Historia* on *L'Internationale SS*, where the story of "Gilbert G…", a Charlemagne veteran who later became active in the OAS, again is exactly his (Piverd 1973, 181). At this point, Gilles's biography seemed unproblematic: A POW in Germany, he had become a member of the Charlemagne in 1944, and *Un ancien SS français raconte* was the narrative of his ordeals in Pomerania in early 1945. Things became more complicated in the late 1990s, when Gilles published a series of books about the campaigns of the Waffen-SS in the Ukraine, claiming that he had participated in such battles as Belgorod, Kursk, and Zhitomir. Likewise, whereas his biography in *Historia* states that he had volunteered for the Charlemagne in November 1944, an interview in "Frankreich" (one of the Internet sites devoted to the French SS) offered a different story: Gilles had joined the Waffen-SS in 1942 already, using a false ID that had made him an ethnic German (*Volksdeutsch*). Thus, the adventures recounted in *SS Kommando, Bielgorod, Citadelle*, and *Shitomir* were his – those of a French who had been a member of an SS Panzer Division before transferring to the Charlemagne.[7] (Interview on http://perso.wanadoo.fr/waffen/interview.htm. 11/5/2004)

While Gilles is discussed neither by professional historians such as Gordon and Giolitto, nor by career soldiers such as Nash and Kennedy, specific aspects of his biography have been questioned on the Internet. In a "note" to Gilles's interview, for example, the webmaster of the site "Frankreich" argued that Gilles does not provide any evidence to support his claim he was in the Waffen-SS, and that his arm does not bear the tattoo, indicating one's blood group, which every SS received during the process of enlistment. Lesseire, the webmaster of Division-Charlemagne.com, had similar doubts about Gilles's joining the SS in 1942. Also pointing out the lack of tattoo on Gilles's arm, he added that Gilles was too short to enter an organization that was still elitist at the time, and that the story of the false ID is most implausible. Finally, Lesseire was concerned with Gilles's photograph in German uniform displayed on the back cover of the first volume of *Un ancien SS français raconte*. Indeed, Gilles affirmed in his *Historia* interview that he was proposed for a 2nd class Iron Cross after being wounded in Pomerania, but that he actually never received

---

[7] The spelling of Russian places is Gilles's. Standard spelling in English are "Belgorod" and "Zhitomir."

his decoration. Yet the photograph to which Lesseire refers, supposedly taken in 1945, shows Gilles wearing an Iron Cross. Is it a photomontage? Lesseire is inclined to think so, even more since Gilles, contradicting his declarations in *Historia*, told him in a letter that he was actually the recipient not of a 2nd, but of a 1st class Iron Cross. Lesseire does not tell whether the decoration on Gilles's chest in the picture he incriminates is a 1st or 2nd class Iron Cross, but LFV and French SS historians Lambert and Le Marec (174) would say that it is a 1st class; the 2nd class was worn "from the second button of the jacket," the 1st, "on the left pocket of the jacket," and Gilles wears his decoration on the left pocket.

Georges Scapini, the World War I veteran and politician sent by Vichy to Berlin as an "ambassador" to negotiate the fate of the French POWs, died too early (in 1976) to contribute to this debate. His memoir, *Mission sans gloire* [Mission without Glory], however, contradicts another, basic aspect of Gilles's story. Reporting his unpleasant exchanges with Nazi officials who insisted that French POWs be allowed to join the LVF or the SS, Scapini maintains that no French POW actually enlisted (142–5). Like most memoirs written by former members of the Vichy government, Scapini's reminiscences are self-serving; the ambassador is anxious to demonstrate that his mission, though "without glory," was still in some respect beneficial to France. It remains that Gilles is the only one not just among my memoirists, but among the volunteers whose biographies I have come across, who claims to have gone from a POW camp to the SS, and that claim alone is sufficient to make inquisitive readers ask questions about the exact nature of the texts he has written. Conversely, taken at face value, Gilles's "memoirs" raise issues about the trajectory of some French POWs; against Scapini's testimony, they evoke the possibility that a few of them might in fact have become members of German units, as some Belgian POWs became members of the Légion Wallonie, and many Russian POWs became members of the army of opponents to the Soviet regime that General Vlasov had organized.[8]

Do the problems of authenticity and discursive genre posed by such works as Sajer's and Gilles's actually matter? The polemics that have

---

[8] In an article about the reasons that led some French men to join the SS, François Delatour quotes from an interview in which a former prisoner explains that he had enlisted while he was in a stalag, after learning that "prisoners could become members of the Waffen-SS" (118). Delatour, however, provides neither the name of the prisoner nor the circumstances of the interview. Christophe Belser, in his study of the collaboration in the Loire-Inférieure area, also mentions a career soldier who went from a stalag to the LVF to the SS, but his information is grounded in departmental archives (316). On the recruitment of Belgian POWs in the Légion Wallonie, see de Bruyne and Rikmenspoel, 114–15; of Russian POWs in the Vlasov army, see Müller, 216–22.

followed the publication of *Le Soldat oublié* and *Un ancien SS français raconte* show that they do. To begin with, the discussions about those works that have taken place in military journals as well as on the Internet confirm what the Wilkomirski affair had already revealed: The distinction between referential and fictional texts is still fundamental in our culture, and offering as referential a text that actually is fictional will be perceived as a breach of contract by most readers when they become aware of the deceit. What these discussions attest to, moreover, is that determining the exact status of a text is sometimes difficult, especially if that text is presented as an authentic testimony but was written by an individual who is not a major figure and whose activities have left few (if any) traces in the public record. In the instance of Sajer's, Mit's, and Gilles's narratives, establishing whether these texts are hoaxes or not would need lengthier investigations than those conducted in the *Army Review* or on Internet sites. More precisely, it would need going beyond the internal criticism of the memoir, beyond a mere search for inconsistencies, such as Sajer's "mistake" about the location of the Grossdeutschland insignia on the sleeve of his jacket. No historian or journalist, at this point, has been willing to undertake for *Le Soldat oublié*, *Carcasse à vendre*, or *Un ancien SS français raconte* the kind of research that Stefan Maechler conducted to write *The Wilkormiski Affair*. Thus, the epistemological status of these texts remains unsettled, because their authors still insist that they are authentic and doubting critics have not come up with the hard facts that would invalidate that claim.

AUTHORSHIPS

The last questions I want to raise about the memoirs produced by the former volunteers concern literary proficiency. If the authors of these texts really were where they claim to have been, and if their works are in this regard genuine, did they write up their recollections themselves? Were they helped by editors or ghostwriters? If they were, what was the extent of this assistance? In short, are the works in my corpus also "authentic" in the sense of "actually written by the person whose name is given as the author's on the front cover"? Such questions deserve to be asked, because conducting a narrative over several hundred pages is no easy task. In French, the difficulty is compounded by the fact that writing a story in a past tense requires the use of a special, literary form that is rarely employed in oral communication: the *passé simple*, with its correlates *passé antérieur* and *subjonctif imparfait*. Of course, the difficulty can be circumvented. Auvray and Larfoux give their testimonies the form of a diary, a strategy that enables them to use the present as well as the *passé composé* as basic tenses for their narratives. Similarly, Rostaing, Rusco, Philippet, Emmanuelli, and the author of *Vae Victis* adopt the so-called "historical" (or "narrative") present, thus making their job as storytellers much easier. Still, most of the authors in my corpus play the game by the rules, pressing their *passé simple* and *subjonctif imparfait* into service with zeal, as Malbosse and Sajer do in the following excerpts:

Je *retrouvai* mon chef de service et lui fis mon rapport. Il *envoya* une estafette à l'officier allemand qui assurait le commandement depuis la disparition du général Puaud, et nous *invita* à attendre sans plus nous tracasser l'arrivée des ordres. Un camion qui, lui aussi, faisait demi tour, nous *lança* au passage quelques colis de la Croix-Rouge. Installés dans un petit bois, nous nous *mîmes à* manger tranquillement.

[I rejoined my Section head and gave him my report. He dispatched someone to the German officer who was in charge since the disappearance of General Puaud and asked us to wait for orders without worrying any longer. A truck that was making a U-turn threw us a few food parcels from the Red Cross. Set up in a small wood, we started to eat quietly.] (Malbosse 15, my emphasis)

Une heure plus tard, notre train roulait, entre deux haies de construction qui, malgré l'absence d'éclairage, nous semblaient plus ou moins détruites. Nous *croisâmes* un autre train moins sinistre que le précédent, mais guère réconfortant. Il était formé de wagons marqués de croix rouges. Nous *aperçumes* par les fenêtres des civières; il devait s'agir de grands blessés pour qu'on les *transportât* ainsi. A d'autres fenêtres, des soldats couverts de pansements nous faisaient des signes d'amitié.

[One hour later, our train was riding between two rows of buildings that, despite the lack of lighting, appeared more or less destroyed. We passed another train that was less sinister than the preceding one, though hardly cheering. It was made of large cars marked with red crosses. Through the windows, we saw stretchers; they were probably holding soldiers who were gravely wounded. At other windows, soldiers who were covered with dressings were waving to us in friendship.] (Sajer 1967, 34, my emphasis)

The literariness in these few lines does not only originate in the use of certain tenses. It also results from the conjunction of those tenses with the first person, a most unusual combination. Indeed, the *passé simple* normally co-occurs with the third person to produce the standard, classical narrative that works of novelists such as Balzac, Stendhal, Zola, and Malraux have exemplified. Many educated French would probably be challenged if asked to tell a story in the first person using the *passé simple*, and to complete that task, they would probably need to rely on

Bescherelle's *L'Art de conjuguer* or on another verb book that provides conjugations.

Two hypotheses account for the ability of the former volunteers to employ the conventions of formal, literary narrative. (I am, of course, not considering the cases of the professional writers Laurier and Saint-Loup, the journalist Leverrier, and the politician Degrelle, who were used to composing texts.) The first one is that the authors were helped by ghostwriters, according to the "X with Z" format of life narrative. Books produced according to that formula are not necessarily less valuable than those with a single author, as evidenced by such works as *The Autobiography of Malcom X*, based on taped interviews of the African-American Liberation leader with the journalist Alex Haley, and the already mentioned *I, Rigoberta Menchù: An Indian Woman in Guatemala*, based on similar interviews of Menchù with the anthropologist Elisabeth Burgos. Yet, as Thomas Couser (37–39) has argued, this type of "ethnographic autobiography" must be distinguished from the "celebrity autobiography," which recounts an athlete's or a show business personality's life "as told to," and whose main purpose is to cash in on the fame of the central character (on the model of the soccer player Zinédine Zidane's *Le Roman d'une victoire* [The Novel of a Victory], Zidane's account of France's victory at the 1998 World Cup written "with" Dan Frank, a specialist of this kind of partnership). In my corpus, Costabrava's *Le Soldat Baraka*, Rostaing's *Le Prix d'un serment* [The Price of an Oath] and Rusco's *Stoï!* were explicitly coauthored. Although the veterans did not collaborate with people trained in oral history, the life stories that they brought out must be regarded as "ethnographic"; authors and publishers aimed mainly to contribute to the history of World War II, as "cashing in" could not have been a realistic goal given the authors' lack of notoriety. Costabrava worked with Frédéric Loeuillet, a student at the University of Nice who explains in an introduction that he met the veteran through a friend, and that his interlocutor was at first reluctant to talk; he eventually did after "mutual respect and shared trust" had developed (3), the result being a book in which the former volunteer reports "just the facts … as he remembers to have experienced them" (4). Likewise, Rostaing collaborated with Pierre Demaret, a journalist familiar with this kind of teamwork and not averse to taking up the case of compromised individuals, such as French Gestapo member Pierre Bonny, whose biography, *Mon père l'inspecteur Bonny* [My Father, Detective Bonny], Demaret helped Bonny's son jot down. The first, 1975 La Table Ronde edition of *Le Prix d'un serment* mentions on its title page "Souvenirs recueillis par Pierre

Demaret," and the latter explains in a preface how, as a writer "with a passion for history," he met Rostaing for an interview that turned into a book (9). The reedition of the book by Irminsul in 2003, however, does not include any reference to Demaret's role, an omission not without consequences. Rostaing now seems to be the only author of the memoir, readers remaining uninformed of the collaboration. As for Rusco, he wrote his book "with" Philippe Randa, a right-wing author and publisher responsible for several works, including a *Dictionnaire commenté de la collaboration française* that shows much empathy with the Vichy regime. *Stoï*'s title page, below the name "Pierre Rusco," specifies "avec la collaboration de Philippe Randa," the editor telling in a preface similar to Loeuillet's and Demaret's how the book was made, in this instance, using the "notes" Rusco had taken and the "reminiscences" he was anxious to share (5). The implicit admission, in these cases, is that the stories of Costabrava, Rostaing, and Rusco were worth recounting, but that the three men needed assistance. How much assistance, we do not know. The coauthors acknowledge their mediation, but they do not specify the exact meaning of "recueilli par" (literally "recorded by") and "avec la collaboration de." Only the tapes of the conversations with Costabrava-Loeuillet, Rostaing-Dumaret, and Rusco-Randa could tell this (if they exist), allowing us to compare the oral and written versions of the same materials, as Lejeune (1980, 229–316) was able to do in his study of the "autobiographies of those who do not write," notably, of *Mémé Santerre* [Grandma Santerre], the best-selling memoir of a seamstress written "with" the journalist Serge Grafteaux.[9]

The second hypothesis is to give the authors the benefit of the doubt, that is, to assume that their education prepared them to write, and that reading other peoples' life stories, especially war memoirs, had made them internalize the conventions of the genre. As far as degrees are concerned, some of the volunteers were university graduates: Bassompierre had studied law, Labat owned a *Licence en lettres*, and Gaultier, a *Diplôme d'études supérieures de lettres classiques*, by and large the equivalent of Master's Degrees in Literature and Classics. Others, like Bayle, Mit, Malbosse, Sajer, and Philippet, were not of college age when they enlisted, but the type of training that students were undergoing in lycées at the time, especially in the area of writing, might have prepared them to

---

[9] In acknowledgments, Levast and Malardier credit the publication of their memoirs to the historian Henri Mounine, a specialist of France's military collaboration who wrote books about the French SS training camp in Sennheim (Cernay) and the battle of Kolberg. However, neither specifies the nature nor the extent of Mounine's contribution.

compose a narrative. Others still received additional practice during the war: Labat (265) affirms that he contributed articles to *Le Combattant Européen* [The European Fighter], the magazine of the LVF, and La Mazière (1972, 20), that he wrote for *Le Pays Libre* [The Free Country], the journal of Pierre Clementi's collaborationist Parti Français National-Collectiviste. Finally, several among the veterans had successful careers after the war: Bayle became a business executive, Leverrier worked for publishing houses, Gaultier and La Mazière had jobs in public relations, and Sajer, as mentioned, turned to making comic strips and graphic novels. Such lines of work involve writing, though admittedly not of the type "life narrative," and their professions, in addition to their readings, might have prepared these former soldiers to become memoirists.[10]

The way some of the volunteers' testimonies were produced remains problematic, however. Emmanuelli, for example, claims to be writing from his exile in Costa Rica when he is fifty-seven years old, after spending several years in jail and in the Foreign Legion (411, 415); he does not explain, however, how someone who describes himself as an uneducated, hard-living man has acquired the skills that enable him to recount his life over 400 pages. The paratext does not answer these questions, either. Laffont, which brought out the book in its series *Vécu*, does not include a "Publisher's note" tracing the history of the text, as it had done a few years earlier for Sajer's *Le Soldat oublié*. It is thus conceivable that *Et j'ai cassé mon fusil* constitutes in fact a "X with Z" type of memoir, though one in which the collaboration is unacknowledged.[11] However that might be, this book remains a prime example of suspicion-raising testimony. Indeed, the performance of the memoirist as a writer does not agree with the idea he gives of his competence, and this discrepancy can only make readers ask whether *Et j'ai cassé mon fusil* is "authentic," in the sense of

---

[10] Although the volunteers obviously had read other peoples' memoirs, it is difficult to pinpoint which ones they might have had in mind when they wrote down their own recollections. Among the numerous historical and literary texts to which they refer in their accounts (see Chapter 5), none can be viewed as a model for a life narrative in general and a war memoir in particular.

[11] Charles Ronsac, who was running the Laffont series *Vécu* when *Et j'ai cassé mon fusil* was published, does not provide any information about the way Emmanuelli's book was produced in his own memoir *Trois noms pour une vie* [Three Names for a Life]. Neither, for that matter, does he comment on Sajer's *Le Soldat oublié* and La Mazière's *Le Rêveur casqué*, which appeared in that same series. He devotes most of his narrative to the series' bestsellers, such as the memoirs of Iran's former Queen Soraya, of French movie star Michèle Morgan, and of Russian dancer (and "dissident") Rudolf Nureyev, explaining how producing those memoirs necessitated the help of up to three "collaborators," who delivered several rewrites.

"entirely written by the person whose name figures on the book's front page as that of the sole author." Such doubts, as is always the case with issues of authenticity, have legal and ethical aspects. From a legal standpoint, it matters to know who did what, if only to find out whether royalties were distributed in equitable fashion – for instance, whether Demaret received his due when Irminsul republished *Le Prix d'un serment* under Rostaing's name alone, as though the veteran had written the book by himself. In the area of ethics, as Thomas Couser points out while discussing coauthorship, unacknowledged collaborations undermine the "truthfulness of the portrayal"; they falsify both the "history" and the "image" of the author, since the latter "did not labor single-handedly" and may in fact not be capable of composing a coherent narrative (50).

While the texts in my corpus reveal a proficiency that is at times surprising given the fact that their authors are not professional writers, not all of them are equally well organized and skillfully written. Problems are especially evident in the case of self-published books or books published at the author's expense, such as those of Gilles. In the area of storytelling, Gilles's works are indeed among the utmost representatives of the paratactic narrative, that is, of a narrative in which episodes are merely juxtaposed or linked to each other with an artless "and then." Thus, the two volumes of *Un ancien SS français raconte* enumerate over 800 pages what happened to Gilles and his unit during the few weeks the Division Charlemagne fought in Pomerania. The narrative proceeds from one event to the next in the way of a chronicle, as Gilles describes places at length but says little about elapsed time. Reading, therefore, soon becomes strenuous, because details accumulate but no plot ever develops that would generate "effects of suspense" (what will happen?) or "effects of surprise" (how could that happen?), as it does in a "good," well-formed narrative (Baroni, 99–100). In one of the appendices he adds to the second volume of *Un ancien SS français raconte*, Gilles explains how the manuscript of this text was saved from a criminal fire (II, 381–2), but he does not contribute any information about its further history. As a result, we do not know whether he submitted his work to commercial publishers before turning to "Gold Mail International Publishing" in Clearwater, Florida, a company that invites prospective customers to contact "Fox and Pitt Management," a distributor based in Charleroi, Belgium. If *Un ancien SS français raconte* was indeed rejected by commercial presses, we are not told whether that decision was due to the controversial nature of the book's subject, to some kind of ostracism toward an author whose past was tainted, or merely to what publishers perceived as problems of writing – problems that the best editors would have trouble fixing. At any rate, whereas the legitimacy of Gilles as a witness has been questioned, nobody, to my knowledge, has doubted that he wrote his books himself. Problems of authenticity, in his case, concern his alleged presence in some corners of the Soviet Union and northeastern Germany, not the authorship of works that few people would claim as their own to begin with.

3

Veracity

Memoirs raise issues of veracity that are even more complex than the issues of authenticity I have just considered. For the basic question that they involve is no longer simply: Was the memoirist really there? It becomes: If the memoirist was there, is he reliable? And this question cannot in most cases be answered in the form of "yes" or "no." Thus, the essential problem about such people as Sajer and Gilles is to find out whether they fought in the Soviet Union or not. If they did not, their writings are definitely disqualified from the discursive and epistemological category "memoir." If they did, the matter is to determine to what extent the stories they tell are dependable, and on what points they can be challenged. In brief, what is at stake now is not the text as a whole; it is part of the text, whose overall status as a valid testimony basically is not at risk. James Frey's best-selling *A Million Little Pieces* (2005), to take another well-publicized example of "fraud," was exposed as questionable not in the area of authenticity, but in that of veracity. Frey undoubtedly had a drug habit; but he made up or exaggerated several items in the account of his journey from addiction to recovery, distortions to which he admitted when confronted with such evidence as police records of his arrests. The new edition of *A Million Little Pieces* includes a "Publisher's note" and a "Note to the reader" in which both the publisher and the author acknowledge the deceit, Frey admitting that he has "embellished many details in [his] past experience."

Whatever the discursive and epistemological status of *A Million Little Pieces* might be, scrupulous witnesses are not necessarily more dependable than Frey when they claim to report what they have lived through "to the best of their recollection." In the early twentieth century, experiments conducted by the psychologist Alfred Binet and his disciples showed how difficult it was for people to retrieve the information they had received and stored. Asked to look at a picture, to listen to a story, and to watch a staged event, most members of a test group were unable afterward to answer simple questions concerning the materials, for example, the appearance and clothing of the people who figured in the picture (Larguier des Bancels 1906). More recent research by such specialists on eyewitness testimony as Renaud Dulong (1998) and Elizabeth Loftus (2000) has led to similar conclusions. According to these scholars, no witness, whatever his/her authority and good faith might be, can be held as entirely reliable; what s/he says on the stand or writes in his/her memoirs must always be probed against other testimonies and other types of evidence. To be sure, the distinction between false and true testimony still applies. But even the most honest witness can err and provide information that must be labeled as "doubtful," because sincerity is not synonymous with perfect recall.

THE FRENCH IN BERLIN

The veracity of what the French volunteers are stating in their memoirs is especially difficult to assess. Unlike Binet and his students, we rarely have the "correct" picture or story, in this instance, a standard, "confirmed by evidence" version of an event, against which the accuracy of the version of that event offered in such texts as *Frères ennemis* [Enemy Brothers] and *Les derniers grognards* could be measured. Nor do the volunteers' reminiscences have critical editions, in which a scholar would assess the credibility of the account that the author is providing; only Marotel's *La longue marche* is prefaced and annotated by an historian, the specialist of France's military collaboration Eric Lefèvre, who adds information to Marotel's text and occasionally amends its inaccuracies. In the case of the French volunteers' memoirs, problems of veracity are compounded by the fact that testifying has an ethical dimension: The witness makes a specific promise, namely that he has seen the event and that he reports it "as he has seen it." Yet the value of a testimony does not depend only on the presence of the witness at a certain time and place; as Dulong has argued, it is also contingent upon his "credit," upon the "trust granted an individual prior to his story" (1998, 15). The question, therefore, is to determine to what extent someone who made choices generally viewed as "wrong" can nevertheless be a "good" witness, in the sense of a witness "reliable in the area about which he is called to testify." In the case of the volunteers, it is to determine whether a veteran of the LVF or the Waffen-SS, who at the start certainly has less credibility than a member of the Resistance or the Leclerc Army, can still be trusted when it comes to explaining, say, why he enlisted and what he actually accomplished in the snows of Belorussia and Pomerania.

The issue of the French participation in the battle of Berlin in late April–early May 1945 constitutes an interesting test case. Participation in itself has not been challenged. Historians of the "last battle," such as Anthony Beevor, Erich Kuby, Tony Le Tissier, Anthony Read and David Fisher, Pierre Rocolle, and Cornelius Ryan, all acknowledge the role of the Charlemagne in defending the German capital. Furthermore, they generally tell the same story. Carried in the chaotic retreat of the German army from Pomerania in February–March 1945, the Charlemagne regrouped in the Neustrelitz area, about 80 miles north of Berlin; of the 7,000 men who had trained in Wildflecken during the winter 1944–45, about 1,000 were left (Mabire 1975, 74). A few of them, led by the SS Brigadeführer Krukenberg, were trucked to Berlin on April 24. After briefly resting in Grünewald, a wooded area in the southwestern part of the city, they moved east to the Neukölln neighborhood on April 25, where they joined the Scandinavian SS Division Nordland. Slowly pulling north, they successively defended the Neukölln city hall, the Hermannplatz, the Belle-Alliance Platz (named in memory of the battle of Waterloo – an ironic situation), and a series of positions along the centrally located Wilhelmstrasse and Friedrichstrasse.[1] On May 2, when General Weidling announced the capitulation of the city (Hitler committed suicide on May 1), they were still holding the intersection Wilhelmstrasse-Prinz-Albrecht-Strasse, two blocks from the Chancellery they were in charge of protecting. Some managed to escape, whereas others were taken prisoner by the Russians and later handed over to the French military police.

While the presence of the Charlemagne in Berlin is uncontested, the question of how many of its members actually took part in the defense of the capital has been widely debated. On this subject, witnesses disagree. Rostaing, the only one of my memoirists with Levast and Malardier who participated in the battle, writes that 125 members of his company "stepped forward without hesitating one second" when Krukenberg asked

---

[1] Like several streets and squares in Berlin, the Belle Alliance Platz was renamed after 1945; it is now called Franz-Mehring-Platz. A journalist and a member of the Social Democratic Party, Franz Mehring (1846–1919) joined in 1916 the recently founded Spartacist League, together with Karl Liebknecht and Rosa Luxemburg. His works include a study of the Thirty Years' War and an exhaustive biography of Karl Marx.

for volunteers on April 24 (186). Yet Rostaing does not tell whether other companies joined his, and Levast (99) does not mention numbers, while Malardier (139) affirms that at least 300 men boarded the trucks that were waiting in Neustrelitz. Fernet, who was in the same unit as Rostaing, states in a *Historia* article that two of those trucks got lost; according to his "estimations," "about 200 men" eventually reached the city (156). Bayle ups these numbers to "350 men" (2008, 179), and Soulat, the secretary of the Charlemagne whose unpublished manuscript some historians have been able to consult, to as many as "500" (Rousso 1980, 227). Yet Krukenberg holds the last two figures to be grossly inflated. In his report "Kampftage in Berlin," he explains that no more than ninety volunteers accompanied him from Neustrelitz to Berlin (1964, 4); the other members of the Division either elected not to join or were left at the camp because trucks were not in sufficient number to transport all the men who were eager to keep fighting. Krukenberg's version has, in turn, been challenged by some of the participants who have surmised that the Brigadeführer intentionally underestimated the number of French volunteers in Berlin. According to Malardier, for example, Krukenberg first used the figure of ninety men when he was interrogated by the Russians after his arrest in May 1945; he stuck to it because he was "acutely aware of the danger of reprisals" faced by Charlemagne veterans (140), and – as a leader most conscious of his responsibilities – he did not want to alert the Allies' justice system to the fact that hundreds of French volunteers had served under him in Berlin.

Historians who have investigated the issue have been unable to establish on the basis of archival evidence which one among these versions is the most reliable. The numbers they are using, as a result, seem to originate less in their research than in their specialization and position on the political spectrum. Mabire, a military historian with a clear admiration for the Waffen-SS and sympathy for right-wing causes, maintains against Krukenberg that among the 700 soldiers scheduled to move to Berlin in April 1945, 350 actually made the trip (1975, 110). More neutral ideologically and less specialized, Giolitto (1999, 249) and Delperrie de Bayac (611) reduce this number to 300. Le Tissier, former governor of the Spandau prison and a scholar of Berlin, writes that Krukenberg brought in "about 350 volunteers, mainly French" on April 24 (130) and "sent for his ninety Frenchmen from the Olympic Stadium" on April 25 (150); however, he explains neither the meaning of "mainly French" (had other foreign Waffen-SS joined the group?), nor the discrepancy between 350 and 90. As for the Occupation or World War II specialists Rousso (1980,

226), Beevor (291–3), and Read and Fisher (380), they follow Krukenberg and settle on ninety. Explicitly justifying his decision, Rousso argues that Krukenberg, as the Charlemagne's commandant, was in the best position to know how many people had come to Berlin with him, and that the former volunteers probably amplified the size of their ranks – together with the importance of their cause – for reasons of "political ideology" (1980, 227).

The matter, of course, is not crucial from a historical standpoint. Whether they were 90 or 500, the French Waffen-SS were too few to contribute significantly to the defense of the capital; they could only accomplish isolated exploits, such as blowing up Soviet tanks with *Panzerfaust* (a weapon that had to be fired from a very close range), a feat for which some of them received last minute Iron Crosses (Rostaing 144–5; Fernet 167–8). Variances of this type, however, confirm the psychologists' experiments about the limitations of memory; they show how difficult it is for people to evaluate in retrospect such things as the size of a group they observed or of which they were part, especially when the information to retrieve is distant in time. For that matter, with the exception of Soulat, who wrote his manuscript in 1949 (Gordon 277), the French witnesses whose testimonies I quoted all testify at least twenty-five years after the events: Fernet in 1973, Rostaing in 1975, Bayle in 1994, and Malardier as late as in 2007 (these dates are dates of publication; no information is available about the time of composition). By the same token, such variances point to one of the historians' predicaments, namely the difficulty of describing an event in a scholarly manner when the only accessible records are testimonies. In this instance, no officer of the Waffen-SS or the Wehrmacht, not even Krukenberg, apparently had the leisure to write a report on April 25, 1945, indicating how many Frenchmen he had at his disposal. Scholars of the Last Battle, at any rate, did not find any document of this type in the archives, since they all derive their numbers from witnesses' statements, the accuracy of which they have no way of assessing with certainty.

POSSIBLY TOO MUCH

Paul Garde, in his study of testimonies about the conflicts that took place in the former Yugoslavia in the late twentieth century, distinguishes among four categories of witnesses: the false witness, who was not there; the pseudo-witness, who was there but did not see anything; the gagged witness, who was there but is not free to talk; and the true witness, who was there and tells the truth, avoiding any imbalance between the facts and the context (67–8). By "true witness," therefore, Garde means someone who focuses his narrative on what he was able to observe and does not overly expand that narrative to include what he learned later about the situation. However, Garde does not consider a case that specialists of testimony regard as quite frequent: that of the witness whose story does not pose problems because he adds information obtained later, but because he includes events that appear unlikely with respect to the circumstances in which they are supposed to have occurred.

Though "true" witnesses in Garde's sense (they were "there" and do not draw too frequently on their retrospective standpoint), several memoirists in my corpus fall into that latter category. To begin with, they seem at times to say too much, that is, to tell more than they actually experienced. Labat, whose narrative usually emphasizes the everyday, tedious aspects of military life, thus tells a strange story that happened to him in Belorussia (88–92). Sent in late December 1942 to pick up the mail and the food supply about twenty miles from the post where he was based, he had to stop in a village on his way back because of the cold. Upon walking into an *izba*, he soon realized it was full of partisans; rifle butts were clearly visible under a curtain, and their number matched, by and large, that of the men present in the room. Recognized as a German soldier, Labat was nevertheless not just spared but invited to eat and drink with the group because it was Christmas Eve: a day of truce for the Russians, at least in areas where the communist regime had not entirely eliminated Christian customs. Though uplifting, this story should raise some doubts. The memoirs of the LVF men who fought in Belorussia (including Labat's) are unanimous on one point: The partisans were merciless with the volunteers, whom they did not just kill after ambushing them, but often stripped and mutilated. Labat's narrative of his sparing thus remains somewhat implausible, insofar as it does not fit in the context that Labat himself provides – that of a merciless struggle between the partisans and the security forces in charge of destroying them.

While bizarre incidents of this type are rare in Labat's memoir, they abound in other accounts, beginning with Mit's *Carcasse à vendre* (which some people, as mentioned earlier, regard as a hoax). In August 1944 in Galicia, Mit helps a Polish woman deliver a child; fellow soldiers bring him water, alcohol, and bandages, he himself cuts the umbilical cord, and then puts mother and child in the chariot of a Polish refugee who providentially was riding by (121–3). In a training camp at Friedenthal in November 1944, he meets the infamous Otto Skorzeny, who had engineered Mussolini's escape from Gran Sasso, the Alpine fortress in which the Duce was jailed (187). Participating in the December 1944 Ardennes offensive as a member of a special commando, he drives a jeep across enemy lines while wearing an Allied uniform and bearing an American paybook (189–94). Wounded and discharged, he spends the last months of the war successively as a *Volkssturm* instructor (201), as a worker in an armament factory (202–3), as an assistant nurse in a military hospital (204–6), and finally with the Americans, who believe him when he explains that he was a victim of forced labor and hire him as an interpreter (209–13). Odd encounters of the Mit-Skorzeny kind are also found in Laurier's *Il reste le drapeau noir et les copains* [The Black Flag and the Buddies Are What Is Left] – a phrase that Laurier states he borrowed from Brasillach in order to describe the situation of the French collaborationists in exile, who must rely on their friends and adopt an individualistic, anarchistic way of life. In Madrid in 1945, Laurier frequently meets notorious expatriates who find themselves in a situation similar to his, having fled France out of fear of the purges: the brothers André and Jacques Tenaille, members of Deloncle's Mouvement social révolutionnaires (MSR) (50); Louis Darquier de Pellepoix (51), the former head of the Commissariat général aux questions juives, a fanatical antisemite and denier whose name was to reemerge in 1978 when he granted the magazine *L'Express* an interview in which he declared that "in Auschwitz, only lice were gassed"; and Charles Lesca (52–3), the former director of the hardcore collaborationist weekly *Je Suis Partout*, who was in Spain trying to move to Argentina, his country of origin (he eventually managed to do so). Certainly, there were French exiles in Spain, and they were likely to meet. But such successive encounters with well-known people smack of name dropping; coincidences are too many, and involve too many (in)famous individuals, not to raise readers' suspicions.

Other stories that the volunteers tell belong to a more generic kind of overreporting. Norton Cru, in his study of World War I testimonies, sets out to expose the false clichés that, according to him, recur in many narratives about the war. Contrasting those clichés with reliable testimonies, he flags as untrue such scenes as the bayonet charge (bayonets were, in fact, rarely used); the stacks of corpses after a confrontation (corpses were, in fact, scattered); and the streams of blood running from bodies (blood was, in fact, hardly visible as it pooled under the bodies and was often covered with soil and mud) (1929, 29–31). My memoirists have their own stock of ready-made tableaux, which they deploy from time to time to account for their deeds. One of the most common could be labeled "fighting in a state of gross numerical inferiority." Terlin writes that in Estonia in late 1944, members of the Division Wallonie "held in front of the town of Kambia at one against twenty and did not give up" (1972, 222). Likewise, Gilles reports that during the thrust of the Charlemagne across Soviet lines along the Baltic coast in March 1945, his unit showed utmost heroism, making its way "at one against fifteen" (II, 249). As for Mit, who was not there and probably draws on the LVF's mythology, he tells that at Djukovo in December 1941, the Russians "came back at 800 against 1," forcing the French to retreat "with unimaginable losses" (8).

Another combat-related cliché to which the volunteers frequently turn is "direct Russian frontal assault." Describing the battle of Starosselie (Ukraine) in February 1944, Terlin emphasizes that the Russians, instead of "crouching down," attacked without any apparent concern for their lives: "We shoot on these enemies who do not seem to be worried about our guns and move forward standing, as in a parade. They are very young recruits, doubtless fanaticized and poorly taught. Do they believe that we do not have enough bullets to kill them all?" (1972, 81). Gilles recounts a similar charge near Neustettin (Pomerania) in February 1945, and he links the recklessness of the tactics to the role of the political commissars who accompanied each Soviet unit: "Most of the men who attacked were wearing civilian clothes and boots taken from European soldiers. It was a wild horde, pushed toward us by political commissars as herdsmen push the cattle toward the slaughterhouse… They were moving forward in close ranks, and our machine-guns made a hecatomb of them in no time … We managed to stop them very easily and to destroy 70% of them" (I, 347). Never concerned about providing odd details, Gilles adds that the French became "nauseated" when they approached the corpses of the Russian soldiers, because those corpses "smelled so much of vodka" (I, 348). From this evidence, Gilles infers that the political commissars had not only intoxicated their troops with communist doctrine; they had also, quite literally, gotten them drunk, in order to make them fight with less awareness of the dangers they were facing. Drawing on stories of this kind as well as on his own experience, Labat boldly claims that the Russians always attacked according to the same "insane" tactics (560). Using the present tense that refers to repeated actions, he writes:

A close, screaming wave comes out running, cut down by the machine guns as it advances … The bodies pile up. Eight, ten waves follow one another. The gunners get tired of killing … Ammunitions are in short supply. Only then, we can see disciplined, properly trained troops advance. They are the Red Guards, the military elite. The real battle can begin at last. The attackers are fresh; our men are tired and out of ammunition; they withdraw. The Soviet army conquers the position, which a normally conducted counter-attack immediately takes back. (560)

Not unexpectedly, Labat concludes his description of this "typical" Russian assault by affirming that the soldiers who make up the first, sacrificed "waves" are, in fact, Asian. They are members of "Kirkhiz and Mongolian tribes," whom a "human rodeo had encircled in the steppe a few weeks earlier" (560). Labat, however, does not cite any source for this latter statement; that is, while he might have witnessed the kind of assault that he recounts and seen Asian soldiers deliberately sent to their death, he does not explain how he knows that those soldiers did not volunteer, but were conscripted by force. We are here in the area of preconceptions about the Soviet army, as Labat has no way of being apprised of the exact circumstances in which "Kirkhiz and Mongolian tribes" were "encircled," and then turned into Soviet troops.

Like most (all?) clichés, the phrases "at one against fifteen (or twenty, or eight hundred)" and "direct Russian frontal assault" admit a part of the truth. In the Ukraine in February 1944, as well as in Pomerania in March 1945, Soviet forces largely outnumbered German divisions and their foreign affiliates. In this regard, the expressions "at one against fifteen" and "at one against twenty" must be understood rhetorically as approximations; they certainly cannot be taken at face value (who was counting during the battle?), but they convey the imbalance between the antagonists at the time, as it was experienced by soldiers on the losing side. The claim that the Russians were conducting direct frontal assaults in the Ukraine in 1944 and in Pomerania in 1945 is more difficult to assess. According to Eastern Front specialist David Glantz, Soviet officers used these tactics at the beginning of the war, especially during the December 1941 counteroffensive near Moscow. But the resulting losses "exasperated" General Zhukov, who on December 9 "issued a directive that forbade frontal assaults and ordered commandants to seek open flanks in order to penetrate into the German rear area" (Glantz 67). Had the Soviets, in 1944–45, returned to strategies they had discarded at some prior point? Were the soldiers who attacked "in close ranks" not just fanaticized but drunk, because they had consumed the "100 grams a day of 40% proof vodka" allotted to every member of the Soviet army by a "government decree of 9 January 1941" (Hill 56)? Or are Terlin, Gilles, and Labat among the many witnesses who, as W.G. Sebald has argued

(80), can only remember events along "stereotyped lines" and thus are unable to communicate an experience that is genuinely "personal?"[2]

However we answer these questions, one thing must be kept in mind when we assess testimonies: As the theorists of French classicism had already observed (e.g., Boileau in his 1674 *Art poétique*), implausible events may be true, whereas plausible ones may turn out to be false. In other words, the boundary between "plausible" and "implausible" is not stable; sports records can be broken that were thought to be unbreakable, and mountains climbed that supposedly could not be. Furthermore, we should not overlook what Dulong calls the "paradox of the historical testimony": The witness is "even more entitled to speak, and more subject to criticism, when his narrative is extraordinary" (68). Such "paradox," in Dulong's analysis, applies to stories told by camp survivors. But there is no reason why it should not also be valid for other categories of "extraordinary" narratives, including those told by people who went through such unusual circumstances as the struggles on the Eastern Front, the retreat from Pomerania, and the battle of Berlin. My memoirists, at any rate, do not seem to have any hesitation with featuring episodes that critical readers might find highly improbable. To put it another way, "narrative desire" in their texts does not take the form of a search for "plausibility," as Suleiman (37) suspects that it did in the memoirs of Resistance members Lucie and Raymond Aubrac. Rather – to stay with Suleiman's vocabulary – it adds to works like Mit's and Gilles's a dimension of "heroic aggrandizement" (37); it renders those works more exciting, though at the risk of causing a few of their parts to jeopardize the credibility of the whole.

AS GOOD IN BED AS ON THE BATTLEFIELD

Leonard Smith, in his study of French soldiers' testimonies of World War I, emphasizes that these veterans are "chaste" and "restrained" when they tell about their sex lives; remaining discreet, they do not conform to the "stereotype" of the "oversexed Frenchman" who boasts of his many conquests (81). Smith's remark certainly does not apply to the World War II memoirs I am considering. While Labat and his fellow volunteers revel in reporting the strange adventures they underwent and the heroic battles they fought on the Eastern Front, they also flaunt their sexual exploits.

---

[2] Against career soldiers like General Foch and novelists like Henri Barbusse, Cru (1967, 63) also lists "attacks in close ranks [attaques en rangs serrés]" among the "legends" of both referential and fictional works about World War I.

The story they repeatedly tell is that, as Frenchmen, they did not have to force themselves on the women they encountered, but that they were more than welcomed wherever the war took their units. In Poland, the French "are very popular … Deprived of affection for months, they find in the company of slender, blond young women all the tenderness of which soldiers dream after exertion" (Rostaing 31). In Belorussia, the *starosta* (elder) heading a village "does his best" to please the French, providing the officers with "a few young women to put in their beds" (Rostaing 96). In another village, the locals happily fraternize with the French, as the men offer tobacco and women "a moment of pleasure"; One of them satisfies in a few hours "two almost complete sections, eighty men, a record" (Labat 87). As for the town of Osjatschitschi, it is known for its female schoolteacher; though a dedicated Marxist, this attractive person "falls for each successive head of the local garrison," causing young officers to compete "ferociously" for being assigned to this location (Labat 154).

To hear the volunteers' stories, the appetite of Russian women for French (and French-speaking) soldiers was insatiable. Terlin reports that a particularly alluring Belgian, in a town in the Ukraine, managed to seduce "the mother and her two daughters" (1972, 92); all three were pregnant when the Wallonie left the area, bearing witness to the virility of the Belgians and the corresponding lust of the local women for them. (Terlin does not ask how townspeople would later treat these women and what was in store for the children conceived with the "enemy.") Even the Russian female soldiers, whom the volunteers describe as particularly bloodthirsty, could not resist the sex appeal of the French. Gilles tells that a few members of the Charlemagne, upon being taken prisoner, were "raped under the threat of a machine-gun by several of these amazons"; kept in the unit of their "mistresses," they then had to fulfill "sweet but tiring duties" as often as their captors wanted to get a "ration of French love" (I, 433). Gilles's narrative here clearly draws on the stereotype of the "rifle woman" analyzed by Klaus Theweleit in his work on the Freikorps (I, 70), but it adds an interesting twist to this male "fantasy." Indeed, Theweleit's "armed," "proletarian" woman is no longer "castrating" in Gilles's memoir. Of course, she takes advantage of her prisoners; but the latter do not seem to mind the "duties" that she imposes upon them, since such work agrees with the image of themselves they are anxious to project.

According to the volunteers' memoirs, however, it is not in the USSR but in Germany toward the end of the conflict that women were most eager to seek Frenchmen as sexual partners. German women, according to Raul

Hilberg (2001, 94), were supposed to have sexual relations with German and "Germanic" men exclusively, and not even with all Germanic men; this privilege was reserved for the Dutch, the Danes, and the Norwegians, barring the Finns, the Swedes, the Swiss, and the Flemish. People found guilty of *Geschlechtsverkehrverbrechen* (crime against the racial laws in the area of relations between the sexes) could be severely punished. Yves Durand, in his study of the everyday life of the French POWs in Germany (1987, 241), points out that the prisoners caught with German women would be sent to disciplinary camps, while the women would be shorn and jailed, just as French women, at the time of the Liberation, were shorn and jailed for having "slept with the enemy." The French volunteers apparently were not aware of the racial laws and the penalties for disobeying them. Indeed, they neither brag about the way they were able to flout those laws nor even mention whether they, at times, had trouble connecting with women, because they did not meet the Nazis' standards in the area of racial purity.

Recalling their love life, the volunteers tell that the relations they had with German women took on different aspects. The most banal, though the one that could bring about the harshest punishment, was the adulterous affair between a woman whose husband was at the front and a French soldier who happened to be in the area. Gilles, for example, explains that the LVF members who regrouped in Greifenberg (East Prussia) after retreating from Belorussia were welcomed by the civilians but not by the German soldiers who were there on leave; too many of them had found "a French volunteer near their wife, when they had come home without warning" (I, 50). That volunteer could have been Rostaing who, near Neustrelitz, before leaving for Berlin, had a brief liaison with the wife of a German army man, in whose country home he had located his office. According to Rostaing, the first move was made by the woman, who blamed her guest for not talking to her and then screamed: "Don't you see that I love you" (184). Sexual intercourse evidently followed, and Rostaing admits that, aware of the "apocalyptic struggles that were coming," he lived these privileged moments "with tremendous intensity" (133).

Such intensity was not only Rostaing's and his landlady's. In the volunteers' version of the waning days of the Third Reich, it characterized most of the rapports between French soldiers and German women during those trying times. Labat points out the "nervous and provoking laughter" of the German women he met in early 1945, a laughter he ascribes to the fear of the approaching Soviet armies; before the foreseeable collapse of their country, these women "sought at any price to give themselves to a man of their clan, to experience love before being raped by some Tartar or Kalmuk horde" (503). Turning moralistic, Labat insists that such attitudes owed nothing to "depravation and vice"; German women, during this difficult period, "seemed to invite love at any price, as if they were aware of the brevity of life, and wanted to keep from the present moment a feminine memory that could nourish their future misery" (508). Saint-Loup describes a similar situation in the Haus Germania in Hildesheim, the SS training school where he was editing the French SS magazine *Devenir* in late 1944. Using terms resembling Labat's, he defines the SS as a "clan" that knew "neither debauchery nor vice," a "healthy environment" in which there were few "sentimental complications," thanks to the women's "independence" (1986b, 85). Saint-Loup explains that he himself had an affair with Guerti, a "beautiful, intelligent, five language-speaking" Dutch who was part of the "babel of blond women" that helped edit the magazines targeted at the foreign SS (84). A skilled writer, Saint-Loup evokes his encounters with Guerti with utmost literary discretion; eliding any explicit description of their lovemaking but using the imperfect tense that refers to repeated actions, he stops on the sentence: "I would squeeze Guerti a little more, she would turn her head backwards, I would see her eyes shine above the lips she was offering to me" (88). (The next, mood-breaking scene is about a meeting with the collaborationist writer and journalist Lucien Rebatet, a contributor to *Devenir*, whom Saint-Loup does not seem to welcome because of his civilian status.)

As grown German women wanted to have what could be their last "good" sexual encounter with Frenchmen, younger, inexperienced women supposedly sought the French for the purpose of losing their virginity before the arrival of the Russians. La Mazière, who pictures himself with complacency as a playboy (he boasts in *Le Rêveur blessé* of his numerous affairs, notably with French star singers Juliette Gréco and Dalida), revels in this kind of story. Thus, he tells that on his way to the Wildflecken training camp in September 1944, he stopped in Heidelberg where he met Inge, a young woman with whom he spent "two marvelous days," though "only nice things" happened between them (1972, 37). One month later, however, guards informed him that someone was waiting for him. It was of course Inge, who had come to "give [him] the most serious gift, that of her purity" (76). Confessing that "Inge is one of the rare virgins I have had in my life," La Mazière adds that there was in her eyes "such a beauty, such a desire to make me realize what she was giving to me, that

I was perhaps more moved than I have ever been since then" (76). Such gifts, according to La Mazière, became quite frequent toward the end of the war. In Körlin (Pomerania) in March 1945, for instance, women were so astounded at seeing French soldiers "defend the Eastern Marches," defend Germany's "past of greatness," that they did not just offer themselves; they offered their daughters, "probably all virgins" and "terrorized at the idea of being deflowered by Mongols or Kalmuks" (1972, 128). By that time, however, La Mazière and his companions were no longer "fresh enough" to collect their "warrior's reward," as they would have collected it "in the ancient city" (129); they had to move on and participate in the hopeless defense of the town.

While some of my memoirists pride themselves on their role as initiators, others claim that they in fact were the ones who were initiated during the war; as green, naive young men, they were taught love's pleasures by German women who had not waited for the French to lose their virginity. Bayle, for instance, writes that he had his first sexual experience at eighteen, while in a military hospital in Konitz (Poland) in September 1944. In the hospital's laundry room, the nurse he was assisting invited him to join her on a pile of towels. Noticing the young man's lack of know-how, the nurse "took things in her hands" (Bayle cannot resist the easy pun), so that everything "went very well"; the happy affair continued for some time, until Bayle's release from the hospital (2008, 155). This initiation narrative of course modifies another of the female stereotypes analyzed by Theweleit: that of the "white nurse." Bayle's initiator is a nurse, that is, a "positive" character who contrasts with the "negative" character of the "rifle woman." That nurse, however, is not the "dead body, with no desire, no sexuality," which, according to Theweleit (I, 90), male soldiers need in order "not to feel threatened." She is sexually active, and Bayle does not seem to sense any "threat" when he entrusts his virility to her in the hospital's basement. Theweleit, for that matter, acknowledges that the figures of the "white nurse" and the "female initiator" are not incompatible. Rudolf Höss, he reports, had an experience similar to Bayle's when he was in a military hospital; it was his nurse who expertly taught him the facts of life, "guiding him quickly to sexual union" (I, 137).

Such stories as having great consensual sex in an atmosphere of *Götterdämmerung*, being asked to take a young woman's virginity, and having one's sexual initiation while at the hospital, pose obvious problems of verifiability and truthfulness. The rape of German women by Russian troops has been abundantly documented, whether in personal testimonies (e.g., the anonymous *A Woman in Berlin*), or in scholarly studies (e.g., Grossmann, Naimark).[3] On the other hand, the sexual activities of French and French-speaking soldiers in places where the LVF, the Frankreich, the Charlemagne, and the Wallonie were stationed or fought, to my knowledge, have not been investigated. Klaus Naumann, in his study of the way the year 1945 was memorialized in German media, mentions that according to the press, the French troops that were part of the Allied armies behaved badly on many occasions; in the Black Forest area especially, they "raped and plundered" just like the Russians did in East Prussia, Pomerania, and Berlin (212).[4] Naumann, however, does not take up the subject of how the media rated the demeanor of the Reich's foreign legions in general and of the French legionaries in particular. It is difficult, therefore, to properly assess such texts as *Les Places étaient chères*, *Le Rêveur casqué*, and *De Marseille à Novossibirsk* in the domain "sexual activities of the protagonists." For we have neither the testimonies (e.g., *A Woman in Berlin*), nor the documents (e.g., Naumann's press reports) that would make it possible to weigh, against other types of archival evidence, the claims that Labat, La Mazière, and Bayle are making about their sexual feats.[5]

Psychologists have argued that people tend to provide their lives with "some semblance of unity and purpose" by construing them as "evolving stories" (Mc Adams 13). That "script theory" of personality might help account for the boastful narratives that the volunteers are producing. Whether they were factual or imaginary, the sexual exploits that the legionaries report – just like the military feats on which they pride themselves – contribute to the construction of a specific masculine identity. Simplified in the extreme, the story that the volunteers tell for the sake

---

[3] The author of *A Woman in Berlin* was outed in 2003 as Marta Hillers, a young journalist who had written propaganda texts for the Nazis. Scholars and journalists describe her as a minor propagandist as well as a kind of Nazi "new" woman, liberated from sexual taboos (Grossmann 291).

[4] La Mazière (1972, 293–4) reports that, while at the Clairvaux penitentiary, he met North African soldiers who had been sentenced for raping German women. They had not, however, committed their crime in the anonymity of the Black Forest, but on the Cathedral Square in Stuttgart, on Christmas Eve. The German clergy had protested, forcing the French to court-martial the disorderly soldiers. No supporter of the justice system of the Fourth Republic and indulgent toward sexual offenses, La Mazière observes that the North African servicemen had been "torn from the bosom of their native land in order to liberate France," and that they, after all, had only committed "what all the other armies had been committing for a long time" (1972, 293).

[5] In *Le Crime d'aimer* [The Crime of Loving], Jean-Paul Picaper examines the fate of the children fathered in Germany during World War II by French POWs as well as by forced and volunteer laborers. None of Picaper's many case studies, however, concerns a child fathered in Germany by a member of the LVF, the Frankreich, or the Charlemagne.

of "unity and purpose" could be scripted as follows: We were on the losing side; but we fought with heroism (e.g., at one against twenty); and at some point, our exploits on the battlefield were rewarded in the form of women obligingly consenting to sex. Whether they agree with the evidence or not, such self-flattering narratives expose a value system that is obviously sexist, uncritically nationalistic, and oblivious to the history of German women. They ascribe to the prestige of Frenchness female attitudes that, in the Polish and Belorussian contexts, point to the fear of being harmed by occupying forces that treated the local population with utmost brutality. Those same stories hardly display more understanding when they describe the behavior of German women. In this instance, the French recognize that women in Pomerania and Berlin, aware that they and members of their family were probably to be violated, wanted to have some choice in the process. But they seem unable to acknowledge that they possibly were not granted sexual favors because of their national origin and reputation as desired lovers; instead, that such favors were part of an explicit or implicit negotiation conducted between unequal parties during most trying times.[6] Furthermore, the French clearly are unaware of the sexual freedom that German women had acquired in the 1920s and were still exercising toward the end of the Third Reich. That freedom, according to Atina Grossmann, could be attributed both to the "modernist Sachlichkeit of Weimar culture" and to the "loosened mores of the Nazi war," including the experiences of "fraternization" that German women had had with POWs and foreign laborers (54). The women with whom the French had *Geschlechtsverkehr*, therefore, had been trained to what Grossmann calls "sexual cynicism," that is, to separating sexual intercourse from "love" and using it as an "instrument" for pragmatic purposes (55), be it for food or mere physical satisfaction.

In his study of the relations between war and gender roles, the historian Luc Capdevila argues that French males underwent a double trauma in the aftermath of France's defeat in 1940, as that defeat affected both their "national and masculine identity" (104). According to Capdevila, the occupation of France by the Germans had several sexual components. French men had not been "man enough" to "defend the territory" (104); almost two million of them had been taken to Germany as prisoners, thus

---

[6] The anonymous author of *A Woman in Berlin* describes bluntly how such negotiations were conducted with Russians, specifically how young, attractive women like herself were able to choose the men with whom they would spend the night and then possibly have a relationship. Assurance to receive protection, food, and other material goods was part of the deal.

symbolically castrated; hundreds of thousands of German soldiers were stationed on French soil, in the position of victors expecting their rewards; and French men were in "direct competition" with those soldiers – a competition that at times caused "scenes worthy of a farce," in which the French were as ridiculed in the bedroom as they had been overpowered on the battlefield (105). Faced with this situation, the Vichy government sought to take measures that would restore the image of France as a virile country. It celebrated the masculinity of farmers, craftsmen, and World War I veterans; promoting physical activities, it set up camps in which young people would exercise as well as work in the fields; and it sought, with the creation of the Légion tricolore, to organize a state-sponsored army that would replace the LVF and represent a "fighting France" in diverse "theaters of operation," beginning with the USSR (Lambert and Le Marec 45). Those measures, however, never met with much success. The project of the Légion tricolore was opposed by the Germans and never materialized. Worse, the occupier ordered the troops that France had been allowed to maintain, the 100,000-men Armistice Army, to be disbanded after the Allies' invasion of North Africa in October 1942; the measure added to the emasculation of France, depriving the country of its last armed forces.

The volunteers' boasting about their sexual exploits with women in general and German women in particular must be understood in this context of a questioned masculinity. The legionaries rarely talk about their family situation, and most of them were too young to have families or even steady partners when they enrolled in the LVF or the Waffen-SS. The only one to mention a household is Rostaing, who bitterly brings up that his wife "has not written since [his] departure" (37), and later briefly announces that his marriage "has dissolved" (88).[7] Rostaing does not tell whether his wife was having an affair with a German, and he seems to take responsibility for the rupture when he writes: "I have made a choice: war. And today, I no longer have a family" (89). Furthermore, Rostaing reports about his first Eastern conquest – a young, attractive

---

[7] Several of the volunteers, notably Bayle, Dupont, Gilles, Lobsiger, and Sajer, had partners in Germany, but none of these relationships survived the war. Dupont's fiancée, for example, was killed during the bombing of Dresden. The only one among my memoirists who found a partner during the war and stayed with her is Philippet; the woman was not German but Belgian, and she was working in the office of the Rexist Party in Liège when Philippet met her; it was love at first sight (I, 182). The last page of *Et mets ta robe de bal* (II, 323) shows the couple, elegantly dressed, walking the street after Philippet's release from jail. Degrelle was married and had children when he left for the USSR, but he never mentions his family in *La Campagne de Russie*.

Polish woman – on the same page that he complains about the lack of letters from his wife, thus showing that it did not take him long to recover his pride as a sexually active male.

While Rostaing's comrades did not have to make up for the failure of a relationship, their insistence on telling about their sexual prowess confirms and extends Capdevila's thesis: French males had something to prove after the defeat of 1940, and finding sexual partners meant more for them than obtaining physical pleasure. In this regard, the volunteers' contention that in Germany they often did not have to look for sex, as women would ask them for it, is particularly revealing. For that claim does not only point, on the part of the French, to a desire for maintaining a reputation of sexual expertise; it also includes an element of compensation and revenge, implying that French soldiers were asked to do with German women what German soldiers had been doing with French women since the beginning of the Occupation. More importantly, perhaps, the fact that the demand for sex, and sex as a favor to the demanding party, is presented as coming from the women reverses the roles played in France since the ceasefire in 1940; for it was France that had been asking for help and "collaboration" and Germany that had been in the situation of granting or not granting the requests submitted to her. Whether they are empty boasts or narratives of actual experiences, therefore, the stories that the volunteers tell about their sex lives constitute a response to the crisis of French masculinity that Capdevila describes; they demonstrate that French males had not been entirely deprived of their manhood by the setbacks they had experienced on the battlefield, as they had no problem proving their virility when the opportunity was there, or when they were called upon to do so.

POSSIBLY TOO LITTLE

While boastful descriptions of their military exploits and feminine conquests occasionally jeopardize the veracity of the volunteers' accounts, the opposite also is true. That is, the memoirists do not always apparently tell "too much"; they sometimes seem to tell "too little," at least with respect to the questions that critical readers may have in their minds. Ansgar Nünning, in an essay about "unreliable narration," has argued that a text may be deemed unreliable because it contains "signals of unreliability," such as contradictions (90). Yet Nünning adds that textual clues alone cannot always account for the fact that a narrative is perceived as unreliable. Readers, in many cases, have misgivings about a text because they process it according to a "presuppositional framework" (95), that is, to a set of information and assumptions that determines what can be taken as reliable and what cannot. Nünning focuses on fiction, but his model can be applied to nonfictional genres such as life narratives. In the case of the volunteers' memoirs, the fact that "presuppositional frameworks" fashion the reception of texts is particularly obvious when readers with a basic knowledge of World War II take up the accounts that former members of the LVF and the Légion Wallonie provide of their activities in Belorussia and the Ukraine. Indeed, those readers cannot be unaware of the studies that historians such as Bartov (1986), Dallin (1981), and Müller and Ueberschär (2009) have devoted to the war in the USSR. More specifically, they cannot be unaware of what Bartov calls the "barbarisation of warfare" on the Eastern Front: of the fact that the laws of war were ignored there, and that the victims of that barbarization were not only the combatants, but also the civilian populations. As part of the Reich's security divisions in charge of controling the rear of the front, the soldiers of the LVF could bear witness to two aspects of the conflict in the USSR: the struggles against the partisans and the relations between the occupying forces and the peasant families that inhabited the areas where the Germans and their foreign allies were stationed. Writing several years after the events, how do the former volunteers describe this trying situation? Did they know about the atrocities committed by the SS, the Einsatzgruppen, and even the Wehrmacht? Did they commit some themselves? And if we readers suspect that they say too little or not enough, what are the assumptions that cause us to have such doubts?

When they begin the narrative of their experiences in Belorussia, the volunteers are prompt to emphasize that they were at first well received by the local population. For one thing, the Germans had taken measures that peasants could only approve; decollectivizing the agricultural system and allowing religious practices, they had redistributed the land and reopened the churches (Dallin 347). The French had applied the same policies with positive results, as Bassompierre observes upon his arrival in Belorussia in the fall of 1942:

The French legionaries are generally well regarded. They maintain firm but human relations with the population, respect its traditions and customs, the holidays and the Sunday rest, make religious services easier, and defend the peasants against excessive requisitioning. When the French representatives de Brinon and Colonel

Puaud visited us in June 1943, they were sincerely cheered in the villages where I was with them and given wild flowers by the population. (142)[8]

Similarly, Philippet notes that in July 1942, the Belgians of the Légion Wallonie were received in the Ukraine with great "kindness" (I, 97). The locals went as far as to "cook meals" for the invaders and "wash their backs" when they bathed, gestures that Philippet traces to the natural "sense of hospitality" that Ukrainians supposedly possess (I, 97).

Whether people in Belorussia and the Ukraine are "naturally" hospitable or were merely trying to adjust to the new conditions, the idyllic situation described by Bassompierre and Philippet did not last for long. The first cause for the quick deterioration of the relations between the locals and the occupying armies was the tendency of the soldiers to supplement their food rations by requisitioning meat, fruit, and vegetables from the peasants, or merely by stealing edibles from them. One page after telling how well the Wallonie was received in the Ukraine, Philippet reports an incident of which he confesses he is still somewhat "ashamed": As his company entered a village, a little girl came to watch them with her flock of geese; the soldiers immediately nabbed the geese, left the girl with just her stick, and then kept marching "as if nothing had happened" (I, 99).[9] Stories of this type abound in the memoirs of the French soldiers stationed in Belorussia. Rostaing mentions simply that "every patrol was an excuse for plundering" (51), while Labat explains at length how that plundering was conducted, detailing exotic techniques such as stealing honey in the hives after killing the bees and shooting chickens with machine guns. Far from apologizing, Labat insists that the French were entitled not to have "scruples"; the food they did not take would have been "seized by the enemy," who was even less principled than the legionaries when it came to stocking up (297).

The relations between the volunteers and the local population also soured because of the presence of partisans. Historians such as Matthew

---

[8] Fernand de Brinon was a member of the *Comité d'honneur* of the LVF; Colonel Puaud became head of the LVF in October 1943.

[9] Photographs such as those published in *The German Army and Genocide*, the catalogue of the exhibit organized by the Hamburger Institute for Social Research to documents the crimes of the Wehrmacht, illustrate these two aspects of the relations between the occupying forces and the local populations. Photo #3 on p. 81 represents smiling Ukrainian women offering refreshments to German motorcyclists. But the photos on p. 105, part of the chapter entitled "Looting the Ukraine," show how the German army "lived off the land," photo #3 portraying a soldier who has just grabbed two geese (as in Philippet's anecdote), and photo #2, a group of soldiers proudly displaying the fowl they have just killed and plucked.

Cooper, Leonid Grenkevich, and Kenneth Slepyan have analyzed partisans' activities in the USSR during World War II, explaining how Belorussia became one of the centers of those activities because its swamps and its forests constituted a favorable environment for guerrilla warfare. Caught between the occupying forces and the underground, the Belorussian villagers had to walk a tight rope. If they "collaborated" with the invaders, they could be punished by their countrymen. Conversely, they could undergo the wrath of the occupying forces if they accommodated partisans' demands for shelter, food, and information. Rusco, for example, reports that a village where irregulars had been allowed to hide was immediately set afire: "Isbas burn quickly... After our departure, nothing was left" (82). Yet sins of collaboration with the underground were sometimes dealt with in a more perverse manner. Labat, who seems to enjoy chronicling the dark sides of the LVF's everyday life, tells about an operation when the discovery that a village had harbored partisans was followed by a deal involving food and women:

Only women had remained in the village ... Terrorized by our findings, they understood that they were at our disposal. That was our only purpose. When we expressed the wish to sit and eat, the table was immediately covered as by a miracle with marvelous riches: a wonderful ham, egg, cakes, honey, crepes, and cream disappeared in a few minutes. Then, regardless of the danger, everybody went about their business in some discreet corner with the woman they had selected. (Labat writes ironically: "avec l'élue de son coeur [their heart's desire].") (325)

It is difficult, in these specific cases, to establish whether the memoirists misunderstood or deliberately underreport the events in which they participated. Do Bassompierre and Philippet really believe in the "natural" kindness of the people who brought them flowers and washed their backs? What happened to the inhabitants of the place that Rusco's patrol burned down? And was the bargain between the legionaries and the village women struck as quickly and peacefully as Labat's narrative seems to suggest? Jean-Paul Brunet, in his biography of Doriot, mentions that in the fall of 1942, the Germans deemed the LVF's repressive policies toward the civilian population to have gone too far. They ordered several legionaries tried because they had "shot children, raped women, and stolen horses" (411); four of them were executed despite the protests of their officers, who argued without success that the volunteers' behavior had not been different from most German soldiers'.

None of my memoirists reports that his unit was disciplined for crimes unbecoming of the Wehrmacht, but the rhetorical strategies to which they turn in the passages I have just quoted are those of perpetrators seeking to justify what they know were wrongdoings. First, they contend that as placed under German command, they were merely following orders. Along these lines, Rusco pictures himself and his company as obedient subordinates when he asserts: "Because this village is a hideaway for partisans, we are ordered [nous recevons l'ordre] to set the isbas on fire" (82). The volunteers also invoke history, presenting their misdeeds as a continuation of cruel but ancient traditions. According to Labat, the "plundering of the peasant by the warrior" is "an old and respectable custom" in the "medieval region" of Belorussia where the LVF is stationed; the Soviets have never established "but a superficial authority" over the "lord-bandits" who reign over this area, and whose activities are comparable to those of the "knight-plunderers" and "Raubritter" of "our Middle Ages" (297–8). Finally, resorting to a scheme I already identified while examining the way they describe their relations to women, the volunteers often deemphasize or even ignore the political context in which the events they recount were taking place. Philippet, for instance, does not seem to be aware that the Ukrainians expected Germany to liberate them from Moscow and grant them "some kind of independence" (Grenkevich 131). "Kindness" arguably was an element of this anticipated bargain, the local populations offering their cooperation in exchange for favors, both immediate and to come.

The most pressing questions that the presuppositional framework of today's readers would make one ask of the legionaries doubtlessly concern the treatment of Jews. Did the French and Belgian volunteers know about the camps? When they were in Belorussia and the Ukraine, did they witness mass killings, such as those perpetrated in Minsk and Kiev by the units (Einsatzgruppen) whose mission was to exterminate the Jews in the occupied territories? And how did they react when they found out that what they had fancied as a crusade against Bolshevism was also a *Vernichtungskrieg* – a war whose purpose was to destroy a whole segment of the population living in the land to be conquered? Some of the veterans had to answer these questions explicitly when they were brought to trial. Rostaing reports that the following exchange took place in court:

The judge asked me:

-You don't regret anything?

-No, Sir, I don't regret anything.

-And the concentration camps?

Ah. Here we are.

-I never knew their existence. Had I known it, I would have acted differently. Because it is not the case, I could only argue in terms of "if." I refuse to do that. Therefore, Sir, I'll ask you to excuse me if I have nothing to add on this subject. (230)

Asked a similar question by a member of the jury (a woman deportee) during his own trial, La Mazière writes that he responded as Rostaing did: "I answered that I wasn't ignorant of the fact that people were being arrested, but that I did not discover the nature of the camps and the 'final solution' before the end of the war" (1972, 250). La Mazière does not tell whether he had to face more queries about the camps while being tried. At any rate, the judge in charge of his case did not seem to be very interested in this subject; his focus was on why La Mazière – who claimed he had gone to Pomerania as a war correspondent – had elected to do a story about the Charlemagne, and not about the French troops that were fighting to liberate the homeland.

Even when they were not asked expressly about the camps upon their return from the front, the volunteers understood that the question "Did you know?" could be on their readers' minds. Some of them, therefore, sought to address it by acknowledging what they had witnessed or what they had been told. Generally, it was very little. Labat and La Mazière admit that they had noticed the existence of a concentration camp, located next to the SS training school they attended in Beschenau, near Prague, during winter 1944–45. But they maintain that they did not have any information about the detainees, Labat assuming that they were "ordinary prisoners [détenus de droit commun]" (518), and La Mazière, "political prisoners" (1972, 92). Labat adds that the deportees were poorly clothed and looked hungry, but that he never saw any case of "brutality or corporal punishment" during the time he lived in the area (519). As for La Mazière, anxious to mark the difference between camp guards and Waffen-SS, he specifies about the former: "Although wearing the SS initials, they did not have the same uniform as we did. In fact, we did not have anything in common with them" (1972, 91). La Mazière also recounts that in Neustettin, while leaving for the front, he saw "a concentration camp on the move," "about a thousand deportees in striped pyjamas," "walking briskly" and "looking fit" (1972, 114): A description that of course does not agree with stories of similar forced departures provided by the deportees themselves, for instance, by Robert Antelme in *L'Espèce humaine*. La Mazière, like Labat earlier, seems intent on showing that all camps were not killing centers (the existence of which he claims he did not know at the time), since the residents of one camp at least were still able to walk "briskly" in March 1945. Rusco makes a similar, politically self-serving statement when he observes that in Vilna, in October 1944, "Jewish prisoners ... identifiable by their yellow stars," were "rushing forward" to board a train loaded with wounded German soldiers (240); the Russians were coming, and even Jews, in Rusco's version of this episode, would rather flee toward the country that has ostracized them than have to deal with the wild, barbarian hordes pouring in from the East.

The volunteers do not have much more to tell about the treatment of the Jewish civilian population than they do about the camps. The author of *Vae Victis* mentions that the SS training quarters in which they resided in Krushina (Poland) during the summer of 1942 was adjoining a ghetto; learning "much later" (how?) that its inhabitants had been used for medical experimentation, he assumes that "none of them had escaped with their lives" (13). Likewise, Labat and Saint-Loup both offer brief descriptions of Jewish life in Minsk, where they stopped on their way to the front. Labat, who was there in July 1943, observes that the Germans had confined the Jews to a "ghetto, an enormous neighborhood closed by barbed-wire fences that looked more symbolic than effective" (176). According to Labat, the Germans were letting the Jews of Minsk live "just as they pleased," treating them "almost like ordinary people, better than the natives," and certainly better than the Jews in Poland, considering the "radical measures" taken there against them (176).[10] Interestingly, Labat traces this favorable treatment to the economic situation; most craftsmen in Belorussia were Jewish, and eliminating Jews would have meant that the population of Minsk, as well as the occupying forces, would do "without watchmakers, shoemakers, tailors, goldsmiths, and coppersmiths" (177). Saint-Loup, who rode through Minsk in the fall of 1942, describes a city in which the Jewish community was supplying the Germans not just with craftsmen, but with forced labor:

We ran to the station. In trenches at the shoulder of the road, Jewish women were working. They were wearing on their backs a number that matched the number of their house in the ghetto. They did not look the least affected by their present

---

[10] According to Hilberg (2001, 104), *radikal* was an adjective frequently used by the Nazis to describe the "measures" and "solutions" adopted to solve the "Jewish problem"; Labat, who spoke German and is sensitive to language, might be quoting here this kind of parlance.

condition. They laughed, they shouted at us from far, they made obscene gestures. (1986a, 151)

Whether Labat and Saint-Loup "did not know" or seek in their retrospective narratives to minimize the hardships endured by the Jews in Minsk is open to question. However that might be, their accounts contrast strikingly with the historians' contention that Minsk was one of the cities in the USSR where the Jewish community was hit the hardest. Hilberg reports that the German military command, upon occupying the area in the summer of 1941, had established a civilian internment camp for almost all the men. Secret Field Police Detachments and Einsatzgruppe B personel then "combed out" that camp, catching in the roundup thousands of "Jews, criminals, functionaries, and Asiatics" (2003 I, 308). Martin Gilbert gives more comprehensive figures. According to the German calculations that he cites, 86,632 Jews were "eliminated" in Minsk between July 1941 and February 1943 (149), out of a ghetto population that had grown to over 100,000 because refugees had streamed into the city. Given these numbers, one can only wonder what Labat was able (or allowed) to see when he describes the size of the Minsk ghetto as "enormous," and its population as authorized to live "as they pleased" in July 1943. Likewise, one may ask what Saint-Loup knew about the situation in Minsk when he confidently asserts that the Jewish women he observed digging trenches were in a merry, joking mood. As attested in such documents as the Einsatzgruppen reports that Yitzhak Arad, Shmuel Krakowski, and Shmuel Spector cite in their anthology, the Germans had taken the "severest defense measures" against the Jews in Minsk who did not want to work (152, 294). The women that Saint-Loup saw, therefore, probably knew that going about their hard, physical job while pretending to be content was the only way to survive, because they would be shot if they refused to do what they were ordered to do. As historians report, the efforts of what was left of Minsk's Jewish community to stay alive by cooperating with the Germans were in vain; together with the Vilna and Lida ghettos, the Minsk ghetto was eventually liquidated in September 1943 (Davidowicz 140).[11]

The only one among the veterans who claims to have witnessed massive liquidations is Emmanuelli. While in a military hospital in Orel in September 1942 (he wanted out of the LVF and feigned to be ill), one day

---

[11] *The German Army and Genocide* treats Minsk as a "case study," showing pictures of the occupation of the city (photo #1, p. 119), as well as of the "relocation" of the Jews into the ghetto (photos #3–4, p. 121; #1–3, p. 122).

Emmanuelli noticed an "unusual hustle and bustle" in the city; the SS were "crisscrossing the streets," "rounding up the Jews," and bringing them to a "large open field behind the hospital" (62). Over six pages, Emmanuelli then describes the gruesome procedure with which survivor testimonies and historical studies have made us uncomfortably familiar. Supplied with picks and shovels, the Jews were forced to dig wide and deep pits; they had to undress and step into the pit using ladders; there, they were shot by the SS, while Russian volunteers sorted out the valuables that the victims had left. Emmanuelli alleges that he was able to watch the whole scene from a window in the hospital, witnessing incidents as horrendous as the killing of a young Jewish woman he knew, employed in the kitchen and used as a sex slave by the SS, who was trying to show that she could still be useful by displaying a potato and a knife:

> They had forgotten her. They got hold of her. The memory of the pleasure they had had with her and the lust of killing possibly had made them remember her. They grabbed her, and she brandished her potato, her knife, showing them as a supplication, as if it were her soul, and trying to make these jerks disguised as soldiers understand that her work was essential, that the potato was not quite peeled, that she had to complete the job ... The sadists ripped her dress as they had ripped her skin. Her breasts and her body shook, horrible shivers and spasms ran through her. Her corpse joined the other dead bodies. (66)

This passage is striking not only because of its lack of counterpart in other memoirs. To begin with, it displays a rare case of shift of point of view; Emmanuelli describes the scene as he saw it from the hospital's window, but he also attributes intentions and feelings to the perpetrators ("the lust of killing") as well as to the Jewish victim ("as if it were her soul"). Furthermore, he condemns the actions of the people with whom he fought for some time in the USSR; the SS are for him "jerks disguised as soldiers," "sadists" whose senseless crimes can only be denounced. Yet that same passage also poses problems of credibility, which add to the issues of authorship I raised in Chapter 2 about *Et j'ai cassé mon fusil*. In this instance, the question is to know whether massive killings of Jews actually took place in Orel during the summer of 1942. Neither Gilbert nor the contributors to the *Holocaust Chronicle* or the editors of the *Einsatzgruppen Reports* indicate that Jews were murdered there during this period. Gilbert does not mention Orel on the maps showing where massacres occurred in the USSR in July, August, and September 1942 (119). Likewise, the *Holocaust Chronicle* does not list Orel among the places where Jews were murdered between June and September 1942, and the name "Orel" does not even figure in the index of that comprehensive study. As for the reports from the Einsatzgruppen, they tell that the Jewish population in the USSR often had fled before the arrival of the Germans; the towns of "Orel, Medyn, and Maloyaroslavets," at any rate, were "free of Jews" when the *Kommando* entered (Arad, Krakowski, and Spector, 258; report of December 15, 1941). True, the whole Jewish population of Orel, in fact, had not evacuated; reports of December 19, 1941 and March 23, 1942 indicate that "several Jews" had to be shot there because they had "started fires" (262), and "a number of Jews and Jewesses," because they had "incited against the German army in an ugly manner" (318). None of the reports that the *Einsatzgruppen* sent from Orel in 1942, however, signals any large-scale slaughter, comparable to the killing of "3000 to 5000 people" that Emmanuelli describes in his recollections (63). One might ask, moreover, whether such massive murders could have been perpetrated next to such a public place as a hospital. According to Hilberg, killing operations were "standardized," the same "procedure" being followed in every city "with minor variations": The site of the shooting was "usually outside of town, at a grave"; the Jews were taken there "in batches ... from the collecting point to the ditch"; and the killing site was supposed to be "closed off to all outsiders" (2003 I, 326), not open for everybody to observe the massacre, as it is in Emmanuelli's narrative.

The Orel episode in *Et j'ai cassé mon fusil*, therefore, constitutes an interesting test case for scholars of the genres "memoir" and "testimony." The problem in this passage is not to determine whether the witness "really was there" and describes the events "as he saw them"; it is to establish whether those events actually occurred, that is, whether the witness's narrative is supported by other testimonies and/or historical evidence. Of course, Orel might have been a place where killings were carried out but went unreported; or it might have been a place where the operations that Hilberg describes were not conducted according to the Germans' preferred "procedure." Given the general difficulties raised by Emmanuelli's text, however, one might surmise that Emmanuelli here combines different accounts, mixing reminiscences of his stay in a military hospital with stories of killings that someone else recounted to him, or which he read about in books on the war. Such mixing, according to testimony specialist Elizabeth Loftus, is difficult to avoid, as witnesses "talk to one another," "overhear each other talk," or gain access to new information "from the media, interrogators, or other sources" (viii). Emmanuelli's account of the slaughter in Orel, therefore, could be viewed not as deliberately fabricated, but as typical of a certain type of distortion frequently encountered in testimonies on any subject. Yet the nature of the distortion in this case would be difficult to assess, and its history difficult to reconstruct. For we would have to find out what newspapers and magazines Emmanuelli read, what books he consulted, and what people he talked to during and after the war – a project that involves locating Emmanuelli himself, enlisting his cooperation, and then checking against other sources the data he might have provided.

The last question that readers proceeding from today's presuppositional framework might want to ask concerns the possible participation of the LVF and the Légion Wallonie in the search for Jews for the purpose of killing them. Do we have reasons to believe that the volunteers are especially cautious in this area – that they tell less than they actually did? As part of the German Security Divisions, the three battalions of the LVF were mainly in charge of protecting roads and railroad tracks against the partisans who were conducting operations of sabotage in order to prevent or slow down the conveyance of German supplies to the frontline. None of the memoirists who were involved in this struggle in Belorussia (i.e., Bassompierre, Dupont, Labat, Larfoux, Leverrier, Rostaing, Rusco, and Saint-Loup) indicates that the LVF might also have been assigned the mission to hunt Jews in general and Jewish partisans in particular.[12] Rusco reports that in July 1942, his unit was moved to the Gomel area, where a group of "irregulars," "composed mostly of Jews," had attacked German quarters, killing thirty soldiers and "locking a few prisoners in an isba before setting it afire" (66). Rusco does not tell what happened to this "mostly Jewish" band of irregulars; ordered to move to another post, his company did not participate in the operations against them. Nevertheless, this passage is significant because of its rhetoric – of the way it emphasizes certain things and passes over others in silence. To begin with, according to Rusco, the task of the LVF was to search for partisans, not for Jews; the fact that those partisans also happened to be Jewish is presented as incidental, although its mention by Rusco tends to accredit the Nazi thesis of a necessary association between Bolshevism and Jews. Then, the war crime committed (prisoners are burned alive) is imputed to the enemy; the reprisals that the Germans doubtless took are not described; Rusco electing here to play the role of the witness who reports only what he saw, not what he might have learned later.

---

[12] The Jewish partisan unit that Nechama Tec describes in *Defiance*, the Bielski otriad, was active in southwestern Belorussia, at the 1939 Soviet-Polish border. The LVF did not operate in this area, and it is unlikely that it ever encountered members of the group that the Bielski brothers had organized.

The same imbalance can be found in most passages where the volunteers tell about their encounters with partisans, whether in Belorussia or in the Ukraine. Indeed, the focus is always on partisans' "atrocities"; the irregulars do not just kill but torture, cutting the Frenchmen's ears, pulling their eyes, emasculating them, and finally taking all clothing and belongings from their dead bodies (e.g., Labat 163; Larfoux 135; Rostaing 67; Sajer 395). It is only on occasion, and almost in passing, that the volunteers also document what most historians regard as the barbaric treatment of Russian soldiers by the SS, the Wehrmacht, and their foreign allies. Sajer, for example, reports that while on leave in Lublin during the winter of 1943, he was called upon to join an SS unit engaged against Polish partisans; he tells how the SS "finished off" the wounded and shot the prisoners (1967, 356), explaining that the laws of war did not apply to "terrorists," who could be "shot on the spot" because they did not wear the "uniform" identifying them as members of a regular army (357). Similarly, Terlin recounts how he and his companions of the Légion Wallonie unmasked partisans disguised as women and shot them. Whereas Sajer is horrified by what he saw, Terlin justifies the actions of his unit as an SS member would do; multiplying "treasons," the irregulars pretending to be women had already killed two Belgians, and they were certainly "hoping to attract more of our boys into their arms," in order to "assassinate them at leisure" (1972, 92).

Examples of the notoriously poor treatment of Russian POWs by the Germans can also be found in the volunteers' memoirs. Sajer, who seems to be particularly sensitive to this kind of exaction, reports that the prisoners whose job was to bury corpses after the bloody battle of Kharkov were prohibited from taking anything off the bodies, even food, of which Sajer admits that prisoners were given "ridiculous rations" (149). When they disobeyed and were caught, the prisoners were immediately killed, often by specialists who seemed to enjoy the task:

Once, these vicious guys tied, under my scandalized eyes, the hands of three prisoners to the bars of a gate. Then they put a grenade in one of the pockets of the victims' jackets. After pulling the cap off the grenade, they ran for cover, while the explosion disemboweled the Russians who up to the last second were asking for mercy. (149)

Sajer acknowledges that he himself, in Belgorod during the summer of 1943, killed Russian soldiers who were attempting to surrender. But he explains that his behavior can be traced to the circumstances – to the fact that he and his companions were "physically destroyed" by the hardships endured during the battle: "We were sleepy, and we knew that we couldn't sleep as long as a Bolshevik was alive. It was them or us. That's why my friend Hals and I, through the windows of a house, threw grenades at Russians who had tried to brandish a white flag" (226). Gilles is less apologetic. Describing the battle of Belgard (Pomerania, early March 1945), he tells how, upon finding four of his men thrown on a pile of manure, tortured and with their throats slit, he supported the German officer's decision to shoot Russian prisoners in retaliation and throw their bodies "on the next pile of manure"; a "just reward," such a measure was the expression of an "immanent justice" that "nobody could contest" (I, 394). Gilles is equally approbative of the reprisals that followed the discovery of German women raped and killed by the Russians in Belgard. As my memoirists frequently do, he blames the "Asiatic" members of the Soviet army, stressing that their savage behavior deserved immediate punishment: "When we happened to see such horror scenes, we couldn't be asked to keep Asiatic prisoners. They were all shot on the spot, paying for their crimes as well as for the crimes of their racial brothers" (410). (I will return in Chapter 5 to this way of singling out the "Asiatic" Russians, a distinction that makes the war into a campaign against the barbarian "East.")

The imbalance, in the volunteers' memoirs, between the report of Russian "atrocities" and of similar war crimes on the part of the legionaries of course begs the questions: Are they telling too little? Could they have told more? And are they deliberately concealing war crimes that they themselves and their units committed in Belorussia, the Ukraine, and Pomerania? Historians such as Bartov (1991, 82–3), Smith (2007, 90), and Capdevila (2003, 226–32) have argued that perpetrators, once peace has returned, are reluctant to tell about their acts of cruelty, whether such acts took the form of mass murders or of occasional exactions. In the case of major criminals – Bartov mentions Rudolf Höss, Franz Stangl, and Adolf Eichmann – archival evidence was available to disprove the exculpating narratives that the perpetrators had provided. Similar documents, however, are not on hand to establish that ordinary veterans such as Sajer, Terlin, and Gilles witnessed more scenes of mistreatments of partisans and prisoners than they actually acknowledge. Even if such documents were obtainable, moreover, the epistemological problems that the volunteers' testimonies are raising would not be solved. As Régine Robin has argued, memory never comes in the "right" amount; depending on the questions we are asking of the past, there is always "too much" or "too little" of it (34). In this instance, the legionaries often seem to tell too little with respect to our knowledge of the atrocities committed on the Eastern Front, as well as to our current concern with the subject of the Holocaust. In short, confirming Nünning's thesis, the suspicions we may have about the reliability of the volunteers' memoirs are traceable to a presuppositional framework. It is important to be aware of the existence of that framework, because it shapes our reception of the veterans' testimonies, accounting for our trust, misgiving, or outright rejection.

Whether they over- or underreport the events that their authors witnessed, the French volunteers' memoirs contribute worthwhile materials to the already abundant corpus of research and testimonies about the war in the USSR. First, they provide more evidence for Bartov's thesis of the "barbarisation" of warfare on the Eastern Front: The transformation of the conflict into a *Vernichtungskrieg*, resulting in an uninterrupted series of horrendous brutalities. In this respect, those memoirs differ significantly from some of the testimonies that Bartov and Capdevila quote, in which veterans concede that they possibly committed atrocities, but claim that they "do not remember taking part in them, or even observing them" (Bartov 1991, 184). More specifically, recollections such as Terlin's, Sajer's, and Labat's contribute – years before the 1995 exhibit – to debunking the myth of a "clean" Wehrmacht that Guderian, von Manstein, and other high-ranking military men had propagated after the war. Indeed, their authors fought in Belorussia and the Ukraine in units that were part of the Wehrmacht at the time, and the accounts that they provide show that acts of brutality toward prisoners and the civilian population were not reserved for the SS and the Einsatzgruppen. While those accounts do not describe mass murders, they document what might be called the "ordinary exactions" of the war; through descriptions that are both meticulous and casual, they reveal what an occupying force is led to do in order to carry out its duties, provide for its needs, and sometimes satisfy its darkest fantasies.

Insofar as the volunteers' memoirs focus on the everyday life of soldiers who were members of small units, they also add to the knowledge of the attitudes and behaviors that prevailed in this kind of environment. More precisely, they testify to the important role that "comradery" played at the front. Thomas Kühne has devoted a whole book to this concept, arguing that *Kameradschaft*, defined as a "steady, family-like, personal bond that was based on trust," linked German soldiers with each other during World War II (12). Some of the passages I have just quoted could illustrate Kühne's thesis, demonstrating that a similar "bond" existed among the troops that were fighting alongside the Germans. But those same passages also confirm another aspect of Kühne's argument, namely that if comradery was a "virtue in the service of care for the other," it could also become an "engine of bestial power" (Kühne 13). Gilles's and Terlin's accounts of the killing of unarmed Russian POWs are, in this respect, most revealing. For Gilles, the fact that "our comrades" were "atrociously mutilated" by the Russians justified the shooting; and for Terlin, the possibility that "more of our boys" could become victims of partisans disguised as women validated the execution of the captives. The words "comrades" and "boys," together with the possessive adjective of the first-person plural "our," here inscribe the solidarity that was one of the main components of *Kameradschaft*. But the two episodes also point to the fact, emphasized by Kühne, that "solidarity" could lead to hideous actions, such as the slaughtering of people who were no longer in the position of defending themselves.

By tracing the killing of prisoners to the demands of comradery, even though demands here are for brutal revenge, Gilles and Terlin seem intent on engaging the audience's support and ensuring its cooperation. Whether readers buy or not into the argument that murder is justified by the requirements of comradery will depend again on their presuppositional framework, more precisely here on their cultural mindset. Smelser and Davies, in their study of the myth of the Eastern Front, have identified "a broad subculture of general readers, German military enthusiasts, wargame aficionados, military paraphernalia collectors, and reenactors" who tend to "romanticize" the German army. Members of that subculture may take "comradery" to be synonymous with "mutual assistance," "emotional togetherness," and "readiness to sacrifice oneself" (Kühne 272), and accept that acts of retaliation be committed in its name. Contemporary readers who think of themselves mainly as members of the "civil society," on the other hand, may deem those acts to show that comradery brings out the worst in people, as it vindicates the "lynching party" type of activities that "bands of males" are prone to undertake (Kühne 272). Wherever we may stand on Kühne's scale of positive versus negative views of comradeship, it remains that the concept was, or had become, an important part of the French volunteers' ideological system. I will take a closer look at that system in Chapter 5, when I examine the cultural references on which the veterans draw when they describe their endeavors.

4

Textualization

The issues of veracity I have just examined obviously are related to issues of writing. The question I want to pose of the texts in my corpus here is: If their authors were "really there" and can be held as dependable, how do they represent what they have gone through? In other words, what conventions of discourse are the authors using when they pass on their reminiscences? Questions of this type are not reserved for literary critics concerned with referential narratives. They are, or should be, equally important for historians, as the data supplied by life stories cannot be exploited without considering the rules that frame that genre. Indeed, experiences do not spontaneously metamorphose into texts just because they are assumedly genuine. They have to be textualized, and the strategies that authors employ during this process must be accounted for because they have epistemological implications. For one thing, some of them entail that the information provided can be verified, while others entail that it cannot; choices in such areas as voice, point of view, and figurative language matter, because they shape the representations of the events that the authors have endured and now are setting out to recount.

The concept of an "experience" that has to be "represented" admittedly must be clarified. By "experience," I mean here what the *Merriam Webster's Collegiate Dictionary* defines as "something personally encountered" (409), in this instance, "something that the witness actually lived through" as opposed to the imaginary pasts that authors of fictional memoirs create for their narrators-protagonists. Describing a testimony as the narrative of "something personally encountered" does not imply the belief in a "natural," "unmediated relationship between words and things," a type of connection that the historian and theorist Joan Scott has exposed in an oft-quoted article (1991, 796). To the contrary, the idea of a process of textualization assumes a mediation between the witness's past and the memoir that represents it. It is on that mediation that I now want to focus, asking what rules, codes, and conventions are at work in texts the authors of which claim to recount actual events and events through which they personally lived.

TOTAL RECALL

In his review of Sajer's *Le Soldat oublié*, Gray wonders how the author can "remember so many details" and concludes that Sajer, who "makes no mention of a journal," must have "reproduced much from memory" (4). Gray's remark is important, as it refers implicitly to a question that can be asked of every life narrative: If the author obviously "remembers," and remembers enough to compose a text, what type of memory is at work in that text? Posed to the memoirs in my corpus, including Sajer's, that question can only yield one answer: The preponderant type is "total recall." That is, the veterans whose reminiscences I am investigating are all, to varying degrees, endowed with perfect memory. Whether they write in the late 1940s or in the 1990s, they have – to turn again to *Merriam-Webster's* – the faculty of "remembering with complete clarity and in complete detail" experiences they had in the past (1246), or at least during the period on which they focus in their memoirs. Moreover, those veterans do not feel compelled to justify how they can retrieve as much information as they do. Some of them (e.g., Auvray, Gruber) signal in prefaces or forewords that they base their recollections on notes taken during the war, while others (e.g., Costabrava, Rostaing, Rusco), as seen in Chapter 1, let their editor explain how he helped them bring back their past and write it up. Most of them, however, provide no clarifications whatsoever, implying – as Gray points out in his review of *Le Soldat oublié* – that they are working "from memory," and that memory in their cases provides an unproblematic access to the past.

Viewed from a textual standpoint, total recall as employed in the volunteers' memoirs has at least two significant aspects. The first one is the presence of highly detailed descriptions of places and activities, as in this account, taken from Rostaing's memoir, of the struggles in Berlin in late April 1945:

Our progression continues. The battle has taken a confusing turn, which won't cease until the end. I can't reach Richard Platz, which is protected by a Russian anti-tank gun. An assault gun is brought. It hits its target. The Russian is now silent. I launch an attack on the Maxim machine-gun that is still blocking the men under the porches. I take cover behind trash containers before I leap again and again. I throw one, two, three grenades. The company following me, I come out onto the square. I've lost contact with the Command Post, which must have changed location. I decide to continue going into the Russian front. A group of young boys from the Hitlerjugend has joined us. A strong enemy troop holds a barricade. We attack it, screaming like madmen. We suffer heavy losses, especially among the Hitlerjugend, but we overwhelm the Russians. We occupy Weserstrasse. (Rostaing 193)

Such descriptions may include the reconstitution of states of mind, the memoirist recalling not just what he did but how he felt, as is the case when Gaultier evokes the moment when he was hit by shrapnel near Sanok, in Galicia, on August 9, 1944:

Vloc! I roll down like a rabbit – what is it? I pick myself up, my mouth is full of blood! What's happening to me? I stand up. Any danger? My comrades have cleared out. I run three meters. My mouth is full of blood. Good God! Where is it coming from? Some tingling behind my left shoulder blade ... My legs no longer support me. That's the last straw! I try to pull myself together. Let's see, what did I decide? My legs are giving out. I am at the edge of the forest ... A blank! I'm laying on two rifles and a tent canvas, uncomfortably lumbering along. (Gaultier 225)

Conventions of total recall are particularly obvious in these two excerpts. Rostaing remembers precisely the names of streets (Weserstrasse) and squares (Richard Platz) where he fought in Berlin in late April 1945, as well as the kind of machine-guns (Maxims) that the Soviets were using during the battle; he also has kept in mind the number of grenades (three) that he threw in these specific circumstances, before successfully storming the Russian barricade with his fellow French SS. Likewise, Gaultier seems to have no trouble reconstructing what he experienced when he was hit by shrapnel; he depicts the physical effects of his wounds (his mouth is full of blood, his left shoulder blade is tingling), while also reporting what he said to himself, whether about his current situation ("That's the last straw!"), or about plans he had made earlier ("What did I decide?"). Total recall is clearly a central component of the narrative in these scenes, as it enables the memoirists to report the particulars of what they lived through at a specific time and place. Whatever problems of verifiability the convention might involve, its use here – as in many similar episodes – definitely increases the readability of the text and accounts in part for the popularity of life narratives about the war with general audiences. More precisely, the strategy makes it possible to include a certain type of fetching personal information ("I threw ... three grenades," "My legs are giving out") that trade historians won't admit in their studies, because it cannot be checked against the available archives, and not even against other testimonies.

In addition to detailed descriptions of events, total recall in the volunteers' memoirs also takes the form of what narratologists have named "reported speech" (Genette 1972, 192). That is, those memoirs include conversations that quote verbatim the words the author has spoken, which were spoken to him, and/or he has merely heard. Such conversations can be extensive. Saint-Loup reproduces over seven pages and 239 lines the discussion he had in Hildesheim with Rebatet on the topic of the "new," federated Europe that the SS were supposedly promoting, against the pan-Germanist program of the Nazi government (1986b, 88–95). Long, didactic conversations of this type are frequent in Labat's *Les Places étaient chères*, where they bear on such weighty subjects as reasons for enlisting (27–30), the situation in Germany in July 1944 after the attempt on Hitler's life (460–4), and the problems posed by the invasion of East Prussia and Pomerania by the Soviets (531–9). They are presented the way they would be in a novel (each reply is granted a separate paragraph), as in the following exchange – an excerpt from the discussion during which a member of Doriot's Parti Populaire Français tries to convince Labat of the need for the LVF to merge with the SS:

– We are confident that the LVF has ceased to live. We will help every one of its members who desires to leave, but as an organization we will remain the last ones if necessary, because we are responsible for its creation; as long as one single man remains in this adventure and is exposed to a risk, all our leaders must help him with all their hearts. We are responsible for souls, and none of our officers will abandon his soldiers and his comrades.
– Even if he must become a member of the SS?
– Even if one must go with him into the fire of hell. And the SS right now is far from hell. But all these distinctions at this stage have little importance. Believe me, it's better to end with a flourish than to slickly get out when the going is good. (475)

The conversation goes on for three and half pages and 116 lines, basically leaving the interlocutors where they were at the beginning. Its function, as in ideologically oriented novels of the 1930s such as those of Malraux, is to introduce different positions, in this instance, the stands of the LVF members who wanted to merge with the Waffen-SS for the sake of efficiency, and of those who refused that transfer because they deemed that it would involve the loss of their French identity. Though less wrenching than the scenes of combat discussed earlier, these lengthy, verbatim reports of conversations nevertheless provide noteworthy data to readers interested in France's military collaboration. Historians generally agree that the French volunteers were contentious, as they often came from different political parties and had enrolled for different reasons. Conversations presented in total recall illustrate that contentiousness, as they give readers an idea of the ideological conflicts that riddled the French units, making them difficult to manage both in the barracks and on the battlefield.

Though the volunteers frequently turn to reported speech, not all of them employ it as often and at such length as Saint-Loup and Labat do. Auvray, Laurier, and Lobsiger, for example, hardly include this type of discourse in their texts, and Gilles indicates at the beginning of his reminiscences that he "won't make his characters dialogue," because he "cannot remember their exact words forty years later" (I, 30). Furthermore, my memoirists sometimes report potentially interesting conversations in "narratized speech" (Genette 1972, 191), treating uttered words as events among other events, on the model "the captain informed us of his decision." The most striking examples are probably the passages in which Degrelle recounts his two interviews with Hitler, to my knowledge the only occasions when a volunteer – granted, not any volunteer – was able to meet Hitler or a major figure of the Nazi regime.[1] Notwithstanding the importance of these moments, Degrelle treats each of the interviews in less than two pages, and he summarizes Hitler's lengthy statements in narratized speech, writing for example: "Soon, he [Hitler] abandoned military considerations and switched to the issue of bourgeois liberalism. He explained to me with an amazing lucidity why the fall of the latter was ineluctable" (380). The only words of Hitler that Degrelle reports verbatim are, at the beginning of the first interview: "You caused me so much worry..." (328), and, at the end of the second, the sentence: "If I had a son, I would wish he were like you..." (381). Degrelle, who hardly uses reported speech in his memoir, may not want to break this self-imposed rule even for the purpose of describing what must have been an exceptional event in his life, given his political beliefs. As a skilled rhetorician (he was supposedly a brilliant speaker), Degrelle may also deem that

---

[1] Rostaing tells that on April 27, 1945 he was invited to meet Hitler and went to the Bunker. Once there, however, he was informed that Hitler was "too busy" and the meeting was postponed. "I will never see Adolf Hitler up close," Rostaing observes regretfully (195).

less is more, in this instance, that reporting his discussions with Hitler with utmost succinctness was the best way of underscoring for the readers the importance that such discussions had for him.[2]

In his contribution to the Internet debates about *Le Soldat oublié* I examined in Chapter 2, Lieutenant Colonel Louis Brown, a "West Point educated scholar and armored officer whose service included service in Germany," notes that Sajer's book contains not just "a lot of dialogue," but also an unusual amount of "quoted material"(http://members. shaw.ca/grossdeutschland/sajer.htm 4/22/2007). Brown does not specify what he means by "quoted material," but he is probably thinking of the extended statements that Sajer incorporates into his book, such as the whole text of a speech celebrating the German enterprise that Sajer's captain, Hauptmann Wesreidau, gave to his troops while in the Ukraine (1967, 258–61).[3] But Brown may also have in mind the letters, sent to his parents and to his woman friend Paula, which Sajer reproduces in their entirety (1967, 211–12, 471), and to which he sometimes adds retrospective comments, such as "I was lying" (211). Similar types of inclusions are found in other books written by the volunteers. Mit also cites complete letters (59, 77–8) and inserts an article, supposedly published in August 1944 in the *Krakauer Zeitung*, praising the "sacrifice" that the Brigade Frankreich had made in Galicia (152). As for Rostaing and Gaultier, they cite statements made on the radio. Rostaing includes Stalin's address of July 3, 1941 calling for the formation of partisan units (41); and Gaultier, who was then in Vichy's Ministry of Information, a speech he gave himself on June 18, 1942 in order to counter the commemoration of de Gaulle's *appel* from London with the remembrance of other events that took place on that same day, in this instance, of several acts of heroism accomplished by units of the French army that were still fighting (104–5).

---

[2] Saint-Loup, who reports these episodes in *Les SS de la Toison d'Or* (299–305), collapses the two interviews into one, quotes the sentence "If I had a son...," and provides additional dialogue. But he does not indicate his sources, and one must assume that he is drawing his information from Degrelle's memoirs, as well as (possibly) from conversations he had with the head of the Wallonie in Spain after the war. Conway, in his brief, scholarly account of the second meeting between Hitler and Degrelle, does not quote any dialogue verbatim, stating dryly that "nothing of substance was discussed" (244).

[3] Bartov (1991, 117), as I mentioned in Chapter 2, uses this speech as an example of the fanaticism that young officers sought to instil into their troops. Focusing on the ideological content of the speech, Bartov does not consider the issues of writing raised by this passage: Sajer's reproducing his commander's words verbatim over two pages and 101 lines involves a major act of total recall, and the original speech has been translated twice, from the German into French by Sajer, and from the French into English by Lily Emmet – the author of the English-language version that Bartov quotes.

The inclusion in memoirs of such material as speeches, letters, newspaper articles, and radio broadcasts has an obvious legitimizing function, especially in texts written by rank-and-file soldiers whose names are not in themselves warrants of authority. This "displayed heterogeneity" (Jeannelle 325) shows that the memoirist can operate as an historian would, specifically that he can supplement his narrative with "documents" that at some point he has produced or received. Yet the presence of these quoted texts pose problems that are not just of memory (how can the author remember?), but of storage in the physical sense of the term; readers may ask how Sajer and Mit saved part of their war correspondence, and Gaultier, the text of a speech he gave in 1942, forty-nine years before the publication of his memoir. Of these questions, the one raised in Rostaing's book might be the easiest to answer. The text of Stalin's call for starting guerrilla activities figures in several studies about the war in the USSR, and Rostaing (or most likely his ghostwriter, Demaret) did not have to look very far to find the speech that they wanted to quote. The same remark applies to the excerpts of historical studies that Bayle and especially Malardier insert into their reminiscences, usually to confirm their version of the facts. Indeed, quoting – as Malardier does throughout his text – such historians and journalists as Amouroux (47), Knopp (90), Brissaud (92), Ryan (169), Kuby (185), Le Tissier (226), and Mabire (447), as well as the former American ambassador to Moscow, Averel Harriman (333), does not pose problems of memory or storage; denoting a concern for grounding one's testimony in other accounts, it only requires access to libraries and/or bookstores.

While the volunteers generally employ the conventions of total recall in their memoirs, it is not always clear on whose recall they are drawing. In his history of the collaboration, Gordon affirms that Saint-Loup's *Les Partisans* provides an "eye-witness account" of the first, unsuccessful battle with the Russians that the LVF fought at Djukovo in early December 1941 (251). Yet Gordon does not specify that the "eye-witness account" here is not the author's. Saint-Loup enlisted in the summer of 1942, and if he may be suspected of sometimes overreporting, he has never claimed to have participated in the attack on Djukovo. The eyewitness testimony to which Gordon refers comes, in fact, from a log book (*carnet de route*) that Saint-Loup admits that he "stole" from a soldier he met at a military hospital in Smolensk (1986a, 50), because he thought that it was a valuable testimony. Saint-Loup states that he is reproducing the log book "as is" ["Je le publie tel qu'il est"], and he is careful to demarcate the passages he cites with quotation marks (50–7, 60–1). Thus, the excerpts from the log book serve as a relay. They enable Saint-Loup to describe the struggles of the LVF in late 1941, that is, events that for him have military meaning and symbolic value, but that he cannot recount in his own name since he was not in the USSR at the time. Moreover, just like Stalin's speech and the *Krakauer Zeitung* article inserted in Rostaing's and Mit's memoirs, those same excerpts have a rhetorical function; as data coming from a source that is not the author, they add to the credibility of the witness's testimony.

Relays, however, are not always as explicitly acknowledged in the volunteers' recollections as they are in the passage of *Les Partisans* I have just examined. Labat, for example, who was in Berlin as an observer in April 1945, describes in most detailed manner some of the combats that took place there during the "last battle," though without always specifying how he became apprised of what he reports:

A German gets lost in the middle of a Soviet company that advances in a tunnel they have just conquered. He pulls the pin out of a grenade in his belt, while following the company. All the grenades blow at once, and their detonation causes the explosion of the grenades that the Reds are carrying. The tunnel is no longer anything but a mass grave, which the SS contemplate with astonishment when they reconquer the tunnel in the evening. (559)

It is difficult, upon reading this passage, to conceive how Labat could have witnessed the scene that he recounts. His report is probably based on other peoples' testimonies, though one might ask "whose testimonies"; the massacre apparently left no survivors, and the SS who "reconquered" the tunnel had no means of establishing with precision what had actually happened. The story that Labat tells here – if one tries to identify the discursive conventions that underlie it – should probably be prefaced with a statement such as: "Here is an example of the kind of tales that were circulating in Berlin in late April 1945, and of the kind of events which those tales were about." In brief, Labat in this passage seems to be reporting a story that someone else told him, and a story that has a generic, symbolic quality. Revealingly, Labat does not say when or where in the vast Berlin subway system the incident that he recounts with so many details actually occurred.

Looking at the passages in Saint-Loup and Labat I have just examined, narrative theorists would say that they are "embedded," whether explicitly (Saint-Loup) or implicitly (Labat). The technique of "embedding," that is, of setting one narrative sequence within another, has been used by such novelists as Joseph Conrad in *Lord Jim* and Vladimir Nabokov in *The True Life of Sebastian Knight,* but it is also found in testimonies, as witnesses often do not recount what they saw themselves, but what other people told them that they had seen. Yet embedding in testimonies has epistemological implications it does not have in fiction. Posing most acutely the problem of transmission that is central for this type of discourse, it entails that the witness is of the type that Holocaust literature specialist Froma Zeitlin calls "vicarious": someone who obviously was not "there," but whose "link to the past … can still be firmly anchored to the presence (and authority) of firsthand witnesses" (130). Admittedly, Saint-Loup and Labat do not have the same "link to the past" as the children of Holocaust survivors whose texts Zeitlin analyzes in her essay. For one thing, they are only vicarious witnesses on occasion; whereas Zeitlin's narrators focus on reconstructing their relatives' past, the volunteers keep their own lives at the center of the stories they are telling. When they shift from testifying to reporting someone else's experience, therefore, they do not aim to "assume the burden of memory, of rememoration, by means of which one might become a witness oneself" (Zeitlin 130). In other words, they do not aim to "become" witnesses; they have been witnesses all along, and their goal, when they draw on the testimonies of others, is to complete their own, necessarily limited narratives, not to make such testimonies (or the quest for them) the subject matter of their enterprise.

In his analysis of the memoirs written by Holocaust survivors, Jared Stark acknowledges that their reliance on such "stylistic and dramatic effects" as the "representation of verbatim dialogue" can "strain factual accuracy" (198). Those effects, according to Stark, lack the "verifiability demanded of historical evidence," therefore bringing "suspicion" upon the value of the testimonies that admit devices of this type (199). To be sure, such instances of total recall as detailed narratives of events and word-for-word reports of speeches and conversations raise issues of memory and documentation: How can the authors remember so precisely what happened years ago? And how could their reports be substantiated so that they would count as Stark's legitimate "historical evidence?" While such questions can certainly be posed about the volunteers' memoirs, they do not disqualify those texts from the ranks of valid, authoritative testimonies. Indeed, rules for writing memoirs must be distinguished from rules for writing historiography, or rather, for writing scholarly historiography. That latter type of discourse excludes factual data the source of which cannot be verified, and it is especially distrustful of reported speech; in this area, it only admits statements and conversations that have been recorded mechanically or attested by several witnesses. Popularizations such as Mabire's histories of the LVF and the French SS, on the other hand, rely on conventions similar to those I have just identified; they include factual items that cannot be documented, as well as conversations that clearly have been reconstructed, provided that they were ever held.[4]

While the epistemological status of Mabire's and similar works can (and has been) debated, memoirs clearly are not submitted to the exigencies of scholarly research and writing. To be sure, falling under Lejeune's "autobiographical pact," the data that they offer can be questioned and challenged. Upon unveiling new documents about the battle of Berlin and exploring press archives, critics could demonstrate, say, that unlike what Rostaing and Mit affirm in their accounts, the Russians did not use Maxim machine guns in Berlin, and that the *Krakauer Zeitung* never published, in August 1944, an article praising the activities of the Brigade Frankreich in Galicia. However, even the exposure of those inaccuracies would not remove *Le Prix d'un serment* and *Carcasse à vendre* from the category "valid testimonies"; it would merely reveal something about the authors, in this instance, that their recall, though total, is not perfect, or that they have a taste for making up details. In other words, as Suleiman argues in her discussion of Charlotte Delbo's and Jorge Semprun's recollections of their experiences in concentration camps, the basic contract that binds memoirs with their readers does not warrant that those texts are "true," in the sense of offering verified data exclusively (2006, 149). It merely warrants that they are "truthful" (149), by which Suleiman means that their authors were "really there," are trustworthy, and recount with sincerity "what things were like" for them at the critical points in their lives on which they have chosen to focus.

Unlike the writers whom Suleiman treats in her study, however, the memoirists in my corpus do not include a metatextual dimension in their testimonies. They may tell where and when their book was composed: Degrelle writes in the "military hospital 'Mola' in San Sebastian (Spain)," between "August and December 1945" (501); Auvray, during the period of "forced leisure" he spent in French prisons after the war

---

[4] The use of dialogs in scholarly works has been debated among historians. Emmannuel Le Roy Ladurie, in his review of Rousso's *Un Château en Allemagne* (a study of the Vichy government's stay in Sigmaringen from August 1944 to May 1945), blames Rousso for "artificially dramatizing his work by cluttering it with endless dialogs," even though such dialogs are grounded in "specific and well explored documents" (240). Conversely, Daniel Cordier writes in a comment on his lengthy, thoroughly researched biography of the Resistance leader Jean Moulin that dialogs for him were "necessary" in a work aiming at completeness; he acknowledges, however, that conversations he includes in his study only reproduce "approximately" what was said at the time (308).

(10); the anonymous author of *Vae Victis*, "from abroad" (227); and Bassompierre, sitting at the "modest table" of the "squalid cell" he occupies in Fresnes, waiting for his execution in 1948 (175). They may also explain some of the principles they will follow while writing up their recollections: La Mazière will report his reminiscences "in no particular order," "as they come back" to him (2003, 18); Auvray "won't use names," because he does not want to invent "strange pseudonyms" (11), as other memoirists and some historians have done; Saint-Loup will recount his experiences in the USSR "with the objectivity, the guarantee of sincerity, and the disinterestedness" he has made his rule during his "ten years of travel throughout the world" (1986a, 145); and Levast, "unlike other memoirists," will tell about his time in Pomerania and Berlin "with a concern for truth and a touch of humor," as he does not want to "make a tragedy out of his adventure," even though "it could have been fatal for him" (12). Finally, they may point to activities (and failures) of memory, qualifying certain statements with such phrases as: "if I remember correctly" (Laurier 80); "I remember this date so precisely for specific reasons" (Lobsiger 146); "I no longer know" (Sajer 1967, 75); "a village whose name I have forgotten" (*Vae Victis* 74); and "while writing, I am furious not to be able to remember ... what was written on the flag of the LVF" (Levellier 51).

Such asides, however, are neither numerous nor provocative enough to constitute a self-reflexive component, in which the volunteers would comment on the conventions of the genre "memoir," especially on the advantages and limitations of total recall. Semprun – to return to one of Suleiman's examples – revisits in *L'Ecriture ou la vie* (published in English as *Literature or Life*) the texts he wrote about his time in Buchenwald, explaining that he rejected "mere testimony" because he wanted "to avoid... the enumeration of sufferings and horrors," a task at which "others would try their hands anyway" (1994, 175). Relying on what narratologists call "disnarration" (Prince 2003, 22), Semprun also states that that he won't report certain episodes in his biography, for instance, the "life changing" moment when the Spanish communist party excluded him from the executive committee, because such stories "no longer appeal to anybody" (278). Finally, and more teasingly, Semprun (46) confesses that he "invented" characters such as Hans von Freiberg in *Le grand voyage* (published in English as *The Long Journey*), and that he is even "fabulating" at the very moment he is disclosing those inventions; recounting how he and a fellow member of the Resistance shot a German soldier, he depicts that soldier "from a distance" as a "blond boy with blue eyes," while they, in fact, could not see the color of his eyes before they had killed him, and then "been able to look at him from close" (42).

Compared to passages like these, the references that the volunteers make to the time when they are writing, the discursive guidelines they are following, and the activities of memory they are deploying appear most faint. Even Laurier, Leverrier, and Saint-Loup, the experienced writers in my corpus, do not seem inclined to play games with their audience, especially games that question the credibility of the story they are telling. Yet this absence of self-consciousness is not unusual in life narratives. Memoirs in general, and war memoirs in particular, do not direct writers to be as mischievous as Semprun is in *L'Ecriture ou la vie*, and readers certainly do not expect veterans to play games with them when they offer their versions of World War II. More basically, life narratives do not require authors to be explicit about the way they have obtained their data, the reasons why they include or exclude certain episodes, and the kind of memory (perfect? partial?) on which they are drawing. On the pragmatic level of writing, moreover, it is difficult to conceive how memoirists could be consistently self-reflexive about their endeavor. If they tried, they certainly would have trouble going beyond the first pages of their manuscript, because the text would soon be clogged with references to sources and comments on activities of memory; and if they nevertheless managed to complete their project, the resulting book would probably only be of interest for scholars obsessed with evidence and specialists in narrative experiments: The flow of the story would constantly be impeded, disrupting the way we read texts in general and life narratives in particular. Yet it is worth noting that the memoirist's discursive and epistemological situation in the area of documentation is ultimately not very different from the historian's. As textual analyses of the most rule-abiding historiographic texts has shown (e.g., Carrard 1986), historians cannot support every statement they are making; sources are not always available, and if they were, quoting them in a consistent manner would soon make the study unreadable.

PERSPECTIVES

If the convention of total recall accounts for the highly detailed narratives that the volunteers supply, it does not explain the presence of other, equally significant features displayed in those memoirs. For one thing, that convention bears on the quantity of data that the witness affords;

but it does not concern the position that the witness occupied as an observer or a participant, a position that both enabled him to have access to the data and limited that access. Determining the vantage point of the narrator-author is important for poeticians who study the memoir as discursive genre, but also for historians who use life narratives to document their studies of the past. For both, it matters to establish what kind of information the witness is communicating, and how that information became available to him. These issues are most significant in the kind of war memoirs I am investigating, as they trigger questions such as: Is the author reporting his own experiences exclusively? If he does, how does he keep readers informed of the larger context? If he does not, does he justify his access to data that were not within his observational range? In short, is he explicit about the way(s) he obtained this additional information, or does he let readers make educated guesses, speculating about the relays that enabled him to report what he did not see himself?

When they consider those issues in fiction, poeticians (e.g., Genette 1972, 206–7; Prince 2003, 31–2) usually distinguish among three types of "focalization": zero focalization, where events are presented "from behind" the characters, from a position that is mostly unlocatable (Tolstoï's *War and Peace*, Thackeray's *Vanity Fair*); internal focalization, where events are presented "with" the characters, from a position that is either fixed (James's *The Ambassadors*) or variable (Joyce's *Ulysses*); and external focalization, where events are presented "from outside," from the standpoint of an observer who reports what the actors do and say without having access to their consciousness (Hammett's *The Maltese Falcon*). These categories obviously are models that do not have "pure" realizations, especially the last two. Most texts move freely from one mode to the other, whether by design when authors play self-consciously with focalization, or by accident when they are unaware of theories about point of view or indifferent to them. Designed initially to account for discursive conventions at work in fictional narratives, these categories can be applied to, or at least adapted for, referential and personal texts. They can certainly be used to describe the texts in my corpus, as memoirs are narratives, and their authors – consciously or unconsciously – had to make choices in the area of focalization, as they did in all other areas of writing.

The historian Stephen Fritz, in his study of the letters, diaries, and memoirs written by low-ranking German infantrymen during or after World War II, argues that those personal texts offer a fresh perspective on the conflict. Contrasting with the works of both historians and high-ranking officers, they present "the view from below" (1), in this instance, an account of the German campaigns as experienced by the *Landser*, Sajer's ordinary, "forgotten" foot soldier. Examining as a historian the texts he has selected, Fritz focuses on those texts' social, political, and ideological content. But he never turns to dissecting, say, a diary as diary – as a genre with its own procedures and conventions. His analyses remain mostly thematic, as he does not consider how specific textual modes may set constraints on the message to be communicated.

Redescribed with respect to narrative theory, Fritz's view "from below" mostly falls under internal focalization. Whether they keep journals or write letters, the *Landser* usually restrict their accounts to their own experiences as well as to the experiences of their fellow soldiers. However, they neither report events in which they did not participate nor enter other peoples' minds without specifying how they know what they know. Most of the memoirists in my corpus were also low-ranking infantrymen, and the standpoint on the war that they offer is similar to that of the *Landser*; it is the standpoint of the ordinary soldier, a lens that generates descriptions usually conducted in internal focalization. In this respect, the accounts that they provide differ notably from those of the high-ranking officers under whom they served, for instance, from the memoirs of German generals such as Heinz Guderian, Paul Hausser, Erich von Manstein, and Felix Steiner. Sajer, in a passage that Fritz quotes in *Frontsoldaten*, complains bitterly about the discrepancy between "top down" and "bottom up" perspectives and points to the exclusions that such discrepancy generates. The subject is the Grossdeutschland's retreat from the Ukraine in the fall of 1943:

Since then, generals have written accounts of these events taken as a whole. They have located catastrophes, writing one sentence or ten lines about the losses from sickness or frost bite. But they never, to my knowledge, have sufficiently expressed the wretchedness of the soldier abandoned to a fate one would wish to spare a mangy dog. They never have evoked the hours of agony added to the thousands of hours of agony, the obvious resentment of the individual lost in a large herd where every man, submerged in his own misery, cannot consider the sufferings of the other. (1967, 257–8)

Comparing top-down and bottom-up accounts of the events to which Sajer refers, namely the retreat from the Ukraine, certainly helps illustrate the gap between perspectives that Sajer bemoans. The SS general Hausser, for example, describes in the following way one of the bloodiest episodes of that retreat – the desperate attempt of German troops (including the Division Wallonie) to break out of the Soviet encirclement at Cherkassy:

> In the area of Army Group South, retrograde operations to the Dniepr River took place until the end of 1943. While the Third Division conducted retrograde operations to Kriwoi Rog, the Fifth Division and starting in November 1943 also the Twenty-Eight Division ("Wallonie") were also engaged in heavy retrograde operations in Cherkassy. (1966, 111)

As far as perspective is concerned, Hausser here plays the part of the military historian and relies on zero focalization. Erasing any reference to his personal involvement, he is content with providing an overview of the events, more precisely with placing the fighting at Cherkassy in the framework of the German withdrawal toward the Dnieper River in late 1943–early 1944. Yet there is no such thing as a description entirely devoid of a standpoint. Hausser's account in this regard is typical of zero focalization, as it does not come from nowhere but juxtaposes two positions: that of the neutral observer, who names places and supplies dates, and that of the career soldier who, more than twenty years after the end of the war, is still using terms that seem borrowed from the reports the German command was issuing in late 1943. Indeed, the expression "retrograde operations" (in the original German: *Zurückkämpfe*) is obviously a euphemism, probably devised at the time for the purpose of reassuring public opinion. Yet Hausser still employs it, to mean that while Army Group South fell back (*Zurück*), it did so fighting (*kämpfe*) rather than merely pulling out. Whether this assessment is correct or not is open to debate, of course. According to the Eastern Front specialists Müller and Ueberschär, Army Group South suffered "heavy losses" while breaking out of Cherkassy, and the battle is described in Soviet literature as "Stalingrad on the Dnieper" (128). The operations conducted there should thus be qualified as full "retreats" (in noneuphemistic German: *Rückzüge* or *Abzüge*), rather than as *Zurückkämpfe*.[5]

---

[5] Hausser is not the only former general to use euphemistic language in his account of the German retreat on the Eastern Front. Von Manstein devotes the last chapter of his memoir, tellingly titled *Verlorene Siege* (published in English as *Lost Victories*), to what he calls "The defensive battles of 1943–1944." The phrase "retrograde operations" is used in *Slaughterhouse: The Encyclopedia of the Eastern Front* (265), and it seems appropriate to render the German *Zurückkämpfe*. Paul Fussell points to the similar phrase "retrograde movement" in his account of the operations of the American army in northwestern Europe in 1944–45, noting sarcastically that it is the Americans' "favored euphemism" to designate retreats of all kinds (129). I owe the explanation of the difference between *Rückzüge* and *Zurückkämpfe* to my colleague (and native speaker of German), Konrad Kenkel.

Hausser mentions the presence of the Wallonie at Cherkassy, and their successful though murderous breakout from the "pocket" has certainly marked the Belgian volunteers more than any other battle in which they took part; Terlin, Degrelle, and Philippet devote, respectively 136, 97, and 71 pages to the Legion's thrust through the Soviet lines, which they recount from the limited perspective of the frontline soldier. Terlin, for instance, provides the following account of combat in the village of Mochny:

> The Russians' attack triggers the only possible reaction from the Walloons. All the officers shout the same order: "We counter-attack!" We must still hold for a few hours the eastern side of the pocket. The Burgundians, shouting and shooting, rush through the burning isbas, trampling the mud and the manure underfoot.[6] The hand-to-hand combat begins in stinking poultry-yards, among cackling chickens that were browned by the fire. A black and acrid smoke gets to our throats. We spit, we cry, we shout. The free-for-all becomes more and more confusing... One has to shout to communicate the order that has just arrived: "Mochny must be held until tomorrow at dawn." (1972, 69)

Unlike Hausser's top-down overview of the operations in the Ukraine, Terlin's bottom-up account of a specific event, the struggle in the village of Mochny, conveys the experience of the ordinary soldier who is exposed to the hazards of the war and has only a limited understanding of the overall situation. The narrative here is "scenic" (it focuses on a specific moment), and the way it is told constitutes a typical instance of internal focalization. That is, Terlin seeks to reconstruct the events as they were lived by the participants, recounting what the soldiers did (they rushed through the village), what they smelled (an acrid smoke), and what they were able to hear in spite of the deafening noise (shouted orders, such as "We counter-attack!"). In this respect, Terlin's narrative can be viewed as an attempt to communicate what Cru, in his analysis of World War I veterans' testimonies, describes as the "material fact" of war: A fact that can only be known "through direct contact," "through the eyes, the ears, the nose, the nerves, and the guts" (1929, 138), and that witnesses can attempt to represent in language, albeit without being able to convey the basic, original sensory experience (the word "smoke" does not have an odor).

Terlin and his fellow Belgians' participation in intensive, large-scale battles was not shared by all the volunteers. It was, in fact, reserved for

---

[6] Terlin names his fellow soldiers "Burgundians" (and not "Belgians" or "Walloonians") in reference to Degrelle's ambition to reestablish the duchy of Burgundy.

the members of the Wallonie and, albeit during a much briefer period, for those of the Brigade Frankreich and the Division Charlemagne. But the soldiers of the LVF spent more than two years in Belorussia hunting partisans, "bitterly disappointed" that the Germans would not let them go to the front (Labat 110). Their narratives, therefore, are very different from the Belgians'; they do not recount real battles (as Terlin's, Degrelle's, and Philippet's chapters about Cherkassy do), but brief, isolated encounters, such as this attack on a German convoy by the partisans on the Mohilev-Bobruisk road, described by the anonymous author of *Vae Victis*:

> The convoy is ready at last. It is made of seven Ford trucks built by the Russians and preceded by an armored car. I step up on a platform, the lieutenant sits next to me ... Frequently we step down from our platforms in order to remove the sawed trees that block the road. We are doing this for the fifth time when we come under violent fire. Everybody is already on the ground, and I remember the precautions I took in order not to tear my new uniform jacket. I find refuge in a ditch. The Germans react violently. I try to aim at a partisan I see behind a tree. I miss him, he misses me and flees. I run after him, but in vain, nobody is there anymore. The silence is oppressing. We make sure we are protected and count our losses: twelve soldiers are dead, four are wounded. (94–5)

The narrator, as Terlin does, turns here to internal focalization in order to communicate his experience of combat. Yet that experience cannot compare with Terlin's, as the legionaries are shot at but cannot really reply because the enemy remains mostly invisible; the only partisan the narrator can detect is hiding "behind a tree," and he soon disappears into the woods. Internal focalization, in this excerpt as well as in several other passages describing encounters between the LVF and the Russian underground, makes for a partial, fragmentary kind of narrative, which evokes adventure novels in which the hero chases elusive adversaries. On a different level, the restricted point of view at work in many accounts of those encounters also inscribes some of the attitudes prevailing in the LVF at the time, such as the anxiety of not knowing where the enemy was hiding and what its next move might be. More generally, the incomplete, partial stories that the volunteers are telling about their encounters with partisans convey the frustration of risking one's life without being allowed to participate in some of the major events of the war.

Most of the memoirs in my corpus are written from a standpoint similar to Terlin's and the author's of *Vae Victis*, that is, from the perspective of an ordinary soldier who is engaged in combat but lacks knowledge of the overall situation. To be sure, some of the volunteers rose in the ranks and were no longer lowly privates by the end of the war. Bayle (2008, 18) and Labat (170) claim that they were promoted to "Unterscharführer" (sergeant); Rusco (254) and Philippet (II, 89), to Oberscharführer (technical sergeant); Rostaing, as the front cover of his book proudly proclaims, to Hauptscharführer (first sergeant); and Saint-Loup (1986b, 76), La Mazière (1972, 98), and Gilles (II, 438), to Untersturmführer (2nd lieutenant).[7] However, none of the officers who commanded one of battalions of the LVF, the Frankreich, or the Charlemagne has left recollections. Some, like General Puaud, were killed in combat (Giolitto 413); others, like Demessine, were executed after the war (Rusco 23); others still were content with giving interviews (e.g., Fernet to *Historia*) or writing introductions to their comrades' books (e.g., Bartolomei to Bayle's *De Marseille à Novossibirsk*); and several, like Cance, Raybaud, and Boudet-Gheusi, quite understandably opted to keep a low profile after the war.

The exception is Degrelle, and his case deserves special attention. None among the politicians and the intellectuals who, soon after June 21, 1941 had called for volunteers to participate in the antibolshevik crusade, were actually eager to go themselves to the battlefield – an attitude that Larfoux, among other memoirists, bitterly denounces when he writes: "It is a betrayal to push others to enlist, to organize large popular meeting and proclaim 'I give the example ... I go!' while staying home, still so patriotic, so unsparing of other Frenchmen's lives and stingy with one's own" (167).[8] The only two political leaders who made their actions conform to their words were Doriot, founder of the Parti Populaire Français, and Degrelle, head of Rex, the proto-fascist party that had been a force in Belgium from the mid-1930s. While Doriot spent one and half year in the USSR with the LVF, he never rose to a position of military leadership and did not live to set down his reminiscences; he was killed, in February 1945, in an air attack on his car by two unidentified (probably British) fighters (Brunet 487–9).[9] Degrelle, on the other hand, fought during most

---

[7] I am using the American equivalents for the German SS ranks proposed in *Slaughterhouse*, viii. Those ranks always included the term "Führer" because of the SS "Führer principle": in this instance, the idea that every unit in the organization should have a leader, who would be responsible for that unit. Gilles (II, 438) claims that he was promoted but never received his epaulette, because he was wounded and had to be evacuated.

[8] The journalist Jean Galtier-Boissière observes derisively in his memoir that collaboration leaders were, in fact, willing to go to Russia, provided that they be given high military ranks. Déat, for example, wanted to be appointed "division general" (1994, 797).

[9] Doriot only testified about his experiences on the battlefield in the course of the speeches he gave during his leaves. See, for instance, "Ce que Jacques Doriot a vu en U.R.S.S. [What Jacques Doriot Saw in the USSR]" (1942, 142), the text of a speech given at the Vélodrome d'Hiver on February 1, 1942. Pierre-François Clémenti, the founder in 1934 of

of the war on the Eastern Front, ending up as Obersturmbannführer (lieutenant colonel) and commandant of the Wallonie, which had become an SS Division in the spring of 1943 (Seidler 170–1). More fortunate than Doriot, Degrelle managed to escape to Spain in May 1945; he spent the rest of his life in that country, sedulously fostering his status as "the last surviving pro-Nazi leader of importance" through interviews, articles, and books expounding his worldview (Conway 281).

While Degrelle became head of the Wallonie, he never commanded whole armies whose moves could affect the outcome of the war, as did Hausser, von Manstein, and the other German generals who later turned out their memoirs. His functions, moreover, were those of an inspirational leader more than of a field commander. On the level of military operations, the Wallonie was run successively by Georges Jacobs, Pierre Pauly, Georges Tchekhoff, and Lucien Lippert; when Degrelle was appointed commander after Lippert's death at Cherkassy, the SS were careful to give him an "assistant commander in military capacity and head of staff," Sturmbannführer Franz Hellebaut, who was in charge of making tactical decisions (Saint-Loup 1975, 353). Whatever Degrelle's exact rank and responsibilities might have been, the fact remains that he spent most of the war at the frontline, sharing the lives of his fellow Belgians. His memoir, in this respect, resembles Terlin's more than it does Hausser's or von Manstein's. True, Degrelle was not especially humble. His fellow Walloons had nicknamed him Modest the First of Burgundy, because of both his vanity and his ambition to reconstitute the large duchy of Burgundy that Philippe III le Bon had established in the fifteenth century – a state that included Franche-Comté, Artois, Flanders, and the Belgian provinces on the top of Burgundy itself (Robert 1619). Yet Degrelle's comrades at the front also acknowledge his bravery, Philippet stating that "every time the Wallonie went to battle, 'le chef' was there" (II, 88), and Terlin, that when Lippert and Degrelle did not have any reinforcements left to send in Cherkassy, "they threw into the brawl the last two combatants they had available: themselves" (84). Degrelle was certainly "there" when the Wallonie was deployed in Estonia in the summer of 1944, having hurried back from Belgium and disobeyed the order "not to return to the front" that Hitler supposedly had issued to him (Degrelle 337). Specifically, he was in a trench near the town of Dorpat when the Soviets attacked

the Parti français national-communiste (renamed in 1940 Parti français national-collectiviste), also spent some time at the front with the LVF, but apparently left no testimony. The only books listed under his name in the catalogue of France's Bibliothèque Nationale are two editions of the essay *Qu'est-ce que le National Collectivisme?* (1938, 1940).

on August 23, 1944 – a day, he states, he "will remember up to [his] death" (355):

> More and more Russians were coming. They arrived from the southeast in small groups of six seven, or eight men, squeezing along the river. I had given the order not to shoot unnecessarily. We had to save our ammunition for a hand-to-hand combat whose imminence was in no doubt. Suddenly, I saw something coming out of the wood, south. A tank! I wanted to believe it was a German tank, which had escaped from Noo. Behind it, came a second tank. Then another. Soon, they were eight. Russian? German? From the distance, we couldn't tell. We were short of breath. The tanks were coming down the hill. Soon, we would know what to make of them: if the Russian infantry, which was massed at the bottom of the hill, fired on them, they were friendly tanks. The tanks reached the first house, behind the water. Not a shot was fired. They were Soviet tanks! (359)

This passage mixes self-importance and communal spirit in a way that is characteristic of Degrelle. On the one hand ("I had ordered..."), Degrelle leaves no doubt as to who was in charge. But he also conducts most of the narrative in the "we" of the group that witnessed the events, maintaining the bottom-up (and in this case, literally bottom-up) perspective of the soldiers buried in their trench. As the author of *Vae Victis* does, Degrelle shows literary expertise in his management of suspense; though he knows the whole story, he tells it by reporting the events as they unfolded for him and his comrades at the time. The long-delayed concluding line: "They were Soviet tanks [C'étaient des chars soviétiques]" also denotes Degrelle's literary culture, as it has an obvious intertext. For readers who went to French high schools when the study (and recitation) of the classics was mandatory, that exclamation can only evoke the famous "C'était Blücher! [It was Blücher!]," which in Victor Hugo's poem "L'Expiation" signals a turning point at Waterloo: The army arriving on the battlefield is not Grouchy's, as Napoléon had assumed, but the Prussian General Blücher's, and that arrival will determine the victory of the (then) Allies.[10]

---

[10] The complete passage in "L'Expiation" reads:

> Sa lunette à la main, il [Napoléon] observait parfois
> Le centre du combat, point obscure où tressaille
> La mêlée, effroyable et vivante broussaille,
> Et parfois l'horizon, sombre comme la mer.
> Soudain, joyeux, il dit: Grouchy! C'était Blücher.
> L'espoir changea de camp, le combat changea d'âme,
> La mêlée en hurlant grandit comme une flamme.

(His field-glass in hand, he [Napoléon] sometimes observed/The center of the battle, an obscure point where vibrates/The dreadful and living scrub of the fray/And sometimes

The way the volunteers recount their experiences on the battlefield using internal focalization calls for three brief remarks. The first one concerns the kind of warfare that is described in the excerpts I have just quoted. Indeed, those excerpts illustrate what Bartov (1991, 12) has called the "demodernization" of the fighting on the Eastern Front: the fact that, a few months after the launching of Barbarossa, the operations the Germans were conducting in the USSR no longer had anything in common with the high-technology *Blitzkrieg* fought in the West in 1939–40. The dispersal of the tank units in three Army groups, the immobilization of those units because of mud and cold, and the stranding of the whole army deep into Soviet territory, meant that the "infantry became the backbone of the front, clinging to it with the same desperation as the men of 1914–18" (Bartov 1991, 18). Terlin and his comrades fighting hand-to-hand in order to escape from the pocket at Cherkassy, Degrelle waiting in a trench for Russian tanks to attack, and the author of *Vae Victis* powerlessly watching his comrades being killed by invisible enemies all bear witness to the "demodernization" that Bartov analyzes. Internal focalization, obviously, is well suited for conveying the experiences of these men, who are no longer involved in large, orderly operations led by armored forces, but find themselves engaged in scattered combats whose purpose is to get away from the Russians or slow down their advance.

On a thematic level, those same excerpts also illustrate the dichotomies that Jonathan Littell identifies in *Le Sec et l'humide* [The Dry and the Wet], his study of Degrelle's *La Campagne de Russie* and the fascist imaginary. To begin with, according to Littell, the men of the LVF and the Wallonie can no longer live by the ideal of the fascist soldier, which is to fight while maintaining an "upright," "vertical" position (39). Duelling with partisans and tanks obliges them to "crouch" and even to "lie down" (39), that is, to adopt a physical posture that denies the image they have of themselves and the goals they were hoping to achieve in the USSR: not just to defeat Bolshevism, but to "organize" Soviet space by "building" erect structures on it (47). Littell also points out that climatic conditions in the USSR force the athletic, sports-obsessed fascist troops to play on a field that does not accord with their standards. They cannot operate on their preferred turf of "hard," "dry" surfaces (35); they are forced to muck about in mud and snow, which means facing "the soft"

the horizon, dark like the sea./Suddenly, happy, he said: Grouchy! It was Blücher./Hope changed side, the battle changed soul,/Screaming, the fray grew like a flame.) (My translation.)

and "the wet" (50) – a type of physical contact that constitutes for them the most painful "return of the repressed" (70).

My last and most extended remarks bear on the memoir as a genre. As literary theorists have pointed out, few stories are told consistently in internal focalization; at some point(s), most shift to another mode, because authors must provide information that readers need even though it was not available to the character(s) through whom the narrative is focalized. Such shifts are likely to be frequent in war memoirs written by ordinary soldiers, insofar as the authors do not just write for veterans and specialists on military history, but for a general audience that they cannot assume to be wholly familiar with the context of the operations that they describe. Thus, the memoirists in my corpus move at times from internal to zero focalisation, because they understand that their readers do not necessarily know about such things as the geography of the Ukraine or the number of Soviet divisions engaged in the attack on Berlin. Rusco, based in Belorussia with the LVF in early 1942, indicates that at that moment, "most of the Reich's forces are concentrated in the South," the objective being "to seize the oil fields in the Caucasus," as well as the "agricultural cultures in the Kuban area" (23). Yet Rusco does not tell whether the LVF was regularly kept aware of what was happening in other areas of the USSR, or whether he is adding this information, which he learned later, in order to provide a framework to his narrative (the one does not exclude the other). Similarly, Bayle supplies an overview of the situation in Pomerania that probably was not available to the soldiers of the Division Charlemagne at the time, noting: "On Saturday 25 February [1945] in the evening, the Russians succeed in breaking through. The 19th Soviet Army rushes northwest toward Köslin and Kolberg, occupies Schlochtau, Hammerstein, and Stegers. Their 3rd Cavalry Corps reaches Neustettin, while their 3rd Panzer Corps occupies Stepen, Bublitz, and Drawelin" (188). Whether the pictures of the larger context that Rusco and Bayle offer in these passages will help nonspecialized audiences or not is open to debate. At any rate, such pictures inform readers of the names for which they should look on maps, though Bayle fails to mention that the map of Germany they use should predate 1945, because most of the territory to which he refers is now Polish and the names have changed.[11]

---

[11] The maps published by Höfer Verlag in Germany help in this respect, as they provide both German and Polish names for the places that, once German, were attributed to Poland after World War II. The map of Polen-Hinterpommern, for example, shows that Köslin is now "Koszalin," and the map of Polen-Westpommern, that Kolberg has been rebaptised "Kolobrzeg."

Presented in the diary form, Auvray's and Larfoux's memoirs pose different problems of focalization. Auvray confesses in his foreword that the actual diary he kept at the front got lost, and the version offered in *Les derniers grognards* is, in fact, a reconstruction, written during the time he spent in prison after the war (10). The pretended nature of Auvray's diary is obvious in the entry of February 26, 1945, which reads: "There are four infantry divisions and one hundred and fifty tanks in front of us" (72). Indeed, it is doubtful that the members of the Charlemagne who were getting out of the train in Hammerstein on February 26 knew with such precision the size of the Soviet forces in whose way they were supposed to stand; Auvray learned this information later, and he is communicating it in order to make readers more aware of the impossible task that the Charlemagne was facing in Pomerania.

Larfoux's *Carnet de campagne* [Logbook] raises difficulties of a different type. Unlike Auvray, Larfoux does not admit to rewriting his text; the printed version of his logbook is supposed to be similar to the text he jotted down during the 1941–42 campaign of the LVF. The problem here is not to determine how the diarist obtained the information that he communicates, but, more concretely, when he found the opportunity to provide a detailed account of his actions on the battlefield. Larfoux's entry of December 1, 1941 is a case in point. Reporting the first, brutal engagement of the LFV at Djukovo over six pages, it ends with notebook #3 as the author and his comrades receive the late-afternoon order to install new telephone lines. The entry continues at the beginning of notebook #4 with the narrative of that installation during the night of December 1 to December 2, concluding with the sentence: "I'm freezing; never mind, I'm going to sleep" (78). Did Larfoux write the first part of his report in early evening on December 1 and the second part at dawn on December 2, while keeping the date "1 December?" But if he had been working on telephone lines for the whole night, how did he still manage to write three and a half pages before "going to sleep?" Larfoux himself does not answer these questions in self-referential manner, prefacing his entry with an indication such as: "In early morning, I find time to take these notes." Therefore, it seems legitimate to assume that Larfoux wrote his December 1 entry later than December 1. How much later, however, is impossible to establish, especially since Larfoux consistently uses the historical present ("I'm going to sleep"), giving the illusion that he reports what is happening, the way a radio or a television journalist would do while covering events "live."

To be sure, the troubles I have described in Bayle's, Rusco's, Auvray's, and Larfoux's narratives are probably perceptible only for poeticians who practice (as I do) a highly channeled type of reading, or for historians who plan to use these testimonies as documents. Such troubles are nevertheless important to identify, because the discursive licences that the authors are taking pose epistemological problems. In this instance, the issue is to decide whether the presence of a few "paralepses" (Genette 1972, 221), that is, of information that is excessive in relation to the point of view the author has chosen, should deprive a text of its status as a valid testimony. Against such exclusion, one could argue that most, if not all, memoirs interweave perspectives as those of the LVF and Charlemagne veterans do, their authors supplementing accounts of events as witnessed with data of which they were apprised later. For that matter, it is difficult to envision how memoirs in general, and war memoirs in particular, could be written in strict internal focalization; the texts would soon become incomprehensible, unless they came with a scholarly apparatus of notes that would provide readers with a wider, more comprehensive picture of the situation in which the memoirists were involved. As for Larfoux's logbook, the unlikelihood that its author was able to write a specific entry on the day he says that he wrote it raises a question that falls under Lejeune's autobiographical pact: Is a diarist contractually bound to recount the events of a day on that very same day, or do the conventions of the genre allow for a delay between witnessing and writing? War diaries clearly authorize some kind of deferment, though how much precisely is difficult to ascertain. Writing after too long a lag would doubtless be viewed as constituting a deceit, especially if the author does not acknowledge the postponement. Eventually, it would make the diary into a memoir or rather into a memoir pretending to be a diary. That latter form is of course hardly acceptable as a legitimate testimony, and Auvray is mindful of possible predicaments when he signals that his original notes were lost, and that his text is, in fact, a reconstruction.

5

Frameworks

If the volunteers' memoirs inscribe specific spatial and temporal positions, they also expose the ideological frameworks from which their authors are writing. Both Clemons and Gray, in their reviews of *Le Soldat oublié*, underscore that Sajer's standpoint constitutes one of the chief interests of the book. Clemons opens his review by stating that "simply as a record of an unfamiliar aspect of World War II – the Russian campaign from a German viewpoint – *The Forgotten Soldier* is fascinating" (37). Taking a more specifically comparative stance, Gray affirms that "though we have several Russian accounts of the war in the East," Sajer's is "the first in English translation from the German point of view" (4). To be sure, Gray's claim is not quite accurate; an English version of Guderian's memoir had been available since 1952, of von Manstein's since 1958, and of letters written from Stalingrad by German soldiers since 1955. But Gray is certainly correct when he insists later in his review that Sajer's perspective is not just German, but also "an outsider's" (4). Indeed, as must be emphasized once again, Sajer was not drafted into the Wehrmacht, as many Alsatians were during the war; he volunteered, and so did the French, Belgian, and Swiss memoirists whose testimonies comprise my corpus. In this respect, those testimonies differ from the personal texts that Fritz examines in *Frontsoldaten* and Kühne in *Kameradschaft*, which were written by native Germans who were not asked whether they wanted to go to the front or not. As far as ideology is concerned, the memoirs in my corpus raise the issue of establishing to what extent their authors did not just fight for Nazi Germany, but also endorsed the values, beliefs, and attitudes that were driving German policy making at the time, particularly in the Wehrmacht and SS environment in which the volunteers were bound to operate. Textual analysis here is particularly valuable, as it can expose stands about race, religion, and politics that are not always explicitly formulated, but are implied in choices made in such areas as vocabulary and figures of speech. Looking at those choices, therefore, will help describe the type of memory at work in the volunteers' recollections, as well as locate that memory on the map of the national memory of World War II in France that Rousso and Robert Frank have drawn in essays that I discuss in Chapter 7.

Viewed from a temporal perspective, the ideological positions that the volunteers take in their memoirs fall into two main categories. The first one includes the assessments that the volunteers make "now," after the war, when they reflect upon their enterprise from the distance, at the moment of writing; the second one, the thoughts that they assert they had "then," when they reacted to events in which they were involved or of which they were apprised. Let us emphasize: that they *assert they had*. Memoirs are always retrospective, and the passages in internal focalization I analyzed in Chapter 4, as well as the stands I am about to review, do not constitute the immediate translation of an experience; they originate in a reconstruction whose faithfulness to the memoirist's actual beliefs at the time no document can confirm or challenge. Leaving the analysis of the first type of stance for Chapter 7, I will focus here on the second: the judgments that the volunteers state that they passed "then," as they were living through certain events or were faced with certain situations.

THE DEMONIZATION OF THE ENEMY

The most obvious area in which the volunteers' memoirs are shaped by Nazi ideology and propaganda is the treatment of the enemy. For the Nazis, the war in the East was indeed both a *Weltanschaungskrieg* and a *Vernichtungskrieg*. That is, the conflict was not exclusively political and economic; it bore on views of the world, as for the Nazis, Communism and National-Socialism were incompatible. That incompatibility entailed military and demographic consequences; the enemy had to be physically destroyed, which means that part of the population had to be slaughtered or displaced. Such destruction was justified both by the need to open space (*Lebensraum*) for German settlers and by racial considerations; the USSR included millions of Jews, and its population as a whole was viewed as "Slav" and "Asiatic," that is, as belonging to inferior, subhuman "races" to which the laws of war would not apply.[1] Accordingly, "dehumanizing" and "demonizing" the enemy (Bartov 1991, 152), German propaganda often represented Soviet soldiers as wild, rampaging Asians – an image that is found throughout the volunteers' memoirs. For Gilles, the Charlemagne in Pomerania had to confront "Asiatic hordes made of rapists, plunderers, and torturers," evoking "the assassins of Genghis Khan" (II, 21). Using the same historical reference, Malardier states that "seeing the face of many of our victors made us realize that throughout the steppes Genghis Khan's irresistible war cry that had terrified all of Europe: 'Mongols, to your horses!' had rung out again" (618). As for the Swiss Lobsiger, he portrays the men the SS Division Leibstandarte had to face in Kharkov as "fierce and ferocious little Mongols, coming from another world" (141), who, upon looting a supply warehouse, are found "sucking tubes of perfumed toothpaste, which they apparently find delicious" (143).

This view of the enemy as "Asiatic" leads the memoirists to conceiving of the war as a conflict between the West and the East, or, in, racial terms, between whites and yellows. Bassompierre, for example, writes that the long-range goal of the campaign against the USSR was to "keep these new Barbarians coming from Asia from overwhelming our old continent" (131). Likewise, when the danger described by Bassompierre had materialized, Rostaing laments that the occupation of Berlin by the Soviets meant that "the Asiatic throngs had won a victory over the white world," over the "Western civilization" for which the volunteers had fought (177). Terlin is no less virulent when he states about a few prisoners taken in the Ukraine: "These Reds are Yellows," adding that such men seem to come from "the very bottom of medieval Asia," and resemble "Gengis Khan's hordes more than Churchill's allies" (34).

While the volunteers generally describe the enemy with contempt, they reserve their most racist, most disparaging vocabulary for the Soviet troops that they encountered in the Ukraine, Pomerania, and Berlin. True, they portray the Belorussian partisans as brutal and merciless opponents; but they also treat them with respect, possibly because Belorussia belongs to the "white," "European" part of the USSR, and the physical appearance of its inhabitants is Caucasian rather than Asian. Thus, Labat insists

---

[1] Before the attack on the USSR, the German high command had already issued orders that removed the actions of German soldiers toward Russian civilians from the actions of military courts and explicitly approved collective reprisal against entire villages, thus providing a shooting licence against Russian civilians. On this subject, see Jürgen Förster 1998a, "Operation Barbarossa as a War of Conquest and Annihilation."

that the struggles in the swamps and the forests of Belorussia could create some kind of warrior brotherhood – a feeling that he describes in a scene where a German, a Frenchman, and a partisan taken prisoner share a boat ride:

> We talked in a quiet, even friendly way. He [the partisan] told me that he wouldn't provide any information that could hurt his comrades. I agreed with him. We were, on this boat, three young men of the same age, whose countries were natural adversaries. And yet, we had the same feelings about almost everything, we lived the same miserable and overproud life, we had almost the same childhood and the same aspirations. (387)

This moment worthy of Renoir's classic *Grande Illusion* did not last, however. The next paragraph reveals that on the following day, the Russian was taken to a camp, and the German was killed by an errant bullet. As for Labat, soon oblivious to the unusual experience he had just had, he resumed hunting the people he calls, in an essentialist, ahistorical manner, his "natural adversaries."

Saint-Loup does not provide an example of fraternization as specific as Labat's, but some of his reflections, in the memoir he published in 1943 about his time in Belorussia, also concern the idea of a political and even existential kinship between enemies. Generalizing the term "partisan," Saint-Loup opens his book with a dedication: "In honor of all the true partisans, fallen in the hope that their conception of the world would triumph" (1986a, 23), to which he adds the epigraph: "Those who took sides with their blood or at the risk of their blood assemble, contemptuous of those who did not take sides and who live" (25). Returning later to the idea of "taking sides [prendre parti]," Saint-Loup explains that the specificity of the war in the USSR for him resides in the fact that it is being fought between "partisans." The term, in his view, should thus not be reserved for the irregulars who harass the German troops in the rear of the front: "The Walloons, the Croatians, the Slovaks, the Spaniards, all the legionaries from Europe" are also "partisans" (94), because they all have made the same gesture: Without being constrained to do so, they have come to the defense of a cause for which they are ready to die. Though forcefully made, Saint-Loup's case for extending the range of the term "partisan" remains somewhat specious. Indeed, the French and the other foreign volunteers who joined the German army could only be regarded as "partisans" in the etymological sense of the word: Having "taken sides," they were fighting for what they believed in. But they were not "partisans" in the concrete, pragmatic sense the expression had in World War II. That is, unlike the men who were operating from the woods of Belorussia, they were not *guerrilleros*; they were regular soldiers, who had been incorporated into the Wehrmacht and, as such, enjoyed several privileges. For one thing, their army uniforms placed them, in theory at least, under the laws of war. They, therefore, were not supposed to be summarily shot like snipers, as actual partisans could be and often were.[2]

Before discovering that some of the Soviet troops they encountered were made of people from the Asian republics of the USSR, the volunteers had already been presented with the idea of the Eastern campaign as a "crusade," though one that initially was directed against Bolshevism rather than against Asia.[3] Upon the attack against the USSR, Cardinal Alfred Baudrillart, a supporter of the Vichy regime and the collaboration with Germany, had stated that the "times were ripe for a new crusade," calling on European people to "rise beyond their narrow interests and establish among them a healthy brotherhood, renewed from the Christian Middle Ages" (Giolitto 223). The LVF was founded on these very principles, as the posters that invited Frenchmen to enroll showed a soldier with a shield, a lance, and a modern German helmet, thus "blending the imagery of the crusader knight with that of the Wehrmacht soldier" (Shields 99).[4] Several of the memoirists also describe their endeavor as a crusade, though some of them do it with more detail than others. Labat is very specific. Depicting the last soldiers who defended Berlin as "new Knight Templars" (554), he links those soldiers not just to crusaders generally speaking, but to the members of a particular military order: the Templars, that is, the knights who, in the twelfth century, were seeking to keep Jerusalem as a Christian kingdom. Connections that Saint-Loup establishes are more comprehensive. Surveying the crusades as a "great historical tradition" (1986a, 38), he likens the "European" troops that fought in the USSR to the "large, international armies of the Continent" that conquered part of the Eastern Mediterranean area in the Middle Ages (38), and asserts boldly that "in the epic of the LVF, something is

---

[2] Saint-Loup is not the only collaborationist who played on the word "partisan." The Radio Paris speaker Jean-Hérold Paquis titled "Words of a Partisan" an article he published on August 10, 1944, in what must have been one of the last issues of the collaborationist weekly *La Gerbe* (Cotta 285).

[3] On this subject, see Förster 1998b, "Volunteers for the 'European Crusade against Bolshevism'."

[4] One such poster is reproduced on the dustcover of this book. The picture of a similar poster encouraging Belgians to join the SS Brigade Wallonie in its "antibolshevik crusade" can be found in Philippet's *Et mets ta robe de bal* (II, 163).

left of these fabulous times, which saw the birth of western culture" (39). What the comparisons used by Labat and Saint-Loup have in common is to reframe World War II as a conflict between the West and the East. That is, for both memoirists, the war is not only a succession of military occurrences; it also implies a clash of values, the French SS defending Berlin against the Soviets as the Templars, several centuries earlier, defended Jerusalem against Saladin and other kinds of "infidels."[5]

The idea of a defense of the West against the East is also noticeable in the way the volunteers account for the causes of the conflict with the USSR. While the Nazis entered Russian territory without being provoked and in violation of the nonaggression pact signed in 1939, they presented the attack as a preventive war, which they had to start because the Soviets were about to do so. Historians generally discount that interpretation, stressing that Stalin, warned of the danger from numerous different sources in early 1941, "was indulging in illusions about the continuing validity of the non-aggression treaty," an attitude that "the Red Army command authorities responsible for the country's external security" were then forced to adopt (Hoffmann 833).[6] Yet the volunteers buy uncritically into the German party line when they refer to the beginning of the eastern campaign. Saint-Loup, always anxious to place events in the "long" time of history, writes that as "the Huns were stopped by the Franks at the 'Champs catalauniques' [a plain located near the French city of Troyes] in 454," "the Slavo-Asian expansion was halted by the Germans in Bialystock and Minsk in July 1941" (1986a, 37). (Saint-Loup writes "stoppée par les Germains" rather than "par les Allemands," characteristically emphasizing ethnic membership at the expense of nationality.) More concerned with the short term, Lobsiger explains that "the Germano-Soviet pact of 23 August 1939 notwithstanding, Stalin had massed the best equipped and trained armies of the Red world at the Eastern borders," and that those armies "were not there exclusively to

---

[5] In 1944, the Allies also described the campaign in Western Europe as a "crusade" against National Socialism. Fussell (5) mentions that just before D-Day, Eisenhower told the soldiers of the Allied expeditionary Force: "You are about to embark upon the Great Crusade, toward which we have striven these past months." Fussell ironically titles his war memoir *The Boys' Crusade*, in reference to both the young age of most American draftees and to Eisenhower's own memoir: *Crusade in Europe*.

[6] On the basis of documents recently made available, the historian Bogdan Musial (2008) has argued that both Hitler *and* Stalin had plans to destroy their opponent. Sooner or later, according to him, the two dictatorships would have faced each other on the battlefield. A Pole naturalized German, Musial has specialized in the investigation of both Nazi and Soviet crimes committed during World War II.

defend the Soviet paradise" (69). As for Labat, who positions himself as a witness ("j'en témoigne"), he assures that the Russians were "ready to attack" in late spring 1941; having seen "the installations that the Soviets had built at the edge of the boundaries agreed upon with the Germans after the occupation of Poland" (564), he can attest that the only purpose of those "installations" was to allow a strike against the West.

The same ideological stand shapes the reactions of the volunteers to the news about the conflict that they receive from different parts of the world, frequently inverting the victors' good-bad dichotomy to which we are now used when we think of World War II. For Rusco, typically, "good news" includes Rommel "seizing Tobruk and reaching Alamein" (58) and Hitler "managing to free Mussolini," that latter report meaning that an "immediately founded Italian Republic will continue to fight alongside the Reich" (96); conversely, "bad news" admits "von Paulus capitulating in Stalingrad" (74) and "Odessa falling to the Red Army" (173), two pieces of information that do not bode well for the German campaign in the East.

In similar fashion, the volunteers often comment on world events with a heavy-handed irony, quoting the words of the Allies to better ridicule and dismiss them. Bassompierre writes that upon crossing the "huge and icy steppes of the Soviet paradise" (117), his stay in Minsk "enlightened" him about the nature of the "government of the people by the people" and the "dictatorship of the proletariat"; perhaps concerned that readers may take his critique for a praise, he adds that it would be "more exact to say 'the exploitation of the masses by a tyrannic minority' and 'the dictatorship of one man'" (139). Similarly, Gaultier sarcastically applauds the bombing of the Renault plant in the Paris suburb of Billancourt (a plant that was working for the Germans), stating: "British energy sparkles brilliantly [L'énergie anglaise éclate de mille feux]. On 3 March [1941], Billancourt is crushed by British bombs. The record is broken: 623 people killed, 1,200 wounded, 200 buildings destroyed" (96). Yet Gaultier is serious when, turning to the Nazi expression *Terrorangriff*, he denounces the "British terror raid" on Dresden (291), and other volunteers employ similar language to indict the Allies' "unscrupulous and sadistic bombing of residential areas" (Bayle 162), which, according to them, caused the "useless, horrible death of millions of women and children" (Lobsiger 202).[7] Adding to a line of questioning that has concerned wholly

---

7 Lobsiger is ill-informed or deliberately exaggerates: Not millions but between 370,000 and 600,000 German civilians were killed in the Allied air raids. Yet seven and a half million people were left homeless, and Lobsiger may be confusing the two statistics when

different areas (why didn't the Allies bomb the railroad tracks leading to Auschwitz?), Bayle observes that the SS training camps that the French attended in Sennheim, Posen, Beschenau, Prague, Tarnow, Schwargenast, and Wildflecken never underwent air attacks, and he asks whether someone can explain why these places were not hit. Bayle's conspiracy theory is that powerful "interest groups," specifically the "armament and construction industries," wanted to "prolong the war"; "sparing soldiers" was thus a cynical calculation, as any extension of the conflict would bring about "an increase in profits" (162).

The way the volunteers reverse the accepted valence of dichotomies is especially noticeable in the comments they make about specific incidents that appear clear-cut in the "judgment of history." The attempt on Hitler's life on July 20, 1944 is a case in point. Historical studies and documentary films have generally praised von Stauffenberg's enterprise, only suggesting that the aftermaths of the putsch had been poorly planned. The letters and diaries that Fritz analyzes, however, show that many German frontline soldiers were incensed when they learned of the assassination attempt; feeling deceived by part of their leadership, they thought that it was their "holiest duty to cling to him [Hitler] even more strongly, in order to make good what the few criminals did without regard for the welfare of the entire nation" (quoted in Fritz, 216). Although the French volunteers did not worship the Führer as passionately as Fritz's native informants did, they tell that they reacted indignantly when they heard the news. Rusco thus writes: "To betray at this point in the war appears to us as a monstrosity. Whatever their reasons might be, the authors are criminals" (241). Labat also denounces the attempt on Hitler's life, and he is especially concerned about the consequences that the putsch, if successful, could have had for the French volunteers, who were then regrouping in Greifenberg, in East Prussia. A few days before the assassination attempt, Labat reports, most German officers had left the camp, and the LVF had been ordered to turn in "all their weapons, including the weapons seized from the enemy and their personal arms" (455). In Labat's somewhat paranoid take on these events, the officers were clearly part of the anti-Hitler conspiracy; and the LVF had been disarmed because the unit was regarded as too sympathetic to the regime, and also – had the putsch succeeded – because it could have been used as a "ransom" in a deal with the Allies (456).

he charges the Allies with being responsible for the death of "millions" of women and children (numbers in Zehfuss 77–8).

Labat and his fellow volunteers reserve their harshest judgments for several of the events that marked the liberation of France. Naumann, in his study of way the year 1945 and its commemoration in 1995 were described in the German press, argues that "liberation" did not mean the same thing to all people at the end of the war. The deportees who were still alive in the camps certainly felt liberated by the Soviet troops that occupied Poland and East Germany in early 1945. The populations of East Prussia and Pomerania, on the other hand, did not experience the Russians' arrival as a liberation, whatever their opinion of the Nazi regime might have been at the time; many people chose to flee, and many others were expelled when the areas where they lived were assigned to Poland after the war (Naumann 91). Similarly, the French collaborationists did not conceive of D-Day and the ensuing advances of the Allies as a liberation of their country from occupying forces, but as the failure of their enterprise as well as a threat against their lives. Hiding in Paris in late 1944, the former LVF member and milicien Mathieu Laurier calls de Gaulle "Charles the Evil [Charles le Mauvais]" and berates de Gaulle's temporary government as "gangsters who have seized power behind American bayonets" (74). (The name "Charles le Mauvais" is obviously coined after the names of kings of France that include an adjective, like Charles le Bel, Charles le Sage, and Charles le Bien-Aimé.) Viewed from the front by the volunteers, the Liberation is similarly depicted as a series of exactions against French citizens who have not committed any crime, since they have supported a perfectly legitimate government. Labat deems news from France to be "even worse than [he] had thought" (457); the Liberation is becoming "an intoxication of revenge and gratuitous murders, bloodier than anything ever seen so far," and the "incoming government seems to be more eager to organize this state of affairs than to put an end to it" (458). Reporting about the situation in Belgium, Degrelle is no less indignant. He writes: "Our friends describe the savage treatment that is being inflicted throughout Belgium in the name of 'Democracy' to thousands of men and women, who are jailed in terrible conditions, scorned, tortured, dishonored, sometimes even assassinated, because they have professed political ideas that are different from those of the 'liberators' of September 1944" (394). "Assassination," for that matter, is the term that some of the volunteers use when they refer to the execution of collaborationists that took place at the time of the Liberation. Gaultier, while teaching French literature to fellow inmates after the war, commemorates the "anniversary of Robert Brasillach's assassination" by making his students read one of the poems Brasillach composed when he was in jail at Fresnes, as well as the personal text he wrote on the morning of his execution (370). Gaultier notes that his audience was receptive, although a warden overheard part of the class and reported the teacher to the administration – a touchy situation out of which Gaultier boasts he talked himself with panache.

Carole Dornier and Renaud Dulong, in their introduction to a series of essays about testimony, argue that one of the functions of the genre is to make readers "reinterpret the event," "question received schemes," and "look critically at history" (2005, xix). Dornier and Dulong probably did not have the volunteers' recollections in mind when they wrote these lines, but the views that my memoirists express certainly force readers used to histories of World War II written from the Allies' standpoint to confront shifts in perspective. By identifying those shifts, I am not trying to make a radically relativist argument; the fact that all judgments depend on a point of view does not entail that all points of view are equally valid. In this case, western historians and philosophers have almost unanimously returned a guilty verdict to Nazi Germany, because the Nazis' endeavors violated shared, commonly accepted ideas about duties and rights, even in a situation as extreme as war. More precisely, they have indicted the barbarous way the Germans conducted war on the Eastern Front, and they have denounced as a gross "distortion" or "inversion" of reality (Bartov 1991, 106) the image of the campaign that Nazi propaganda sought to convey in order to conceal the crimes committed by the SS and the Wehrmacht. And yet, it is also true that scholars and theorists have by now also taken up some of the issues that the volunteers had raised, such as the bombing of the German cities and the treatment of the collaborationists in France and Belgium at the time of the Liberation. The historian Jörg Friedrich, the political scientist Stephen Garrett, the philosopher A.C. Grayling, the literary theorist Dagmar Barnouw, as well as the novelist and essayist W.G. Sebald have questioned the morality and strategic purpose of the Allies' air war, generating heated debates on both sides of the Atlantic. Similarly, the historians Philippe Bourdrel and Marc Olivier Baruch have investigated how the purge was conducted in France, asking what actually happened during the "uncontrolled," extrajudicial "cleansing" [épuration sauvage] of the summer of 1944, and whether the people who collaborated formed a mere "handful of scoundrels [une poignéee de misérables]" – an expression that de Gaulle used in a speech of October 14, 1944, and that Baruch picked up as a title for the book he edited.

The volunteers' rants on such subjects as the Allies' "war crimes" and the "assassinations" committed by members of the Resistance certainly cannot match these scholarly studies in terms of precise data and sophisticated arguments. For one thing, my memoirists abusively equate civilian deaths resulting from bombings and the execution of collaborationists with the systematic massacre of whole populations, or they use the former as an excuse for the latter. They also fail to mention that the Nazis, as Naumann (55) has argued, could have brought the war to an earlier conclusion, thus stopping the senseless dying of women and children. Nevertheless, the passages in which they discuss such subjects as the bombing of the German cities and the fate of the collaborationists constitute vehement, if not quite convincing, interventions into the memory wars that started at the Liberation, and that of course are far from over; Friedrich's, Grayling's, Barnouw's, Sebald's, Bourdrel's, and Baruch's studies were all published in the 2000s, as were several of the life narratives included in my corpus.

FRENCHNESS

While the memoirs of the French and French-speaking volunteers point to the ideological indoctrination of the foreign troops by Nazi propaganda, they also reveal how some of those troops resisted the German way, especially in the areas of discipline and organization. That resistance, according to my memoirists, was particularly strong in the LVF, where the volunteers asserted their Frenchness by displaying stereotypically Gallic attitudes. As a career soldier, Rostaing thus observes (and deplores) that his countrymen should cultivate demeanors like "we don't give a shit [j'm'en foutisme" (33) and "anger and grumbling [rogne et grogne]" (29), to the extent that some of them had to be sent back to France as "unfit for serving in the uniform" (39). "Uniforms," for that matter, was a domain in which the French soldiers' resistance to German desire for discipline and conformity was particularly noticeable. More indulgent than Rostaing, Labat describes the legionaries' attire as "picturesque bohemia" (327), a description whose accuracy is confirmed by photographs. The picture on the front cover of Rusco's *Stoï!*, for example, shows four members of the LVF's elite "hunting section [section de chasse]," whose uniforms are tidy but mismatched; the soldiers sport two different kinds of boots and four different kinds of hats, and they wear their pants and jackets in two different styles; even Rostaing, the would-be disciplinarian, does not carry a helmet but a *shapka*, the Russian fur cap that many legionaries had adopted, because, though offering no protection, it kept their heads warm.

The volunteers also complacently report practical jokes that they played both to affirm their Frenchness and to challenge the alleged seriousness of the Germans.[8] The novelist Antoine Blondin, in his review of Labat's *Les Places étaient chères*, submits that readers will "enjoy the narrative of the huge pranks with which these men supplemented the perhaps debatable luxury of making war in a private capacity" (116). Whether readers will "enjoy" those narratives or not is a question of taste, of course. Upon telling the story of an officer who, at the training camp in Wildflecken, "fired four or five bullets 50 centimeters above the head of a soldier who would not wake up in the morning," Gilles admits that "such pranks are difficult to understand for people who have not known dangerous periods of military instruction" (I, 124). Gilles nevertheless keeps telling about similar antics, such as exploding a bottle of ink in order to soil the new long johns of fellow soldiers (125), or stealing their pants when they had a woman in their bed, thus forcing them to walk to the morning call in coat and underwear (136). Gilles also treats as jokes violations of military discipline, for instance, leaving the camp to go partying in town (112) or (a double violation since wild game was strictly protected as "Reich's game") to go hunting in the woods, a hunt whose product was then consumed in the camp's basement, conveniently made into a kitchen (118–9). According to Gilles, such getting around the rules only confirms that Frenchmen are "born clever [nés malins]," that they know how to make everyday life more pleasant in difficult circumstances. Incidentally, such passages also show that whereas some French members of the SS sought to emulate German discipline, others steadily held out; the stunts that Gilles reports all took place at the SS training camp in Wildflecken, where the French supposedly were to learn how to leave their bad habits and attitudes behind. The Bavarian journalist and right-wing politician Franz Schönhuber, who was at Wildflecken as an instructor and a translator, tells in his memoir that the French sought indeed to assert their individuality by breaking the rules. They would, among other acts of mischief, add a "personal touch" to their uniforms by sporting both "German and French decorations," wearing

---

[8] I am saying "alleged" because all German soldiers did not endorse the antihumor position of the SS officer who wanted to remove cartoons from the journal intended for the French volunteers. As the documents used by Fritz show, the *Landser* used humor "as a form of comfort and escape," "poking fun at the conditions around them" and even "ridiculing those in authority" (74–5).

"colorful scarves," leaving their collars "open," and wearing their caps in a way that was "bold" though it did not "conform to regulations" (117). Schönhuber also recounts that one of the Charlemagne regiments insisted to be commanded in French (123), and that supporters of Pétain, Darnand, and Doriot were engaged in constant "squabbling" and even in "brawls"; Krukenberg sought to contain these excesses by making the French take the oath to Hitler, and by requiring that "a portrait of the Führer be hung in every room" (120–1).

If the volunteers take delight in telling about the acts of indiscipline they committed and the practical jokes they played, they also have no qualms recounting dramatic events in a sarcastic manner. In his bizarre celebration of Hitler's Germany, *La Gerbe des forces* [The Sheaf of Strengths], the future collaborationist writer Alphonse de Châteaubriant maintains that one of France's main liabilities is "Voltaire's smile," and one of Germany's strengths, the fact that "in Germany, there is no Voltaire's smile" (1937, 119).[9] Confirming Châteaubriant's thesis of a clash of mentalities between the two cultures, Saint-Loup reports that when he was in Hildesheim editing *Devenir*, the journal of the French volunteers, the SS officer who was in charge of supervising the publication would not tolerate the inclusion of any humorous text. That officer became indignant when he saw that cartoons soldiers had sent from the front were reproduced in *Devenir*, telling Saint-Loup: "You do not understand anything of the SS spirit" (1986b, 80). Clarifying his position, the officer then explained that the SS were "professors of aesthetics and nobility," whose mission was to promote a "physical ideal" (80); as teachers in charge of advancing that ideal, they could not accept the "grotesque representation of the human person" that comes with comical genres in general and cartoons in particular (81).

When they write up their recollections, however, most of the French volunteers display no desire for abandoning Voltaire's manner and adopting what Châteaubriant holds to be German earnestness. The anonymous author of *Vae Victis* obviously delights in reporting a tragic incident (the French and the Germans have mistakenly fired at each other) in derisive fashion:

The Germans silently encircle Martianowitchi. Fifteen of us are assigned to head to Martianowitchi at dawn, making as much noise as possible. When they hear

---

[9] Though certainly not politically aligned with Châteaubriant, Denis de Rougemont makes a similar remark in his "Journal d'Allemagne." Attending a Nazi meeting in Saarbrücken on March 11, 1936, he notes about the discipline and the earnestness of the crowd waiting for Hitler: "Nobody gets impatient, nobody has a joke" (319).

us, the partisans will leave the village and throw themselves into the Germans'
arms. We set off, smoking cigarettes. Complete success. The disarray is such that
the German get us mixed up with the Russians. We are attacked from everywhere.
We vigorously defend ourselves. Outcome: the Germans have wounded a gunner,
we have killed two of their men. When we finally recognize each other, similar to
heroes of Antiquity, we insult each other from one front to the other. Of course
all the Russians have escaped. Captain Bridoux is one of the planners of this brilliant feat of arms. We are happy, upon this strange combat, to have beaten the
Germans on points, and even our wounded man is not the last to revel in this
success. (163)

This narrative is indeed Voltairian, as it combines the dry objectivity that
lets readers draw their own conclusions ("Outcome: the Germans have
wounded a gunner"), the biting irony that indicts the incompetence of
the officers ("Captain Bridoux is one of the planners of this brilliant feat
of arms"), and humor that defamiliarizes the situation by describing it
through a reference to the world of sports (the French have beaten the
Germans "on points"). From Châteaubriant's perspective, this passage
could of course be viewed as one more instance of the French inclin-
ation to take everything lightly. If we read "with" the text, however,
that same passage does not mean that war is something frivolous, and
that the French are conducting it as a form of entertainment. War here
is clearly indicted, albeit in a Candide-like manner, for the author con-
fronts the gravity of the subject by "pretending," in this instance, that the
bloody incident of friendly fire he is reporting does not deserve thought-
ful consideration.

The war, or more precisely the way the Charlemagne was used in
northeastern Germany, is similarly denounced when Auvray titles the
chapter of *Les derniers grognards* he devotes to this subject: "Les loulous
de Poméranie [The Pomeranians]." The rhetorical weapon here is pun-
ning. "Loulou" can designate a small lap dog or a delinquent youth, but
also constitutes a term of affection ("mon loulou" = "honey"). Auvray
clearly plays on these different meanings of the word, as he suggests that
the outnumbered, poorly equipped French soldiers in Pomerania can be
compared to harmless pets fighting aggressive animals (Russian bears?),
to young outlaws who, if they are not killed, will be brought to court in
their own country, and (the pun here also involves irony) to people who
find themselves the privileged objects of warmth and tenderness.

Of course, not all the works in my corpus adopt that caustic tone, nor
are *Vae Victis* and *Les derniers grognards* written entirely like the passages I have just quoted. Still several of the memoirists like to mockingly
expose the absurdity or the hopelessness of the operations in which they

were engaged, as they like to report examples of another Voltairian attribute, namely, wit: the supposedly typical French capacity for resolving a problem or handling a situation with a *mot d'esprit*, however difficult the problem and dangerous the situation might be. Wit may first be a way of quickly and cleverly addressing a question that would need a detailed answer. Labat, who avidly collects instances of his fellow soldiers' verbal skills, reports a rejoinder of this type. When, upon arriving at a new post with his detachment, he asked how the sleds had to be arranged, the officer in charge merely answered: "Facing west, right now it's the only sensible strategy" (81). Playing with readers the game that the officer had played with him, Labat does not here bother to unpack the witticism. That is, he does not explain how the officer, while preferring black humor to a direct response to the newcomer's query, nevertheless had supplied plenty of information: The LFV unit stationed at the post was in no position to repel a Russian attack; it had to be ready to withdraw quickly; and things were under control, as he, the person in charge, knew what measures had to be taken immediately (the sleds should "face west") if the future evacuation of the post were to be successful.

Examples of wit that the volunteers report also bear not on a situation but on a person whom the *mot d'esprit* derides and belittles. Patrice Leconte's popular film *Ridicule* (1996) has familiarized audiences with this type of wit, which it contrasts with gentle British humor and presents as typical of the way French noblemen (and noblewomen) would mercilessly duel with each other in the eighteenth century ("You are not, Sir, as stupid as you first appear." Reply: "It's the difference between you and me."). Labat fondly collects statements of this type, even though he himself is often the victim of higher-ranking officers who rely on wit to make him accept new, clearly unwelcome assignments:

One morning, he [the officer] asked me smiling if I knew how to ride a horse.

- I do not know, Sir, I've never tried.

His smile opened out.

- Legionary Labat, a soldier must be able to do everything. Your company commandant, who is a seaman, is obliged to frequently fall on his head because regulations say he is entitled to a horse. There is no reason why your insignificance should protect you from this kind of trouble. Go to the stable. I've recommended that you be given the wildest nag of the company. (122–3)

- The Battalion informs me, Sergeant Labat, that the German team which was operating the 152-mm gun will be removed as soon as they have trained a group of French men to manage the cannon. Gunners are few in the Company. You know nothing about it, which in the army is an almost absolute criterion for qualification. Therefore, you will be the head of this group, and you will yourself select your assistants. (254)

Labat's officers, in both cases, impose upon their subordinate tasks for which he has no taste and is at any rate ill-prepared. But they make protest difficult, as they justify their decisions with the help of witticisms: of a universal truth that they present as accepted while they are making it up ("A soldier must be able to do everything"), and of a paradox that they employ to disguise their autocratic manner ("You know nothing about it, which in the army is an almost absolute criterion for qualification"). Although Labat is a casualty in the game his officers are playing with him, he hardly objects. For he admires the way they are playing it – the way they are not merely telling him what to do, but are toying with him and exploiting the situation to display their verbal skills.

Games between officers and subordinates, however, sometimes take on a more pleasant tone, as when Labat's captain receives a few men returning from a patrol with the words:

– Here you are, valiant warriors! You've brought desolation to the enemy, dismayed by your audacity. His jovial and ironic smile was in itself a reward.
– Jaffeux, bring something to drink. The gods are thirsty! (223)

As Labat does not react to the arbitrariness of his officers, he does not comment on the fact that he and the other participants in the patrol are not formally congratulated for their work (they have just spent several hours in the snow, positioning mines). To the contrary, he deems the captain's "ironic smile" and his pastiche of epic greeting to be enough of a reward. Earnest congratulations probably would have been perceived as gauche, at least in the code by which Labat and the officers in his unit had been trained to abide; for games of this kind, in the 1920s and 1930s, were frequently played between teachers and students in the French school system, and young people going to the army were used to dealing with figures of authority who communicated with them in both playful and despotic manner. Most of my memoirists, for that matter, were in their late teens and early twenties when they enlisted, and their frame of mind was still largely that of students.

THE LENS OF CULTURE

The education that the volunteers received and the attitudes that they developed during their school years account for another aspect of the

Frenchness of their memoirs. Ruth Amossy, in her critique of Cru's work, has argued that there is no such thing as the direct, transparent way of telling one's story in which the author of *Témoins* sees the mark of a "good" testimony. Witnesses, according to Amossy, always make sense of things by drawing on "preexisting models and schemes" that "mediate" between the experience and its textualization (20). The volunteers' memoirs certainly bolster Amossy's thesis. Indeed, their authors frequently evoke what they endured on the Eastern Front by turning to "preexisting models and schemes," in this instance, to the French cultural framework they had acquired during their school years. Under this label, I mean a body of knowledge that includes not just the culture of France, but the materials that young people would learn in French schools between the wars, or with which they could become familiar by reading books written for teenagers, by attending concerts and exhibits, and by going to the movies. Labat shows he is conversant with ancient epic diction when he reproduces his officer's congratulatory speech verbatim, and some of his fellow legionaries flaunt their literary proficiency by inserting lines or sentences from famous writers into their texts: Dupont quotes from Musset (104); Mit, from Villon (68) and Verlaine (176); Leverrier, from Giraudoux (239) and Saint-Exupéry (240); the author of *Vae Victis*, from an anonymous Japanese writer (164); and Malardier, by far the most addicted to citations among my memoirists, from people as diverse as Carlyle (146), Allais (168), Hugo (224), Caesar (438), Bernanos (467), Éluard (467), Montesquieu (583), Pascal (584), Goethe (586), Kipling (586), and the medieval epic *Chanson de Roland* (539). Yet the Frenchness of the legionaries' memoirs is especially noticeable in the way that the authors describe what they experienced on the Eastern Front by referring it to the cultural framework they had acquired through their education. Labat, Saint-Loup, and the author of *Vae Victis* are the volunteers who draw most frequently on that framework, but the other memoirists are not averse to displaying what they had learned in lycée (in some cases, at the university), as well as to flaunting the extracurricular knowledge they had picked up during their free time. The references to which they turn include:

1. Literature and history of Antiquity: In Berlin, after one of his men was killed, Rostaing is like "a new Achilles, crying over the body of Patrocles" (Malardier 144); silence on the front foretells "the great disasters depicted by Tacitus" (*Vae Victis* 148); climbing a mountain in the Caucasus from which the sea can supposedly be seen, the soldiers of the Wallonie "remember the 'Thalassa! Thalassa!' of the *Anabasis*" (Degrelle 180); the name "Bobr" (where 600

LVF men temporarily stopped the Russian advance in June 1944),
"five centuries before our era... would have been 'Thermopylae'"
(Leverrier 170); the level of the LVF recruits has decreased, because
the Germans now accept "all those whom Suburrhe and Ergastule
are spewing out" (Labat 243).[10]

2. Medieval and classical literatures: A volunteer writes to his war
   godmother, "as he would to a Beatrice" (*Vae Victis* 151); resembling life according to Macbeth, Europe in the summer of 1944
   is "full of sound and fury" (Auvray 8); where Belgian soldiers are
   housed, the appearance of two young women makes the scene shift
   from a "play by Corneille to a play by Marivaux" (Terlin 1972,
   176); the title of Leverrier's memoir: *C'était pendant l'horreur
   d'une profonde nuit* [It Was During the Horror of a Dark Night]
   quotes the first line of a celebrated monologue: The main character's "dream" in Racine's *Athalie*.[11]

---

[10] Suburrhe was a lower-class neighborhood in Rome, and Ergastule was a place where
slaves were housed or imprisoned. Labat refers here to Antiquity by (probably) quoting
a line from "Après Cannes," a poem by the Parnassian writer José Maria de Hérédia.
Describing the anxiety in Rome after Hannibal's victory over the Roman legions in
Cannae, Hérédia writes:

> Et chaque soir la foule allait aux acqueducs,
> Plèbe, esclaves, enfants, femmes, vieillards caducs,
> Et tout ce que vomit Subure et l'estragule;
> Tous anxieux de voir surgir au dos vermeil
> Des monts sabins où luit l'oeil sanglant du soleil,
> Le Chef borgne monté sur l'éléphant gétule.

[And every night the crowd went to the aqueducts,/Plebeians, slaves, children, women,
rickety old men,/All those whom Suburrhe and Estragule are spewing out,/All afraid to
see appear on the vermeil back/of the Sabines Mountains where shines the bloody eye
of the sun,/The one-eyed leader mounted on the North African elephant.] The elephant
is "gétule," which means that he was provided by the Gétules, a tribe from North Africa
that had contributed troops to Hannibal's army when the Carthaginians invaded Italy
and defeated the Romans at Cannae in 216 BC.

[11] In this dream, Athalie first sees her dead mother and then is stabbed by a child. The passage from which Leverrier quotes reads:

> Un songe (me devrais-je inquiéter d'un songe?)
> Entretient dans mon coeur un chagrin qui le ronge.
> Je l'évite partout, partout il me poursuit.
> C'était pendant l'horreur d'une profonde nuit.
> Ma mère Jézabel devant moi s'est montrée,
> Comme au jour de sa mort pompeusement parée.

[A dream (should I worry about a dream?),/Maintains in my heart a sorrow that erodes
it./I avoid it everywhere, it pursues me everywhere./It was during the horror of a dark

3. Modern French literature: On a work site in the town of Osintorf, the engine whistles "like the famous engine in Malraux's *Man's Fate*" (Saint-Loup 1986a, 161); seen by the captain Barthes de Montfort, the war becomes "the kingdom of Père Ubu" (Labat 388); in Smolensk, an elegant building surrounded by a snowy garden evokes Verlaine's line "Dans le grand parc solitaire et glacé [In the large, solitary, and icy park]," as well as Mallarmé's landscape of "frozen lakes and swans" (Leverrier 79, 80).[12]

4. French, British, and American adventure novels: The Russian partisans are "true Sioux" (*Vae Victis* 141); hunting them is like being "in a sequel to the stories we read in our youth: Fenimore Cooper and Gustave Aymard" (Labat 356); furnishing an isba means making "a compromise between the room of Louis XIV at Versailles, a compartment of the P.L.M. [the Paris-Marseille-Lyon train], and Robinson's cabin" (*Vae Victis* 143).

5. Films, especially westerns: Because trucks must be protected from partisans' attacks, "they are placed in a circle, as at the time of the conquest of the West" (Rostaing 68); a Russian soldier threatens the French prisoners, "drawing his gun, like a cowboy" (Costabrava 160); chased by the Russians in a trailer hooked to a tank, members of the Walloonie "seem to reenact the movie *Stagecoach*," as the vehicles become "two wagons of the American West dashing through a swarm of Indians" (Terlin 1972, 76); a refugee in Tangiers, Laurier thinks of himself as living the "Hollywood common place" of the "good guy who is unfairly chased and flees," "wants to start a new life but is stalked by society," and at some point, out of money, must choose between "crime and submission to social rules" (Laurier 49).

6. Painting: In a village near Briansk, the long, white face and dark hair of a young woman evoke "Holbein's portrait of Anne Boleyn" (*Vae Victis* 67); in a post, the scene of tired soldiers resting on the floor "would have inspired a Dürer to a masterly etching" (Labat 110); as the Walloons feast on fruit and honey in the Ukraine, their bivouacs remind of "paintings by Bruegel the Elder" (Philippet I,

---

night./My mother Jézabel appeared in front of me,/Pompously arrayed as she was on the day of her death.]

In Leverrier's text, the "horror" is that of a military hospital in which men can only "suffer and die" (84).

[12] Leverrier's quotation from Verlaine is inaccurate. In Verlaine's poem, "Colloque sentimental," the line reads: "Dans le vieux parc solitaire et glacé."

101); on Russian markets, "children escaped from Goya's dreams" are on the lookout for anything they can eat or use (Saint-Loup 1986a, 152); in a forest near a lake over which the moon is shining, the scenery evokes "Gustave Doré," the author of the illustrations in Jules Verne's original Herzel edition (*Vae Victis* 140); on the snow, the silhouettes of the soldiers, the horses, and the sleds loaded with equipment, bring forth "Raffet's engravings" (Labat 109); in Pomerania, the French "resemble the soldiers of the Empire, as they are represented in paintings and in the illustrations of our history books" (Rostaing 162).[13]

7. Music: The soldiers of the LVF, in Belorussia, have turned into "Offenbach's carabineers," chasing uncatchable outlaws as the *carabinieri* do in the opera *Les Bandits* (Saint-Loup 1986a, 111);[14] in Berlin, the boyfriend of a French woman who sought to sell birds "has nothing of Papageno, the tuneful 'lustig' in *The Magic Flute*" (Leverrier 203); in Pomerania, burning towns make "an arc of a circle designed by a pyromaniac Wagner" (Auvray 96); Saint-Loup titles his memoir about the end of the war in Germany *Götterdämmerung*, a predictable reference that recurs in several other memoirs.

8. Napoléon's Russian campaign: Following ("Route Napoléon") the Emperor's very itinerary, the legionaries arrive in the village of Ucholody, "which Napoléon and the Great Army had crossed in the past" (Rusco 225); Smolensk is "used to being in ruins," since "it was burned on 17 August 1812" (Saint-Loup 1986a, 139); Auvray titles his book *Les derniers grognards*, after the name ("grumblers")

[13] Like Labat, Rostaing probably has in mind the military paintings of Raffet, who left numerous works representing Napoléon's armies. Cru points out that Raffet, born in 1804, "never saw Napoléon's soldiers during one of their campaigns," and that "his first military lithographs are from 1830" (1929, 6). Those lithographs, according to Cru, show how art can shape our image of war, even when the artist was not an eyewitness of the events that he depicts.

[14] Saint-Loup quotes the whole text of the carabineers' chorus, which in French reads:

> Nous sommes les carabiniers
> Gauche, gauche,
> La sécurité des foyers,
> Gauche, gauche,
> Mais par un fâcheux z'hasard
> Gauche, gauche,
> Nous arrivons toujours trop tard!

[We are the carabineers/Left, left/The security of the homes,/Left, left/But by an unfortunate accident,/Left, left/We arrive always too late.]

given to Napoléon's faithful old guard, and he weaves the connection throughout his text: The Charlemagne's retreat in Pomerania calls up "the throes of the Great Army" (84); taken to Russia as POWs, the French follow "the trail of shilly-shallying [valse-hésitation] of 1812, when Napoléon was pretending to look for Kutusov, who did not yet feel like finding Napoléon" (146); in the chilly wagons, they are likely to catch cold, as were "the grenadiers before Borodino" (161); later, the train that carries them back to France "joins the great East-West route which, from Moscow to Berlin and from the Moskwa River to the Berezina River," was "the Stations of the Cross of two invaders" (165).

9. Colonial times in North Africa: In Belorussia, fighting an enemy that is both "always present and invisible" is a type of operation that "General Lyautey himself could have conducted" in Algeria and Morocco (Saint-Loup 1986a, 113); the Soviet partisans are "bastards" (Labat 163) and "*Chleuhs*" (Saint-Loup 1986a, 134, 169, 173), two terms used to label the "unsubdued tribes" that colonial troops were fighting during the Rif Wars of 1920–26;[15] indicted with the help of the same colonial vocabulary, the Free French Movement in London is a "dissidence," and such people as de Gaulle and René Pleven are "dissidents" (Gaultier 93, 126); the men who serve under Lieutenant Bollet acknowledge his qualities as a "*blédard*" (Labat 193), that is, as a man who fought in the rural regions (*bled*) of North Africa, and is thus especially qualified to lead an antiguerrilla unit in Belorussia.[16]

If cultural critics of the twenty-first century were to consider the volunteers' memoirs, they probably would condemn not just those texts' offensive politics, but also the conspicuously euro- and gallocentric biases of the reference framework on which they draw. Characterizing activities conducted in Eastern Europe in terms of western culture, as Monika Fludernik puts it while describing similar schemes at work in general autobiographies, would testify to an attempt to "recuperate alterity," to "reintegrate centrifugal material of the past and memory into the fold of recognized continuity and identity" (264). In other words, it would testify

---

[15] In a strange way, the word *Chleuh* came to designate the Germans during the Occupation. In volunteers' talk, however, it always refers to the Russian partisans.

[16] To honor the tradition of fighting irregulars and the earlier accomplishments of such men as Colonel Puaud in the colonies, a vast operation against the partisans organized in early 1944 was named "Operation Morocco"; the Germans deemed its relative success to be worth of an official Wehrmacht communiqué (Giolitto 290).

to an imperialist, colonial mindset, which is as troubling as the explicit pronouncements that aggressors make in order to justify their invasion of a foreign country.

While it is difficult not to agree with this assessment, I would maintain that the volunteers reveal more than ideological positions when they draw on western culture to describe their experiences on the Eastern Front. First, as with their stories of combat feats and sexual prowess, their allusions to literature, history, and the arts contribute to the construction of the image they want to give of themselves. By referring to Dante, Shakespeare, or Verlaine, the legionaries show that they are not, or not only, brutish warriors intent on ridding Europe of Bolshevism; they are also educated people, who can place a reference to Mallarmé in their memoirs as they could drop this famous poet's name in a conversation with their former teachers. By including Jules Verne and *Stagecoach*, the volunteers also signal that they still remember (and value) their teenage years, and that their culture is not limited to what they learned in class. Costabrava is particularly explicit on this subject, stressing that when he was in lycée in Nice he also played soccer and went to the movies "with passion"; it was "the golden age of Hollywood film," and teenagers were especially fond of "detective movies, epics, westerns, and musicals," whose favorite scenes they would "replay" after doing their homework (25–6). In this respect, the references that the memoirists make to Fenimore Cooper and John Ford next to Homer and Tacitus can be viewed as appeals to an audience that might not share their political stance but has the same cultural background and is ready to be drawn into a game of allusions that mixes high- and lowbrow cultures. Priding oneself on being familiar with both cultures, for that matter, was a typical attitude among young educated adults in the 1920s and 1930s, and it can be found in the personal writings of some foremost French intellectuals who grew up during this period. Jean-Paul Sartre and the author of *Vae Victis*, for example, clearly did not make the same political choices; still, they like to show off in similar ways their knowledge of both the classics and popular art forms, in a gesture whose purpose is to appeal to insiders as well as to challenge the cultural establishment. The diaries Sartre kept and the letters he wrote in the 1930s and 1940s, at any rate, attest to his delight at reminding himself and his addressees that he reads both Martin Heidegger and Dashiell Hammett, and that he enters both concert halls and movie theaters.

The volunteers' cultural framework is intriguing for another reason, namely for the way it exposes some significant contradictions in the memoirists' attitudes. To begin with, the volunteers do not seem to read the works of the main representatives of what David Carroll calls "French literary fascism." They may mention the names of Brasillach, Céline, Rebatet, and Drieu la Rochelle, that is, of intellectuals who share their convictions. But they never use Céline or Drieu, as they use Corneille or Defoe, to describe people and events with respect to a passage they might recall from, say, *Mort à crédit* or *Le Feu follet*. They apparently do not read the French "literary fascists" or they have not become familiar enough with the latter's works to make them part of their framework. An even more interesting contradiction can be observed about the relations between the volunteers and Nazi Germany. On the one hand, the legionaries buy without apparent reservation into Nazi propaganda; they present the Russian campaign as a necessary preventive operation, talk about the enemy in a scornful manner, and describe the last battles in Pomerania and Berlin as battles of the West defending itself against Asia. On the other hand, the main absentee from the volunteers' reference system is not the culture of Eastern Europe or some culture of the "other," as we would probably insist today; it is *German* culture, on which the volunteers hardly draw when it comes to accounting for their experiences during the war. I am not vouching that the volunteers' memoirs do not include more allusions to German cultural past than those I have identified (specifically, to Dürer, Mozart, and Wagner). But the great names of German literature are conspicuously absent from those memoirs, as are the great names of German history and mythology, of which the Eastern Campaign could have reminded the legionaries. To take just one example: While the volunteers often designate themselves as Crusaders, only one of them, Terlin (1972, 10), compares the 1941 attack on the USSR to one of the earliest drives of the West against the East: the invasion of Russia by the Teutonic Knights in the thirteenth century, an invasion (and its repelling) that is the subject of Sergei Eisenstein's 1938 classic film *Alexander Nevsky*. As for the other memoirists, they remain with the image of a crusade intended to liberate the Holy Land, or, as Saint-Loup does, of battles fought in Central and Western Europe against intruders coming from the barbarian East.

The volunteers' neglect of German culture might be traced to a variety of causes. School training clearly is not one of them, as young people in France had to learn German language and study German literature in the 1920s and 1930s – which of course does not mean that they became proficient in either. Among the memoirists, only Labat (whose mother was Viennese) and Lobsiger (who had spent time in Germany before the war) claim to be fluent in German, and many admit that they had difficulties communicating with the German soldiers who did not speak (some) French. It remains that the volunteers were acquainted with German literature and history, and that the absence of these fields in their memoirs seems to be related less to a lack of knowledge than to a resistance to things German, generally speaking. In the military area, as discussed earlier, most soldiers of the LVF and even some members of the French SS were reluctant to comply with the German exigencies of order and discipline, affirming instead the "French" prerogatives to challenge authority, as well as the "French" virtues of cleverness and resourceful-ness (*débrouillardise*). The scarcity of references to German culture in the volunteers' memoirs must probably be understood in relation to a similar Gallic value system, which in this instance remains implicit. Indeed, the legionaries do not reject German culture as deliberately as they mock German military rules. They do not, for example, specifically designate Goethe's or Schiller's works as unable to convey their experience of the war, explaining why those of Xenophon, Racine, and Defoe are better suited to serve that purpose. In short, they do not expressly spurn German art, literature, and history. They merely leave them out, showing, more fundamentally perhaps, that such domains are not part of their mindset and thus are unavailable when it comes to describing their experiences in the USSR – and even in Germany toward the end of the war.

Insofar as they deride German discipline and shut out German culture, the volunteers' life narratives occupy a most distinct place on the map of the memory of the collaboration. On the one hand, those narratives differ from the personal texts of a writer such as Brasillach, who in his "Lettre à quelques jeunes gens [Letter to a Few Young People]" published on February 19, 1944 in the collaborationist newspaper *Révolution Nationale*, describes his attachment to Germany in emotional terms that the prosecution later used against him at his trial; proclaiming that he will "never forget" the "love affair he has had with German genius," he states that the French who "more or less slept with Germany" during the Occupation, will keep a "sweet memory" of this relationship (quoted in Amouroux IX, 243). But the veterans' reminiscences also depart from the memoirs of former Vichy officials such as de Brinon and Benoist-Méchin, whose collaborationism was grounded in a comprehensive knowledge of, and admiration for, German history and culture. De Brinon had trav-eled to Germany as a journalist, interviewing Hitler in 1933; he also had been one of the founders of the Comité France-Allemagne, whose function was to promote the reconciliation between the two countries.

This background, he explains in his memoir, accounted for his conviction that France and Germany had to cooperate, justifying his activities in Paris as "General Delegate of the French Government in the Occupied Territories." Benoist-Méchin was equally familiar with Germany, whose armed forces he had studied in his monumental *Histoire de l'armée allemande*, first published in 1936. Like de Brinon, he endeavors in his memoir to defend the pro-German policies he had advocated when he was a member of the Vichy government, arguing that Germany was more of a "natural" ally of France than England and the United States were, and expressing his disappointment in the face of Hitler's reluctance to accept the offer of a more comprehensive collaboration that France had made in the spring of 1941. Unlike Brasillach, the volunteers have no amorous feelings for a "German genius" that they largely ignore; and unlike de Brinon and Benoist-Méchin, they have no cultural or intellectual affinities with a country for which they are fighting, but in whose army they still feel like outsiders. One might thus ask, given this lack of empathy for Germany and its people, why they elected to enlist, and why they were still on the battlefield in early 1945, when the war was obviously lost. My next chapter should provide tentative answers to those questions.

6

Bearing Witness

Reflecting on the "remnants of Auschwitz," Giorgio Agamben submits that any examination of the Judeocide can only lead to an "aporia of historical knowledge" (12). That is, it can only lead to the identification of an irreducible discrepancy between our awareness of the "facts" on the one hand and our "comprehension" of those facts on the other (12). Agamben restricts his analyses to the aftermaths of the Holocaust, and the gap between knowledge and understanding that he describes is certainly most observable in the case of "Auschwitz," because the event seems to resist any attempt at historical contextualization. Yet we may encounter similar though admittedly less profound gaps when we read books, watch documentary films, or listen to testimonies about other aspects of World War II, and have trouble apprehending why the participants acted the way they did. The presence of hundreds of thousands of foreign volunteers in the German army is a case in point. Nowadays, that presence can only produce, as Estes puts it, "both curiosity and consternation" (chapter 1, 1); the cause was evidently criminal, and why so many people chose to defend it on the battlefield, and to defend it to the end, appears incomprehensible in our time. The memoirs of the French who joined the LVF and the SS are most valuable in this respect. Indeed, they provide partial answers to a certain number of questions we may have about the volunteers' motivations, attitudes, and beliefs. Before examining those answers, I want to emphasize once again that memoirs are written from a retrospective standpoint, and that in the case of the texts in my corpus, we generally cannot measure against other sources the veracity of what the authors are reporting. The problem is obvious in the veterans' descriptions of their military and sexual feats, whose credibility I sought to assess in Chapter 3. It arises again, however, when the memoirists account "now" for decisions they made "then," and no document is available to establish to what extent the explanations provided can be held as genuine. Reviewing some of those explanations, I will take up three questions that they explicitly or implicitly address, beginning with the most obvious: Why did Frenchmen choose to fight alongside the Germans, that is, for the "hereditary enemy" who had just humiliated them during the May-June 1940 campaign, was occupying part of their homeland, and in whose culture – as we have just seen – many of them apparently had so little interest?

ENLISTING

George Mosse, in his work on the "myth of the war experience," has asked why people would "rush to the colors," that is, why they would volunteer to join an army when no conscription forced them to do so. Initially, according to Mosse, volunteers were involved in wars of "national unity and liberation" (1986a, 175); they decided to fight for their country when the latter was attacked, was seeking to spread its political system, or was intent on consolidating, as was the case in the wars of the French Revolution, the Napoleonic wars, and the wars for German unity. In the twentieth century, however, nationalism gave way to "ideological and political" considerations (180); beginning with the Spanish Civil War, volunteers joined one side or the other because they believed in a specific doctrine, whether Fascism, Socialism, Communism, or Anarchism. According to Mosse, men in the foreign armies of the Third Reich belonged to that latter type, with one restriction; many of them were also nationalists, as they were hoping that their involvement would "secure the survival of their particular nation in Hitler's Europe" (181). Whatever the circumstances might have been, Mosse concludes, common themes run throughout the history of volunteers. By "joining," individuals have sought a "purposeful life," "meaningful personal relationships," "submersion in a moral cause," as well as the satisfaction of being "in the thick of things"; their ultimate aspiration has been to create a "new man," one whom the brotherhood of combat would transform, and who would be radically different from the types that dominate "existing society" (181).

Historians of France's military collaboration have distinguished among different categories of volunteers and the reasons they had to go fight in the USSR. Investigating the LVF, Giolitto (61–84) submits that members of extremist organizations such as Doriot's Parti Populaire Français (PPF) and Déat's Mouvement Social Révolutionnaire (MSR) enrolled to assert their political beliefs; fervent Catholics, to defend Christian civilization; some career soldiers, to show what the French army was capable of; other military men, to fill easy administrative jobs in the rear; unemployed or poorly compensated people, to get a decent paycheck; criminals, to escape justice; and adventurers, to experience something new in a far, exotic country. In sum, Giolitto explains, the LVF was made up of one-third political militants, one-third career soldiers, and one-third adventurers (71). As far as age and social class were concerned, young people, employees, factory workers, and farmhands constituted the majority of the LVF, showing that the organization had mostly recruited in the "très petite bourgeoisie" and the "lumpenproletariat" (74).

Not unexpectedly, the categories listed by Giolitto are not all represented in the memoirs I am considering. Members of the "très petite bourgeoisie" and the "lumpenproletariat" usually do not write, or they write with assistance that, in this case, they did not receive. We do not, therefore, have the recollections of a volunteer who enlisted on financial grounds, nor those of a criminal whose objective was to stay out of jail, nor those of a career soldier whose main goal was to do paperwork in one of the LVF's many offices. Furthermore, and most importantly, the veterans' reminiscences are prime examples of the discursive situation I described earlier: Their authors account for their decision from a retrospective standpoint, and we do not have the documents that would enable us to compare the version of enlisting that the volunteer provides "now" with another, "then" version of that same event, for instance, with a letter or a journal entry that he jotted down when he was about to join the LVF or the SS. La Mazière states that he thought of sending a letter to his father before going to the recruitment office of the Waffen-SS in August 1944, but that he gave up because he had neither the time nor the "inspiration" to write it (1972, 26). The only volunteer to introduce this type of record is Dupont, who reproduces the text of the message he left on his father's desk before departing: "In London, people get involved for the benefit of uncontrolled capitalism [capitalisme sauvage] and international Jewry. In Paris, they get involved in order to crush Communism and ensure the coming of a new order. Don't be angry with me, I have made my choice: I've enrolled in the Légion des volontaires français contre le bolchevisme. I will write shortly" (71). In addition to the general issues of genre and authenticity I raised in Chapter 2 about *Au temps des choix héroïques*, the problem here is that the document originates with

Dupont himself (did he keep a copy?) and not with a more neutral source, such as the departmental archives in which Belser (315–16) and Rousso (1992, 177) have uncovered similar correspondence. In other words, the document in this instance does not provide a confrontation of contemporary and retrospective perspectives; it merely repeats the arguments that the author himself has provided in the preceding pages, making the two perspectives coincide in a way that raises suspicion because it is typical of the coherence that people often bestow upon their lives when they turn them into narratives.

Giolitto's "political soldiers" have several representatives among the memoirists, though surprisingly only two (Cisay and Costabrava) expressly claims allegiance to Doriot's Parti Populaire Français and none to Déat's Mouvement Social Révolutionnaire – the two parties that, according to Giolitto, contributed the largest number of volunteers. In my corpus, the politically committed memoirists tend to come from the small, "anticonformist" parties that had proliferated in France during the 1920s and 1930s, as well as from more recently created collaborationist organizations and even from the Vichy government. Laurier and Labat were members of Clémenti's Parti Français National Collectiviste; Bassompierre, of Pierre Taittinger's Jeunesses Patriotes and Eugène Deloncle's Comité Secret d'Action Révolutionnaire (the infamous "Cagoule"); Leverrier, of an unnamed organization close to Italian fascism; Saint-Loup, of Châteaubriant's Groupe Collaboration; Gaultier, of Paul Marion's Ministry of Information; and Larfoux, of the school that trained leaders for the Centres ruraux de la jeunesse, an institution typical of the "back to the land" Vichy politics. Bassompierre, Gaultier, Levast, and Marotel also belonged to the Milice – the paramilitary force established in 1943 by Vichy in order to protect its supporters and fight the Resistance. Commenting upon his and some of his fellow miliciens' decision to enlist, Gaultier writes that the point was to make one's actions agree with one's beliefs; that is, it was to establish a "distinct, concrete correspondence between what we had said and what we were about to do" (175), a gesture that would send a message to the many collaborationists who called for France's reentering the conflict but remained themselves in the comfort of their Parisian offices. Using similar language, Leverrier states that as an avowed "fascist" (though not one belonging to any party), he had to "get involved" (28); after "playing the tough guy," he felt morally obligated to "put his money where his mouth was [mettre sa peau au bout de ses idées]" and join the troops that were leaving for the USSR (32).

The category "political soldiers" also includes the Swiss and Belgian volunteers who wrote their memoirs and who are especially explicit about the grounds they had for enlisting. Lobsiger describes over sixty pages (3–65) his prewar activities in Switzerland and in Germany: his involvement in the proto-fascist Swiss Front National, his contacts with the SS during a stay in Württemberg from 1937 to 1939, and his clandestine crossing of the border in June 1941, several days before Germany's attack on the USSR.[1] Terlin does not recount the circumstances of his enrollment but mentions, while telling about an encounter with Degrelle, that he has known "le Chef" "since the tough political battles of the 1930s," when he, "with some fellow workers in Liège, was an activist for the Rexist movement" (231). Philippet supplies more details, explaining that he was an enthusiastic member of the Gamins de Rex [Kids of Rex], and decided to enlist when he was seventeen, after a political rally in Liège during which Degrelle had given a particularly inspiring speech (I, 8). Gruber had a similar trajectory; a supporter of Rex during his teens, he volunteered to go work in Germany after Belgium's defeat, and then enrolled during a leave (35). As for Degrelle himself, he points out that his purpose when he organized the Légion Wallonie was both to help the Germans and to serve his own country; whereas Belgium's attempts to establish a genuine collaboration with Germany were going nowhere, participating in Barbarossa provided the opportunity "to force the Reich's respect," eventually making the Belgians into "the companions and the equals of the victors" (14). For Degrelle, in other words, the presence of Belgian troops on the Eastern Front served a nationalist purpose; such participation ensured that Belgium would not be left out or reduced to a satellite state at the end of the conflict, but had a place in the new, "saved" Europe that the Nazis were planning (14). That "hope," as Mosse has argued (181), was not particular to Degrelle and the Belgians who had joined the Légion Wallonie; it was shared by thousands of volunteers, who expected that their respective countries would be rewarded for contributing to the German war efforts. Whether the Germans, had they been the victors that Degrelle foresaw, were intent on offering rewards of this type seems doubtful, to say the least. As historians such as Burrin, Gordon, and Jäckel

---

[1] It is worth noticing that, among the "political" volunteers, Lobsiger is the only one who had spent a long period of time in Nazi Germany. Bayle, Degrelle, Leverrier, and Saint-Loup had briefly traveled to Germany and/or to Italy in the 1930s, and Labat, the son of a diplomat, had lived for a few years in Vienna. But none of these men had Lobsiger's specific, firsthand knowledge of life under a strong, nondemocratic regime, such as German National Socialism or Italian Fascism.

have shown, Hitler was not interested in establishing a fascist Europe; his only concern was to expand German *Lebensraum* and exploit the occupied territories. The Nazis' "new" Europe, therefore, would have been a "patchwork" (Burrin 2000, 268), in which France and Belgium became "rump states [pays croupions]," with "amputated" territories and economies whose sole function was to fill Germany's needs (271).[2]

While career soldiers, according to Giolitto, accounted for one-third of the membership in the LVF, only one of them has published his memoir. Rostaing's *Le Prix d'un serment* is the sole testimony written by a volunteer whose profession was "serviceman," as the other representatives of that group either did not survive the war, were not interested in testifying, or were never asked to bear witness to their experience. Self-consciously playing the part of the simple soldier, Rostaing asserts from the first lines in his "Prologue" that he has nothing in common with the men who joined the LVF because they were supporters of Doriot or Clémenti; having never "been involved in politics," he has always "distrusted people who were involved in it," and the fact that he participated in "important events of a political nature" is one of the "contradictions" in his life (15). Briefly describing his personal trajectory at the beginning of his memoir, Rostaing insists it is one of a serviceman; A member of the feeble Armistice Army [Armée d'armistice] authorized by the Germans, he had joined the Légion Tricolore, only switching to the LVF when it became clear that the former would never be sent to the front. That decision, he explains, was made easier by a message in which Marshall Pétain, then head of the "legal" government and almost unanimously regarded as the savior of the nation, had told the legionaries: "You are holding a part of our military honor," and "by participating in the Crusade that Germany is leading, you will win quite deservedly the gratitude of the world" (22–3).[3]

---

[2] The *Generalplan West* presented to Hitler by Wilhelm Stuckart and his team in June 1940 is in this respect particularly revealing. According to this plan, Wallonie, Luxemburg, Alsace, Lorraine, as well as the industrial areas of northern and eastern France (about 50,000 square kilometers) were to be annexed to the Grosses Reich in postwar Europe. Stuckart was "Secretary of State for Border Questions and Annexions" in the German Ministry of the Interior, a title that leaves little doubt as to the Reich's intentions. Schöttler (2003) provides a copy and a thorough analysis of the "Generalplan West," tracing the history of this curious document, which had disappeared for fifty years before Schöttler was able to locate it in Canada, in the library of the University of New Brunswick.

[3] The complete text of the "message" sent by Pétain to the volunteers on November 5, 1941 is reproduced in Giolitto (29–30). According to Giolitto (31), that message might have be written by de Brinon, then a member of the LVF's Comité central, and Pétain might have signed it without reading it, as he supposedly signed many documents.

Rostaing returns frequently to the concept of "serving," which, according to him, accounts for most of the decisions he has made throughout his life. He uses it no less than four times in the brief statement he claims he gave to the court during his trial, when he asserted: "I am a servant of my homeland... I've been at France's service since I was eighteen .... I've served in the French army for fifteen years ... My motivation is simple: it's always been to serve" (230). Rostaing, in short, maintains that his driving force consistently has been patriotism, though without the political calculations that the term includes for such people as Degrelle. Indeed, Rostaing never argues that he fought alongside the Germans so that France might have a place in Hitler's reshaped Europe, nor does he advocate a form of government that for him would be especially well suited for his country. His sole motivation, he insists, was to show the world that the rout of 1940 was an accident, as French soldiers were ready to return to the battlefield and fight with courage.

Giolitto's "adventurers" have more representatives in my corpus than the veterans of the French army. The most typical is the anonymous author of *Vae Victis*, who describes the circumstances of his enrollment in the sarcastic manner that constitutes one of the trademarks of his memoir. Specifying that the story he is about to tell begins in May 1942, that is, at a time when "smart, realistic" people could have no illusions as to how the war would end, he writes:

I am making no claim to wisdom, and I would despise myself for being rational in this Paris where the Ride of the *Valkirie* and Liszt's *Preludes* resound, and where the radio, the papers, the movies, the posters, and boredom are telling me about a country where cities have names like "Tarangog" and "Diepropetrowsk." For a week I've known that I am about to leave, but I only understand that my decision is irremediable after I've signed my enlistment in a non-descript house in the rue Saint-Georges. I've signed on my honor that I was neither Jewish, nor a Freemason, nor a convict. After which, I am deemed worthy of entering the Queen's barracks in Versailles. (8–9)

The author of *Vae Victis* claims that his activities at the front were still those of a dilettante, who thought of himself as a participant in an adventure novel. Typically, he recounts that he and his friend Raymond planned to "cross the Russian lines" and "seek to reach the Republic of the Kirghiz," a project that retrospectively he still views as "doable" (123). Likewise, he describes his excitement at the idea that the name of the partisans' leader the LVF was hunting in a certain forest was "Nikitine," asking how people could still "believe in the 3% life annuity" offered by some French retirement systems, when there were opportunities "to be bandits in the woods, command a horde, and be called Nikitine" (130). That same author never mentions other, more serious reasons he might have had to enlist, and he acknowledges that his offhand manners came with a price: His comrades traced his attitude to his social class, chiding him for being "a likeable dreg [déchet sympathique] of the ruling classes of the Third Republic" (189). Yet he makes no further reference to his privileged background – a background that is obvious not just in his affected aloofness, but in the numerous, pointed references to high culture that he strews throughout his text.

Other representatives of the adventurers are Auvray and Emmanuelli. Less provocatively disengaged than the protagonist of *Vae Victis*, they seem to act out of a drive to be, as Mosse puts it in his description of this type of volunteers, "in the thick of things" (1986a, 181). Auvray concedes that he did not enlist in the Milice "just after D-Day" in order to help defend the Vichy regime against the Resistance; the Milice was only "one stop" on the road to the Waffen-SS (7), in which eager young men like himself would have the opportunity to satisfy their yearning for commitment:

The height of this war had caused so much excitement in the imaginations of the young generations that the school, the office, or the workshop had become burdens of an unbearable triteness; clear-headed decisions to serve reasonably well had given way to a frenzy of serving at any price. (8)

The phrase "serving at any price" here is particularly revealing. Contrasting with Rostaing's repeated statement "I've served France," it points to a mere desire for participating, for being at the place where important events supposedly are taking place. In this respect, it also contrasts with the attitude of miliciens such as Gaultier, who affirm that they enrolled for ideological reasons; Auvray does not profess having any beliefs, or at least any beliefs upon which it would be worth elaborating because they account for his joining the German side when the latter had obviously lost.

Whereas Auvray sets forth that he was anxious to get to the battlefield, Emmanuelli describes his enrollment as fortuitous. A Corsican from Marseille, he explains that he joined the LVF in the summer of 1942 in order to do a favor to fellow Corsicans. More precisely, he felt called to go to Russia and retrieve François Sabiani, the son of Simon Sabiani, a prominent member of Doriot's PPF and the president of the "delegation" appointed by Vichy to govern Marseille after the dismissal of the socialist municipality. Arguing that it is easy, after the facts, to ask "Why did you

go to Berlin and not to London?", Emmanuelli maintains that joining the
LVF for him was "an affair of heart, of feeling, of Corsican solidarity," as
he himself did not belong to any political organization (33). Risking one's
life out of regional allegiance, however, proved futile, as it turned out that
François Sabiani had been killed in combat. According to Emmanuelli,
all the unfortunate events that then occurred to him: being jailed in
Germany for ration card trafficking, jailed in France for his participation
in the LVF, signing up with the Foreign Legion, and failing in diverse business endeavors were due to similarly ill-considered decisions. Explicating
at the end of his book the title *Et j'ai cassé mon fusil* [And I Broke My
Gun], he confesses that the phrase falls under wishful thinking: "I should
have taken my gun and broken it ... yes, I should have broken it ... but
I'm a coward ... I've always let myself be made to do things..." (410).
Furthermore, whereas Auvray and the author of *Vae Victis* take responsibility for their actions, however unmotivated they might look to them
from a retrospective standpoint, Emmanuelli concludes his reminiscences
by affirming that he did most of what he did by accident; he is someone
who is incapable of saying "no" (410), as he was incapable of saying
"no" to the Sabianis when they made their fateful request.

While the volunteers who wrote their memoirs are not representative
of all the types that Giolitto lists in his study, the reverse is also true.
That is, those volunteers sometimes trace their involvement to motives
that Giolitto does not identify. Some of the very young men who joined
the Waffen-SS, for example, claim that they did so because they were
enthused by that corps and the values that it represented. La Mazière's
testimony in *Le Chagrin et la Pitié* is revealing in this respect, as the
former member of the SS does not only explain his enrollment by his
political beliefs and family background (his father was a career officer
and staunchly antirepublican), but also by his admiration for the German
army's physical appearance:

And Germany was triumphant. Wherever their armies went, they were victorious.
I must say that the German army at the time made a great impression on young
people. The sight of those German soldiers, stripped to the waist ... For the first
time we saw an army which was all we had dreamed ours might be. The French
army was made of rather sloppy recruits – not exactly the kind of soldier that
puts fear into the heart of the mob. It is a terrible thing to say, but it must be said.
It is the truth. (Ophuls 49–50)

Bayle and Mit account for their enlistment in similar fashion, explaining that their wonderment at the view of the German troops that were

stationed in France made them join when they were barely sixteen years old. Bayle writes that, being from a family of gymnasts and circus artists, he became a member of the SS out of a fascination for the athleticism, cleanliness, and discipline of that corps. To illustrate the connection, Bayle includes pictures of bare-chested SS soldiers exercising in shorts next to a photo of himself performing on the trapeze with his father, part of an act in one of the best-known French circuses – the Médrano (n.p.). Continuing the link between sport and war, Bayle also justifies his decision to get involved by turning to Baron de Coubertin's famous statement: "The main thing is to participate," adding that he felt obligated to engage "in any possible way," because "wait-and-see was not the proper attitude for an athlete" (58). Bayle, who had attended the 1936 Olympic Games in Berlin with his family, does not indicate whether he was aware of Coubertin's political views – of the baron's support for the strong, authoritarian regimes that alone could ensure that their populations become "healthy" through physical education.

More provocatively than Bayle, Mit traces his decision to join the Waffen-SS to the lure of not just those units, but of Germany in general: "What aren't people standing in line saying about the Waffen-SS? They kill, rape, they have the power of life and death. I laugh at this rubbish. The homeland of Goethe and Schiller, of Beethoven and Bach, attracts me like a magnet. The die is cast: I will join the Waffen-SS" (9). Mit's germanophilia, however, remains confined to these few lines. The names "Goethe" and "Schiller" never reappear in *Carcasse à vendre*, and the book does not include a single mention of another "great German." When Mit recites poetry, it is a piece by Verlaine (176); when he sings with his comrades during combat, it is *La Marseillaise* (126–7); and when he sings in German for the nurses at the military hospital where he is treated, it is the translation of "J'attendrai [I shall wait]," a hit song by the French crooner Tino Rossi (180). In this regard, his initial pronouncement notwithstanding, Mit resembles the memoirists whose "French" reference system I examined earlier – the volunteers who fought for Germany but never account for their experiences in terms of German culture when they write up their recollections. Mit is also among the French recruits who were not infatuated with the SS for very long; upon discovering the rigor of German discipline at the training camp in Sennheim, he and most of his recently enlisted countrymen quickly returned to Gallic ways of resisting a system they had admired from a distance, but with whose exigencies they were not ready to comply.

If Mit ignores Germany while professing to be enamored with it, other volunteers proclaim loudly that they never liked that country and did not relish the idea of becoming members of its armed forces. The soldiers who had participated in the hapless 1940 campaign were especially reluctant to join, as Germany for them was still "the enemy." Describing his state of mind at the time, Rostaing writes: "I had just come out of this war against Germany, and I was not particularly anxious to put on the uniform of yesterday's foe and to fight at its side" (23). Bassompierre, who turns to the historical present, spells out the hesitations he had in the summer of 1941 in a similar manner: "For me, the question is to know whether I will enroll in this antibolshevik legion whose principle I approve, even though out of gut feeling [sentimentalement], and without knowing them, I don't like the Germans. Rationally, I think that at some point we'll have to get along. But is it a reason for wearing their uniform? I can't resign myself to that" (132). Rostaing, Bassompierre, and the other volunteers eventually had to "put on German uniforms" and to do so in the most literal sense of that phrase. Because France and the USSR were not officially at war, the presence in the USSR of soldiers wearing French outfits could have caused diplomatic incidents. The volunteers, therefore, had to be content with wearing an insignia on the sleeve of their jacket, the only mark of their national origin (Giolitto 92). As an additional vexation, the French were also required to pledge fidelity to Hitler, which they would do not by repeating the text spoken by a German officer, but by raising their right arm "as a sign of acceptance" (Rostaing 40).

While the volunteers enlisted for diverse reasons and with varying degrees of enthusiasm for Germany, they nevertheless shared a certain number of beliefs. The most widespread were anticommunism and, to a lesser extent, faith in the new Europe that an Axis victory was supposed to produce. Statements about the evils of Communism and the need to fight it abound in virtually every memoir: "I am leaving for Russia to fight the enemy of all civilizations: Bolshevism" (Rostaing 25); "The enemy now is Communism, it's Stalin... Europe must unite against this scourge, and France must be present in this struggle" (Dupont 73); "In 1941 the Wehrmacht launched an assault on Russia... I was jubilant and decided to help the Germans to destroy Bolshevism" (Laurier 26). Rostaing, to describe his feelings toward the USSR, uses the phrase "visceral anticommunism" (23), and that phrase may serve to characterize the political stance of most volunteers when they resolved to enlist. Indeed, none of them justifies his decision to fight on the Eastern Front with arguments against the social, political, and economic aspects of the Soviet system. They can state that their beliefs were confirmed when they saw what Russia was like, as Bassompierre does when he observes that most people in Minsk, resembling "human animals," live in "horrible, small wooden hovels" (138). But they never seek to make a reasoned case against Communism, listing the grounds on which they reject that doctrine and favor others. In this regard, their texts sound like excerpts from the editorials that the collaborationist press was running after June 22, 1941, such as Doriot's of June 27, 1941 in *Le Cri du peuple*: "From lies to betrayals, from betrayals to crimes, Communism has placed itself outside the conscience of civilized men from all the countries of the continents ... Communism will pay. And, we hope, it will pay dearly" (quoted in Cotta, 107). However simplistic and stereotyped, reasons the volunteers give to justify their decision to go fight "Bolshevism" are nevertheless "political," as they imply the exercise of power, more precisely the rejection of a system and the attempt to suppress it. In this regard, they differ from the reasons for their engagement that the Germans who fought on the Eastern Front offer in their memoirs. As Smelser and Davies have shown, generals such as Guderian and von Manstein, as well as rank-and-file soldiers such as Koschorrek and Scheiderbauer, focus "almost exclusively on operational questions" when they recount their campaigns (137). Avoiding "any discussion of the political and strategic" (137), they claim that their only motivation was to defend the homeland; they do not explain how they found themselves involved in a war of "conquest and annihilation" (138), that is, in a war that was as political as there ever has been.

As the volunteers resort to clichés to justify their hostility to Bolshevism, they explain their endorsement of a new "Europe" in a language that is equally formulaic. On this subject, their statements often take the form of assertions that no argument sustains: "We are at a turning point of history. I feel European. France must abandon her nationalism and accept to be integrated into a larger European organization, following the example of Germany" (Rusco 17); "For me, one thing is clear. I must act. Since 1936 I've known that my ideal is a united and supranational Europe, which can only be built by fighting Bolshevism" (Bayle 52); "Chauvinistic nationalism is obsolete on our continent. If we don't want to be dominated by Russian Bolshevism or Jewish-American plutocracy, or even by both, we must defeat them, and in order to do so we need a united Europe" (Dupont 189). Again, the volunteers' crude affirmations seem to originate in texts of propaganda, such as the lines on a poster inviting the French to join the SS: "With your European comrades-Under the sign of the SS-You will be victorious" (reproduced on the front cover of

Mit's *Carcasse à vendre*), or those in an editorial published in the collaborationist newspaper *La France au travail* on June 23, 1941: "For us, the war between Germany and Russia is an episode in the struggle for a European federation, for a large community in which France has a place, with a significant role to play if she so wants" (quoted in Cotta, 108). In fact, one can ask whether the volunteers recall "how they felt" at the time of their enrollment, as Rusco contends that he does, or whether they merely remember (and reproduce) statements that they had read in the press or heard on the radio. The passages in which my memoirists rage against Communism and clamor for a new Europe could thus be viewed as examples of what Scott and Amossy hold to be the necessarily filtered nature of experience: the fact that what we live through is always interpreted through a network of mediations, beginning with language. In this instance, one may regret that the volunteers could only describe their beliefs by resorting to well-worn slogans; but the alternative was to employ a different vocabulary, for instance, one borrowed from theorists more sophisticated than the editorialists of *Le Cri du Peuple* and *La France au Travail*, as there is no way of representing one's feelings and beliefs in direct, transparent manner.[4]

While the volunteers employ ready-made phrases to account for their support of a "united," "federated," "supranational" Europe, they do not specifically describe what they were hoping for at the time, nor what they possibly knew (and thought) of German plans on the subject of "Europe." Only Saint-Loup claims an awareness of such plans, which he discusses in the "The Monastery of the Black Men," the chapter of *Götterdämmerung* he devotes to his stay at the Haus Germania, an SS training school in Hildesheim. In late 1944, according to Saint-Loup, the German leadership was deeply divided about how to reshape the continent after the German victory. The more traditionalist among its constituents supported Pan-Germanism; their aim was the union of all German-speaking people and their native territories into a single German state, under which the other states would be subsumed. Yet younger, more "progressivist" members of the SS organization had a different goal; they wanted to build a borderless, decentralized Europe, which would extend from the Atlantic to the Ural. In Hildesheim, Saint-Loup reports, that progressivist wing had a

---

[4] For a study of the work of these theorists (e.g., Marcel Déat, Bertrand de Jouvenel, Francis Delaisi, Jean Luchaire), see Bruneteau, 2003. Bruneteau analyzes in detail the "illusion" of intellectuals who thought that the Nazi endeavor, deemed to be contingent and provisional, would make the constitution of a new, supranational Europe possible.

most articulate representative in Obersturmführer von Dahnwitz. This SS officer and theorist advocated the unification of Europe through the elimination of nation-states, their replacement by communities grounded in "ethnicity," and the grouping of those communities into "an SS federation with a common ethics of race, of power to the best, of fundamental inequality, and of submission of the individual to the people" (1986b, 94). In a note, Saint-Loup affirms that von Dahnitz's "pan-European, supranational, anti-imperialist" conception was adopted by the SS in the fall of 1944, "under the pressure of student officers coming from fourteen different nations" (94). The "levers of revolution were thus in place" (94), though, Saint-Loup regrets, circumstances kept them from ever being pulled.

Obviously impressed by the SS "European" project, Saint-Loup has frequently returned to it after the war. He has published a series of novels under the banner "the rebirth of carnal homelands [la renaissance des patries charnelles]," a series that includes such titles as *Plus de pardon pour les Bretons* and *La République du Mont-Blanc*. He has also written essays in which he clarifies his position with respect to Europe, showing that he has remained deeply convinced of the merits of the Hildesheim project. In an article published in 1976 in the right-wing journal *Défense de l'Occident*, for example, he describes a plan for reorganizing the continent that is very close to von Dahnwitz's: Nation-states and their political borders are artificial and must be abolished; they should be replaced by "carnal homelands," that is, by "natural" entities grounded in "biological givens" like "blood" and "territory" (the old Nazi motto *Blut und Boden*); keeping their cultural trademarks, those entities should constitute a federation; and that federation should be centralized in the areas of economy and defense, in order to ensure its protection against the "assault" launched by billions of Asians and Africans – an assault that for Saint-Loup will "fatally" take place (1976, 73–4). Maps occasionally included in texts by or about Saint-Loup show what the new Europe would look like, Brittany, for example, becoming a "carnal homeland" under the name "Armorique," and the French Haute-Savoie, the Italian valley of Aosta, and the Swiss canton of Valais, being merged to form "Les pays du Mont-Blanc."[5]

Saint-Loup, however, is the only one among my memoirists to advocate such a specific reshaping of the continent. Other volunteers may proclaim, as Rusco does (17), that they "feel European," but they do not

---

[5] One such map can be found on http://www.jeune-france.org.

indicate whether they would support projects as radical as von Dahnwitz's and Saint-Loup's. Furthermore, if some of the "political" members of the French and Belgian units assert that they enrolled in order to save a place for their country in the new, Nazi-dominated Europe, they never indicate that their goal was to bring independence or autonomy to their region. None of them belonged to the Bezen Perrot, the pro-Nazi unit made of separatist Bretons, nor to the Alsatian independentist party, that is, to groups whose members expected that their engagement alongside the Axis would incite Germany to grant their province autonomy after the war. In other words, none of the texts I am considering illustrates what the historian Francis Arzalier calls the "fascist drift" of autonomist and independentist movements during World War II: the assistance provided to Nazi Germany by some of those movements, in the hope that the favor would be returned later in the form of political sovereignty.[6] As for Saint-Loup, he presents his discovery of the SS program for a Europe reorganized along ethnic lines as a late confirmation of the correctness of his ideological choices, not retroactively as one of the reasons he joined the LVF. Indeed, he could not have known at the beginning of the war about plans that had not yet been formulated. When he explains, in 1943, why he enlisted in the summer of 1942, he traces his decision to his anticommunism; he does not mention, however, that one of the happy outcomes of a German victory could be the disappearance of "France" to the benefit of such entities as "Armorique" and "Pays du Mont-Blanc."[7] The only thread that runs from *Les Partisans* to *Götterdämmerung* to the article in *Défense de l'Occident* is Saint-Loup's belief that Europe must be refashioned under the auspices of National Socialism, or of a regime that is situated in the legacy of that doctrine.

FIGHTING TO THE END

What, the historian Michael Geyer asks in an article he devotes to the topic of "catastrophic nationalism" (2003), may cause individuals and nations to keep fighting when a war is obviously lost, leading to self-destruction?

---

[6] On the promotion of ultra-regionalism among right-wing organizations after the war, see Duranton-Crabol. The author examines in particular the activities of the GRECE (Groupement de recherches et d'études sur la civilisation européenne).

[7] Two lectures that Saint-Loup gave in May and October 1941: "Jeunesses d'Europe unissez-vous" and "Les jeunes devant l'aventure européenne" are not more explicit; Saint-Loup advocates a unified Europe, though without providing details about the structure of this new entity. The two lectures are included in *J'ai vu l'Allemagne*, a collection of texts by Saint-Loup published in 1991.

In the instance of World War II, what made Germany struggle to the end, the country losing more men between the summer of 1944 and May 1945 (400,000 a month) than during the big battles of 1942–1943? And why did the last months of the war also witness an enormous number of mass murders, the "marches to death" being the most gruesome example of this type of carnage? Scholars, according to Geyer, have researched and identified the reasons why people seek to avoid death and suffering. But they have not investigated why whole nations would self-destruct, specifically in the case of Germany, why this country inflicted so much pain upon itself when any hope for a military victory had vanished long before.

The question "why fight to the end?" is even more relevant when we consider the case of the foreign volunteers. German soldiers, at least, were defending the homeland, which was being invaded and faced with occupation. In Germany's eastern provinces they also were protecting the local populations, whose flight they were covering before the arrival of the Soviet troops. Moreover, given the Allies' demand for unconditional capitulation, Germany was left with few alternatives; either it surrendered or it kept fighting until it eventually collapsed. Yet foreign volunteers were in an entirely different situation; they were not defending their national territory, had no countrymen and women to shield from invaders, and were not directly concerned with the conditions under which the war would end. Given these circumstances and the inevitability of defeat, why didn't they do what many a German soldier did (though at the risk of being caught and shot): put on civilian clothes and return to where they came from, taking advantage of the chaos reigning during the last months of the conflict to slip home unnoticed?

In the case of the French volunteers, one might first ask why some of them enlisted in 1944 after D-Day, that is, when it had become clear that Germany would definitely lose the war because it could not fight on two fronts. In other words, one might ask not exactly why some volunteers fought to the end, but why they enrolled to be there for the end – for what could only be the last battle(s). Auvray, as seen earlier, does not elaborate on this subject, tracing his decision to join the Milice and then the SS to the "frenzy to serve at any price" that had seized many young people during the summer of 1944 (8). La Mazière provides more details. Beginning his narrative in August 1944, he explains that several options were then available to him. Compromised because of his collaborationist activities, he could have "disappeared from France," or, "better, done the Resistance a few favors" that would have made up for his mistakes (1972, 12). Yet,

La Mazière insists, using metaphoric language, "it is precisely when the house is on fire, and when one could escape from it taking advantage of the catastrophe, that it must be defended with even more energy" (12). In short, it is when the cause we have endorsed is about to be lost that we must support it most determinedly, if we want to be true to ourselves. La Mazière adds an anecdote to make his point. In the newsroom of the magazine that employed him, he had met a young worker who, about to join the SS, had told him: "Reading your articles made me understand the road to a more upright future [le chemin d'un avenir plus propre]" (22). This young man, La Mazière concludes, "was not just following my convictions"; he was "leading the way," "showing me what example to emulate if I did not want to live in fear and shame" (22).

Neither Auvray's nor La Mazière's enrollment for the last battles, therefore, illustrates a theme that Bartov (2000) has treated in "Grand Illusion," an essay devoted to France's Occupation, and Louis Malle (on a script by Patrick Modiano), in his film *Lacombe Lucien*: that of the contingency of choice, of the fact that the young people who, in 1944, desperately wanted to "participate," could join the collaboration as well as the Resistance. Indeed, Auvray and La Mazière are no Lacombe Lucien. If Auvray merely wants to be "in the thick of things," he does not find himself on the side of the collaboration because he was rejected by the Resistance, which deemed him too young and questioned his motivations. As for La Mazière, he never considers becoming an eleventh-hour member of an organization he has attacked in his journalistic writings. To the contrary, he strives to "make his actions conform to his beliefs" (1972, 15), the Malraux-like formula that Gaultier also uses to account for his involvement. Employing similar language, Marotel recounts that, being from a family of soldiers, he received an offer to join the Resistance by one of his father's former officers, but that he refused, because "only cowards can resort to this kind of way out"; betraying his comrades from the Milice when everything seemed to be lost, he maintains, would have meant "betraying oneself," and "life thereafter would not have had any significance" (38).

The ethical imperative described by La Mazière and Marotel is also the main reason that some of the veterans provide in order to justify their continuing presence on the battlefield when the defeat was unavoidable. Like the German soldiers whose attitudes Kühne studies in *Kameradschaft*, the French volunteers claim that the demands of comradery, the commitment they have made, as well as the "opportunity to prove themselves" for a last time, keep them from giving up, even "when faced with the downfall

[Untergang]" (Kühne 144). The Catholic and law-and-order-minded Bassompierre asserts that he cannot "leave [his] fellow volunteers, when things are taking a turn for the worse" (155); Levast, that although he "no longer has illusions," he wants to go to Berlin in order to "die in combat" rather than being "killed in a ditch by a bullet in the neck" (99); and Terlin, upon arriving in Estonia, that he wants to do everything in his power "to block the road to the enemy," out of respect for the SS motto "My honor is loyalty [Meine Ehre heisst Treue]" (1972, 242). Rostaing does not invoke that motto, but the theme of the oath and the responsibility for it are already present in the title of his memoir: *Le Prix d'un serment*. It recurs throughout his text, for example, in this passage, which follows the news of D-Day, learned in July 1944 as the LVF was regrouping in Greifenberg:

I had sworn an oath and I was determined to remain faithful to it. If, as some were doing, I quit when faced with defeat, I could never more look at myself in the mirror when shaving in the morning. A few of us were thinking of deserting and surrendering to the Americans, as a way of redeeming themselves. This idea never crossed my mind, as I had never thought that a man can find a new reason to live before finding a new reason to die. And the only reason I had was to continue my crusade against Bolshevism until one of us disappeared. It looked like it was going to be me, but I remained optimistic. (145)

Toward the end of his narrative, Rostaing also reports that his loyalty to the oath made him turn down an offer to serve in the Russian army (which had taken him prisoner), as well as honestly fill out the questionnaire that the French Red Cross had handed out to him upon his liberation from the Russian POW camp, acknowledging he had fought with the LVF and the SS. The ladies from the Red Cross, Rostaing complains, turned immediately hostile, treating him like a pariah because of his membership in these organizations (219–20).

For other volunteers, however, fighting to the end was less a sign of loyalty than a way of continuing the adventure, as they had fancy plans about their future after Germany's collapse. Labat, documenting once again the offbeat sides of the LVF, mentions that in Saaletsch in the fall of 1944, a few members of his unit were thinking of "crossing the forests, the steppes, and the swamps, Europa and Asia, and resurfacing in some corner of China" (468). Labat also reports that about the same time his friend De Witte suggested that they desert, telling him: "I want to keep going east, towards elsewhere, following the first pleasant opportunity. Just to have a good time, because here it won't be fun. I need adventure.

I may end up as a political commissar with the Soviets or as a eunuch at the Great Vizir's. I don't give a damn, I just want to see the country" (489). Labat states that he declined De Witte's invitation, though not because he did not like the plan. He just deemed De Witte to be too much of a loner, and he was concerned about undertaking an adventure during which he certainly would soon have to fend for himself.

In his preface, Labat quotes Otto Abetz, Germany's "ambassador in Paris" during the occupation, who in 1941 had toasted to the LVF officers about to leave for Russia with the words: "I drink to your beautiful artist gesture [geste d'artiste]" (11). That toast, Labat comments, had been misunderstood at the time, embarrassing the journalists and politicians who were attending the reception. Yet Abetz spoke perfect French, and his reference to the aesthetic nature of the LVF endeavor, according to Labat, looks even more accurate if viewed from a distance. The LVF was of little political and military use, and its activities were "artistic" in Kant's well-known definition of the term: They were "disinterested," serving no practical purpose but affording "pleasure" (Labat says "joy") to those who were exercising them. For the LVF, according to Labat, such pleasure resided both in the "approval of oneself" and in the "drunkenness of having no hope" (12). A component in most of the French volunteers' undertakings, it became even more noticeable during the last months of the war, when defeat clearly could no longer be avoided. Thus, asked to cover the retreat of German troops near Vilnius in August 1944, the French accepted, because "to fullfil an impossible mission has such a charm, constitutes such a temptation, that it cannot be resisted" (Labat 43). Describing the bloody struggles of the Charlemagne in Pomerania, Auvray also points out that the French seem to "delight in defeats," "provided that they are sumptuous" (73). The last word appropriately belongs to Labat, who toward the end of his book confesses that he has never had much sympathy for the Germans, but that he appreciates them "now that they are losers"; for "lost causes" as more appealing than winning ones, as "too many bastards swagger around the victors" (551).

In the case of Germany and World War II, the theme "fighting to the end" is closely associated with one specific location, namely Berlin. Literary critics would in this instance talk of what Mikhail Bakhtin (1981) calls a "chronotope": a place in which temporal and spatial series intersect, as in (to stay with World War II) "Pearl Harbor," "Normandy," and "Hiroshima." Berlin was certainly not the only spot in Germany where "last battles" were fought in late April and early May 1945. But it was the capital of the country, the headquarters for many Nazi organizations, and its defense played a symbolic as well as a military role. That defense has been studied exhaustively by such historians as Beevor, Fischer, Le Tissier, Mabire, Rocolle, and Ryan, and I won't describe it once again. But some of the French volunteers found themselves in Berlin during the last months of the war, and their accounts pertain most directly to the topic of fighting to the end.

As I signaled in Chapter 3, the only ones among the memoirists who actually participated in the "last battle" are Levast, Malardier, and Rostaing. Other testimonies exist, notably the milicien and Hauptsturmführer Henri Fenet's who, under the transparent pseudonym Henri Fernet, tells about his experience in Berlin in the issue of *Historia* devoted to "L'Internationale SS."[8] Fenet and Rostaing were in the same unit, and both recall the strange ceremony during which Fenet, in the basement of a Friedrichstrasse bookstore in the night of April 30–May 1, gave Rostaing the First Class Iron Cross he had been awarded but had never received: a ceremony that Rostaing, about thirty years later, cannot remember without feeling "a lump form in [his] throat and [his] eyes fill with tears" (200). Levast and Malardier report similar emotional episodes of bestowing decorations, but the bulk of the three men's narratives is devoted to the account of what the title of Malardier's book designates as a *combat pour l'honneur*: a combat that has to be fought although its outcome has been known for some time, as a losing athlete insists on finishing the race. Describing the state of mind of the French SS who have just destroyed several Soviet tanks in Friedrichstrasse on April 29, Rostaing writes:

This series of victories warmed our hearts, although we knew that they were useless. We felt that everything was lost, that everything was dying around us. But we were determined to fight to the end, to the extinction of our strengths and the exhaustion of our stock of ammunition. A kind of warrior's rage was driving us not to cede a single parcel of land without defending it with an energy I have trouble imagining today. (197–8)

Although Rostaing and his men had sworn "never to surrender" (199) and "to die in combat" (203), they only fought to the end in the sense of "to the extinction of their strengths" and "to the exhaustion of their stock of ammunition." They were taken prisoner by the Russians on May 2 in the Kaiserhof subway station, hiding behind a pile of baskets that

---

[8] Fenet's testimony was probably solicited and written up by Mabire, who figures among the main contributors to this issue of *Historia* (sometimes under the pen name Henri Landemer), and whose style is strangely similar to "Fernet's."

they hoped would screen them from the enemy and allow them time to plan an escape (Rostaing 207; Fernet 171).[9] Levast and Malardier, under different circumstances, were also taken prisoner by the Russians, and they soon joined Fenet and Rostaing on the road to France – and to the charge of the French justice system.

Several tourist guides (e.g., Kopleck, Roth and Frajman) and scholarly studies (e.g., Ladd, Heesch and Braun) focus on Berlin as a site of memory: a place that has both retained traces of its past and erected additional markers, whose purpose is to commemorate particular aspects of its history. The concept "site of memory" of course begs the questions: "memory of what?" and "whose memory?" Current concerns now privilege the locations once occupied by the Third Reich's repressive apparatus, whose victims are remembered in numerous plaques, steles, and monuments. Yet Rostaing's and Fenet's accounts of the Battle of Berlin point to the existence of alternative sites, as well as to the polysemy of certain locations that so far have been associated with one type of remembrance exclusively. Memories, for example, compete in the case of Grünewald, a large wooded area in Southwest Berlin. The Grünewald train station was one of the three deportation points in the capital, and thousands of Jews were marched to that station before being taken to the East, where most of them were murdered; a large concrete block, a stele, a plaque, and a series of iron plates have been installed nearby in remembrance, the old track that carried the trains being integrated into the plates "as both historical artifact and artistic metaphor" (Roth and Frajman 89). Grünewald, however, plays an entirely different role in Rostaing's memoir. It is the place where he and his comrades stopped on their way to Berlin in the night of April 23–24, 1945, that is, the place where they were able to do such ordinary things as "rest," "sleep," and "wash" for the last time before the battle (Rostaing 188).

Similarly, Prinz-Albrecht-Strasse (now rebaptised Niederkirchnerstrasse, after Käthe Niederkirchner, a communist resistance fighter killed in Ravensbrück in 1944) was during the war the address of the Gestapo Headquarters, of the Reichsführer SS, and of the Reich Central Security Office; denoting the most hideous aspects of the Nazi past, the ruins of the buildings that rose there (only parts of the basements are left) now

---

[9] The Kaiserhof subway station was named after the Kaiserhof, a luxury hotel that the Nazis appreciated because it was close to the Chancellery and other government buildings. That hotel was destroyed during the war (the embassy of North Korea now occupies its former site), and the subway station has been renamed "Mohrenstrasse."

constitute the permanent exhibit "Topography of Terror." Yet this area, too, has a wholly different significance for Rostaing and the few men of the Charlemagne who were still with him at the time. Prinz-Albrecht-Strasse for them stands for "Reich Aviation Ministry," the large building across from the Gestapo and Central Security Offices that they reached in the early hours of May 2. More precisely, it stands for the end of the adventure, since it is there that the German officer in charge of the Ministry informed them that Hitler had died and that the city "would capitulate at 8 a.m." (Rostaing 205).[10] To be sure, posing the question "whose memory?" about such sites as Grünewald and Prinz-Albert-Strasse does not mean that the remembrance of a few dozen soldiers who fought in Berlin by choice is on the same level as that of tens of thousands of innocent victims whom a criminal regime tore from their homes by force. In other words, to take a relativist perspective and state that there are different types of memory does not mean that all types have the same significance. Todorov's "social consensus about good and evil" (43), in this case, cannot be bracketed off to save the volunteers; it is difficult not to see them as people who were certainly courageous, but who at some point made wrong choices and found themselves held as coresponsible for the criminal activities of the side that they had joined.

Additional accounts of the "last battle" are provided by Labat and Saint-Loup, who were in Berlin at the time, though they did not actively participate in the defense of the city. Labat, unwilling to be sent to Pomerania for what he foresaw would be a "laughable butchery" (531), switched to propaganda and asked to be assigned to Berlin, where he spent March and April 1945. Saint-Loup was in the capital from September 1944 to early 1945, busy editing publications that would bolster the spirits of the French volunteers. The pages that both men devote to their time in Berlin illustrate Auvray's thesis of a French taste for the aesthetic dimension of defeat. Labat, whose main goal was to see "how the capital of the Reich was preparing itself to receive the Russians" (552), was not disappointed. He writes:

As soon as I arrived in the city, I was overwhelmed by such a surprising, such a tragically poignant atmosphere, that for several hours I was dazzled and incapable of understanding. In the last two weeks of April, the drama of Berlin, which had been thickening for months, and whose intensity was going every day beyond the peaks reached the day before, got to a level of which only the word ART,

---

[10] Unlike the other buildings on Prinz-Albrecht-Strasse, the Air Ministry was hardly damaged by bombs. Restored, it now houses the Federal Ministry of Finance (Koplek 15).

written in capital letters, can give an idea ... One million people were living on a plane of an upsetting irreality, were aware of it, and most selflessly placed their lives and their last sources of energy at the service of the image they had of the way it is appropriate to be defeated. (552)

Saint-Loup is no less admiring than Labat, but his feelings of wonder go to the new cityscape that the Allies' bombings have created. Acknowledging that he has never liked Berlin in spite of his frequent visits to the city, he explains:

For the first time in my life I was discovering Berlin, and what I was discovering was beyond me: Berlin had become beautiful! As far as I could see, there was nothing but disemboweled palaces, department stores reduced to their silhouettes in stone, columns lying on the sides of the avenues. Everywhere pyramids and porticos were springing up. All that was marvelously sculpted by the fire, worked on by the scatter bombs, with unforeseen angles, suave roundings, bas reliefs, and, on tablets made of stone, the mysterious hieroglyphs of the phosphorus. Every ruin had its specific character, as though generations of artists had worked there with the love of cathedral builders, as though time had then completed the masterpiece, brought in the irreplaceable work of erosion produced by the water from the sky and the tears of praying women. (50)

The aestheticization of Germany's end is particularly noticeable in these two excerpts. Labat turns the situation in Berlin into a play whose topic reads "grandiose defeat" and whose actors are the image-conscious inhabitants, striving to perform their roles as well as possible and to leave evidence of their talent to future generations. Saint-Loup is less concerned with people than with architecture, but his point, like Labat's, is to show that Berlin at the end was beautiful. His rhetorical strategy here is to "see as," namely to describe ruined buildings and monuments as architectural artifacts that for our society are valuable, such as "pyramids," "porticos," and "bas reliefs." It is also to depict "as though," that is, to pretend that destruction is in fact the work of skilled artists or the outcome of natural phenomena, such as erosion. In both Labat's and Saint-Loup's accounts, the perspective is clearly that of an outsider. Historians have commended the stoicism of the Berliners, but to my knowledge they have never claimed that the inhabitants of the capital, concerned about the way future generations would look at them, were self-consciously playing the part of the nobly defeated. Similarly, numerous photographs show that several areas in Berlin had been reduced to ruins by 1945. But it is doubtful that the people who lived there could view the rubble as art, as they were busy clearing it and could hardly find any aesthetic, disinterested pleasure in the contemplation of their devastated neighborhoods.

To join aesthetics and politics, it could be argued that Labat and Saint-Loup, by celebrating what they portray as the made-for-theater attitudes of the civilians and the beauty of the devastated cityscape in Berlin, buy into the Nazi promotion of a fabulous *Untergang.* That is, they implicitly endorse Hitler's idea, described by Albert Speer in his recollections, that since Germany could not win the war, it had to disappear in a spectacular inferno: All industrial plants, electrical facilities, water and gas works, food and clothing stores, all bridges, railway lines, waterways, ships, freight cars, and locomotives had to be destroyed, irrespective of the cost in innocent human lives (quoted in Richie, 574). Of course, that scenario was not consistently enacted. Breslau, designated as a "fortress [Festung]" to be held at any price, was defended until May 6 and almost entirely destroyed, because the people in charge – General Hermann Niehoff and Gauleiter Karl Hanke – unswervingly followed the instructions they had received. But Halle underwent little damage, as marine officer and World War I hero Felix von Luckner, together with mayor Karl Huhold, negotiated a deal with the Americans; declared an open city against Hitler's order to resist to the last man, Halle peacefully surrendered on April 17.[11] Investigating the way the press covered the 1995 commemorations of the year 1945, Naumann has shown that accounts of the end comparable to Rostaing's, Labat's, and Saint-Loup's are now taken as representative of the wrong stance. In press commentaries about the events of 1945, the bad soldiers are those who elected to fight to the end, and whose fanaticism jeopardized the communities they were purporting to defend; conversely, the good soldiers are those who understood that resistance was pointless and surrendered or fled, thus sparing those same communities from destruction and suffering (Naumann 133–5).

A few among my memoirists qualify as good soldiers in Naumann's sense. The most representative is Sajer, who describes the Grossdeutschland Division as fighting desperate battles in East Prussia in early 1945, but also as seeking to save the civilian population, terrorized at the prospect of the arrival of the Russians. Using metaphorical language to describe how he and his fellow soldiers attempted to help people get to boats in the harbor of Gotenhafen, near Danzig, he writes:

We assisted old people whom younger ones had already abandoned to the Soviets. In the night lit by the war, we once again performed our duty. We held and carried old men and women toward the harbor, where a boat was waiting for them. Planes unfortunately attacked us, dropping death on our commitment. We tried

[11] On the events of April 1945 in Breslau and Halle, see Peikert and Bock.

to make the old people dive to the ground with us, but some of them could not do it. Still, we saved quite a few. With my friends we managed to lift them on a trawler. We helped to cram them into the crowd, and meanwhile the boat slipped its moorings in order to escape from an air attack. (1967, 527)

In Sajer's antiheroic narrative, such words as "duty" and "commitment" do not define the warrior's devotion to his trade, as they do in Rostaing's memoir. They apply to the soldier's responsibility toward civilians, which here drives Sajer and his comrades to act the way they do. To be sure, the helpers are also concerned with their own survival; they embark on the boat together with the people whom they assist, holding on to the passes that allow them to board as firmly as they hold on to their guns. Furthermore, they themselves will fight to the end, surrendering to the British near Kiel after a trip that takes them to Denmark and then back to northwestern Germany. Sajer, however, does not describe this journey as a glorious last stand. Unlike Labat and Saint-Loup, he also finds nothing to admire in the behavior of the populations he comes across, nor any beauty in Gotenhafen and the other locations through which he and the remnants of the Grossdeutschland make their way during their retreat along the Baltic coast.

The questions "what memory?" and "whose memory?" must therefore be asked again, albeit within the memoirists' community. For, if several of the volunteers fought to the end, they did not do so at the same time, at the same place, or under the same conditions. More important, they do not remember that last moment in a homogeneous, unified fashion. What their reminiscences eventually have in common is that they are those of survivors. In other words, it is that they are reminiscences of people who fought "to the end" but not "to their own ends," of people who lived on to tell their tale. Agamben, in an oft-quoted passage of *Remnants of Auschwitz*, has argued that testimonies from survivors of the death camps lack the ultimate "authority"; only the dead could provide "true," "complete" testimonies, since they are the ones who "touched bottom" (34). Leaving to Holocaust specialists the task of discussing Agamben's work, I will only point out that the circumstances of the surviving soldiers who fought "to the end" are deeply different from those of the surviving deportees. People were sent to death camps for a specific purpose – to be murdered. In this respect, to testify about death for them would be to testify about *the* experience – about the very finality of their presence in the camp. But soldiers were drafted to fight, and getting killed for them was a risk, not an objective that their superiors had set from the start.

Similarly, volunteers had enrolled to defend a cause; but if they were, as they claim, ready to die for that cause, dying was not the goal of their endeavor. In brief, death for them was not the experience that both made them unique and unable to tell about that uniqueness. It was a threat, to be sure, but one that they had chosen to face and that at least they had the possibility to actively confront.

TESTIFYING

While the memoirs written by the volunteers provide valuable data about France's military collaboration with Germany, they also tell about the reasons their authors had to jot them down. In this regard, they answer a question that most readers familiar with the French scene are probably asking: Why, after endorsing a cause that they knew most of the world regarded as the wrong one, did some of the veterans decide to speak up? Why, in other words, did they choose to call attention to themselves when their tainted past had probably been largely forgotten? For one thing, the volunteers' reclamation had been difficult already. Because of his youth, Costabrava was freed a few days after being sentenced to six months in jail (212); on the same grounds, Sajer and Bayle were allowed to join the French army immediately after the war, as a way to redeem themselves for their mistakes (Sajer 1967, 545; Bayle 2008, 247–51). Others, like Rusco, Laurier, Degrelle, Saint-Loup, and the author of *Vae Victis*, managed to live underground or to escape abroad, some of them coming back to France after an amnesty. But Auvray, Gaultier, Gilles, Gruber, Labat, La Mazière, Levast, Leverrier, Lobsiger, Malardier, Marotel, Philippet, Rostaing, and Terlin spent several years in jail, and to return to civil life was not always easy for them. As a former convict, La Mazière had trouble finding work and was obliged to slave away at les Halles, carrying boxes and cases with other marginalized people (2003, 7–9). Likewise, Rostaing could not practice the only profession he knew, soldiery. Prohibited by law from living in Paris, he had to move to southern France, where he became a mason (241–2). As for the Belgians, they needed a "certificate of good citizenship [certificat de civisme]" in order to get a job (Gruber 422), a requirement that created a catch-twenty-two situation for the collaborationists who had completed their term in jail but were still regarded as "inciviques."[12] Testifying, therefore, was risky

---

[12] *Inciviques* was the code name given to collaborationists in Belgium after the war, *civisme* referring to the quality displayed by people who had been members of the Resistance or at least had not collaborated.

for the former volunteers, as revelations about their past could cast a shadow over their public and professional lives. Sajer recounts that his disclosures caused his firing by *Pilote*, one of the comic strips magazines that employed him after the war (interview on http://www.brusselstour. com, 12/16/09).[13] Bayle reports that after several years as a manager with an oil company, he was let go when one of the directors learned about his employee's past as a member of the SS (2008, 244). La Mazière claims that his appearance in *Le Chagrin et la pitié* had severe financial consequences for him. After some difficult times, he had become the head of a successful firm in the entertainment sector, International Relations Press; but the revelation that he had been a member of the SS caused most of his clients to take their business elsewhere, and he had to find another line of work (2003, 207–8). The danger of designating oneself, or of exposing someone else, as a former military collaborationist accounts for a specific aspect of the texts under consideration: the fact that they were sometimes written under a pseudonym, and that the characters they stage were also occasionally either given pseudonyms, or left nameless. For that matter, even historians such as Mabire, Lefèvre, and Saint-Loup (in his "historical" studies) resort to strategies of this type, claiming that they do not want to compromise individuals who have made a new life for themselves, and whose employment or status might be jeopardized by revelations about their pasts (Mabire 1973, 7; Saint-Loup 1963, 10).

Why then, knowing the chance they were taking, did some of the volunteers nevertheless elect to turn their reminiscences into what we now would call "coming-out stories" (Smith and Watson 108)? Ory, in the analysis of the "rétro satanas" that followed the release of *Le Chagrin et la pitié* in the 1970s, traces the publication of *Le Rêveur casqué* to shrewd marketing. In the publisher's mind, La Mazière's testimony would meet the needs of an audience eager for texts about the darkest sides of the collaboration, as Patrick Modiano's novels and the memoirs of such compromised people as Victor Barthélémy, René Belin, and Lucien Combelle did (Ory 1981, 111). Similarly, the eloquent Resistance spokesperson Marie-José Chombart de Lauwe charges publishers with cashing in on the "mode rétro" in the 1970s and "flooding kiosks" with a dangerous

---

[13] In *La BD*, Sajer gives a different version of his firing: It was due to disagreements between him and the editors of *Pilote* about his freedom to draw up his own scripts (Dimitri 1999, 115). This alternative version is consistent with *La BD*, a text in which Sajer never refers explicitly to his past, only alluding to such things as "a painful period in [his] youth" (114).

"brown tide": books depicting German soldiers as "pure heroes" and propagating "a value system easy to identify," when we know that their authors are frequently "former members of the LVF, which became the French SS Division Charlemagne" (50–1).

Chombart de Lauwe does not mention names, but whomever she had in mind, her periodization and characterization are inaccurate. Indeed, dates of publication indicate that the volunteers' memoirs owe little to the 1970s taste for collaborationist memorabilia. Only Emmanuelli's, La Mazière's, Malbosse's, Rostaing's, and Terlin's books were published during this period. But Mit's, Degrelle's, Laurier's, and Bassompierre's works date from the late 1940s–early 1950s (as does *Vae Victis*), when there was little interest in this kind of work; Sajer's and Labat's, from the 1960s, the moment of repressed memory and national consensus that Rousso (1987a) sees as having been imposed by de Gaulle; with regard to the other memoirs, Gilles's, Rusco's, and Lobsiger's were brought out in the 1980s, Auvray's, Bayle's, Gaultier's, Gruber's, and Philippet's in the 1990s, and Costabrava's, Dupont's, Larfoux's, Leverrier's, Malardier's, and Marotel's in the 2000s, that is, at a time when the "mode rétro" had largely subsided. Publishers may certainly have encouraged former volunteers to speak and/or write, as the prefaces to Rostaing's *Le prix d'un serment* and Rusco's *Stoï* make clear. But most of the texts in my corpus do not qualify as "rétro satanas" or "brown tide," in the restricted sense of "1970s literature aimed at a wide audience" defined by Ory and Chombart de Lauwe. The most recent, in particular, were brought out by small, specialized publishing houses such as Lore, Arctic, and L'Homme Libre, which run a limited number of copies and target a specific readership.

While the former volunteers might have been enticed to "tell" by astute publishers, the reasons they themselves give for testifying ultimately – and oddly – differ little from those of camp survivors and members of the Resistance. If they speak, it is to bear witness, to assert: I was there, and what I experienced is worth recounting and preserving. The historical worth of their testimony may be proclaimed in the paratext by a publisher worried about the nature of the book's materials. The Librairie Académique Perrin, for example, inserts a careful "Publisher's warning" before the first chapter of Gaultier's *Siegfried et le Berrichon*:

Did we need to publish this testimony, in which the author seeks neither to justify himself nor to convince? Doubtless not, if it were a solitary experience. But it happens that thousands of Frenchmen participated in the same adventure. Therefore, whatever feeling it may inspire, the voice of these vanquished of history deserves to be heard. What Léon Gaultier recounts in his own way accords with a reality that numerous men have experienced. Doubtless we must judge, but to ignore serves no purpose. The pages that follow, given without alterations or comments, provide a form of document that must be appreciated as such. (9)

Yet the author himself may also affirm the factual, referential value of his testimony. The function he assumes is that of a privileged witness who sees his task as being to establish (and often to reestablish) what happened in actuality. It is doubtful that Bayle has ever read Walter Benjamin's "Theses on the Philosophy of History," and his purpose is certainly not, as it is Benjamin's, to engage nineteenth-century "historicism" in the name of "historical materialism" (Benjamin 256). However, he complains in terms close to Benjamin's about the fact that history is generally written from the standpoint of the victors, then goes on to state (in the third person) his intention to set the record straight and provide readers with information formerly concealed:

As everybody knows, official history is written by the victors. Woe to the vanquished. What was yesterday (and still is today) war propaganda becomes the objective version of history, the version that will be taught but does not agree with historical truth. The author intends neither to rewrite history nor to justify anybody. He merely wants to communicate knowledge that has been withdrawn from the public, whether by design, neglect, or opportunism. Above all, he wants to describe the reasons for which the volunteers enlisted, the European dimension of their fight (they came from more than forty nations), their training, their campaigns, and the consequences of their involvement, such as their captivity in the USSR. (2008, 17)

Gilles, too, claims that he intends neither "to convince anybody," nor "to plead a cause"; if he is speaking up, it is because the stories of soldiers "of all fronts" must be told, so that audiences can form an opinion "with serenity" (I, 31). Although Bayle and Gilles assert that they do not write in order to "justify" or "convince," one of their main goals remains in fact to validate endeavors that they know have been disparaged. Several of the volunteers, for that matter, assert explicitly that their reminiscences supply not just data, but also explanations and validations. Thus, Lobsiger traces his decision to speak up to a telephone call he received "on 22 March 1979 at 13:22," during which an anonymous party told him to "leave Switzerland immediately or commit suicide," because it was known that he had served with the SS (10). That call, Lobsiger submits, gave him the idea that if he could not be "successful in his life," he could at least "answer for that life" by recounting it (10). He, therefore, started immediately to "take notes" (10), first on the threatening call he had just received, then on his recollection of the events he had endured forty years prior.

Not unexpectedly, the volunteers' attempt to validate their involvement on the German side has produced a certain number of critical comments. Mosse, in one of his essays on the memory of World War II, points out that most efforts to rehabilitate the SS has originated not with the Germans, but with "past members of the international brigades" who had enrolled in that corps, beginning with Saint-Loup (1986b, 499). None of the volunteers-turned-memoirists, Mosse observes, has called for the resurrection of the SS state. Instead, they have sought "to transform an evil into a respected past, laundering history rather than calling for its repetition" (499). This new myth, for Mosse, must be distinguished from the old myth of the "war experience," with its "cult of the fallen soldier," its "ideal of camaraderie," and its picture of war as "a test of manliness" (499); such apologists of the SS as Saint-Loup do not strive to glorify the past, but – knowing that it is "unpalatable" – to make it "acceptable" to readers who may have a Manichean view of World War II (500). The two myths analyzed by Mosse are not incompatible, however. Most of my memoirists seek to validate their undertaking, but – just like the German soldiers whose attitudes Kühne describes in *Kameradschaft* – they also celebrate comeradery, attend to the dead, and believe that war has increased their manliness.

While the veterans explain why they decided to testify by the need to supply historical information and justify past choices, they insist that speaking up also fulfills for them an ethical and therapeutic function; by telling, they can come to terms with a past that they elected to self-censor, or that their environment forced them to repress. (Again, the parallel with the postwar experience of camp survivors is striking, however incomparable the journeys of the two groups might have been.) Sajer writes on the last page of his book: "My parents imposed a total silence on me, and a conversation about what could have relieved me was never considered" (545). Likewise, Rostaing states toward the end of his narrative: "My past was buried in my heart. I often thought of it; I never talked about it. Could my countrymen understand the struggle I had joined, or were they at least willing to try to understand? I thought that they were not willing, that the time had not come yet" (242). For Sajer and Rostaing, therefore, testifying had the function of what psychologists call an "anamnesis" (Suleiman 123); by telling, they were able to lift the repression, to restore a part of themselves that they

had been compelled to blot out. A similar process is described with elo-
quence by La Mazière. Explaining why he agreed to be interviewed in
Le Chagrin et la pitié, he states: "I had put the past behind me in a way
that I thought was definitive. Still, I was not going back on my past; I
have not gone back on anything, but I thought that it was behind me –
ancient history, just an old album to leaf through among insiders, and
not too often" (1972, 145). La Mazière returns later to the subject of
this interview, spelling out that if he eventually, against his best judgment and the advice of his friends, accepted Harris's invitation, it was
to obey "an inner voice":

Nobody, from then on, could keep me from answering not Harris's call but the
call from an inner voice that day after day became more demanding, more pressing. That voice told me that by confessing, explaining, and questioning, I would
recover my lost dignity and my identity; and also that I would do justice to all
those who had fallen on the Eastern Front and who deserved, because they had
remained faithful to the cause they had embraced, to join the long cohort of the
men who wanted to change history. (2003, 202)

　　La Mazière's reference to his comrades "fallen on the Eastern Front"
points to another important issue raised by any testimony: that of determining who the witness is speaking "for," in the different senses of that
preposition. None of the memoirs in my corpus has a specific "witnessee,"
a term that Waintrater (42) coins after "addressee" and "narratee": an
individual or a group to whom the witness tells his/her story *in presen-
tia*, as he/she does during a therapy session or in court to the people in
charge of deciding the case under investigation. But some of these texts
have particular addressees who are named in the paratext, usually in a
dedication. Those addressees may include fellow combatants as well as
other people, "for" whom the book is written even though they did not
necessarily fight alongside the author:

To my son, so that he understand his father better.
To my comrades, so that they know that I remember.
To my countrymen, so that they understand that courage was not
　　the exclusivity of one side. (Rostaing 7)

To all those who, in the German, American, British, or Russian uniform,
　　insured that the reputation of France's warriors be respected.
To all those who, for the sake of that mere glory, put their Honor in
　　the loyalty to causes that were not theirs.
To all the desperados whom an undeserved defeat revolted.
None of them was wrong. All sacrificed themselves to the Glory of
　　their Country, without hope and without calculation. (Labat 9)

In those instances, the author may explain later why his text is dedicated to a person who was not a combatant. Rostaing does so indirectly when he traces his decision to bear witness to a question that his son, who was engaged to a German woman, asked when the family was in Berlin for the wedding. According to the story he tells in his "Prologue," the party was walking by the Staatstheater (now the Konzerthaus) on May 2, 1970, twenty-five years to the day since his surrender to the Russians, when the following dialogue between father and son took place:

> – What is wrong, dad?
> – Twenty-five years ago, I was fighting here.
> – Tell.
> – Not today. Perhaps one day.
> The day has come. (16)

Rostaing returns to this episode in the last paragraph of his book, stating succinctly that his son's request: "Tell" made him change his determination to keep silent, and concluding unassumingly on the sentence: "I hope that I have not been wrong" (242).

Dedications, however, may also be restricted to the people with whom the author fought in the USSR or elsewhere. Degrelle addresses his *Campagne de Russie* to fellow Belgian volunteers exclusively:

> To the memory and to the glory of the two thousand five hundred Belgian volunteers of the Légion Wallonie, who died as heroes on the Eastern Front, from 1941 to 1945, in the struggle against bolshevism, for Europe and for their Homeland. (9)

The inclusion of battlefield comrades as addressees of the dedication denotes an essential function of the testimony: To represent the group. "To represent" here may be ascribed the two meanings analyzed by Gayatri Chakravorty Spivak, admittedly in a different context: "to describe" and "to speak for" (275). Indeed, Rostaing, Labat, Degrelle, and the other volunteers-turned-memoirists want to report their own experiences. However, they also want to convey the experiences of the soldiers in the unit of which they were part and for whom they would act as spokespersons. None of the texts they have written continues in the form of the address that may have been used in the dedication, the author recounting to his comrades what they are (or were) doing in the second-person plural ("You attacked the Soviet position..."). But their narratives frequently shift from the first-person singular to the first-person plural, "we" referring in these cases to "I, the author + they, the men who were with me at a certain time and place":

We are five. We have crossed the dry stream whose bed marks the end of the forest. We have run up the hill, but from its top we see nothing but the edge of the
wood. Is there a better spot? A place from where we could see and be protected?
All five we set off again, two in front, I, and two behind me. (Gaultier 224)

To "represent," in this excerpt, clearly means to "describe" the men
with whom one has fought and to "write in their name," because, it
is assumed, they lack the ability to express themselves or died on the
battlefield. More precisely, it means to stage the "we-community [wir-
Gruppe]" (Assmann 2006, 21) of which the author was part at the
time, to describe both its physical activities ("We have run up the hill")
and what the author takes to be its members' thoughts at a particular
moment ("Is there a better spot?"). That community obviously is small,
as is the case in most war memoirs written by ordinary soldiers (Cru
23). It includes the author and the few men who were with him at the
time, "we" corresponding here on the level of enunciation (who speaks?)
to the use of a limited perspective on the level of focalization (who per-
ceives?). It is for this restricted we-community that the memoirist writes
above all, intent, as Ricoeur puts it, on "paying his debt," that is, on ful-
filling his obligations "toward those who are no longer but who were,"
on maintaining the latter's "legacy," and drawing up the "inventory" of
their endeavors (Ricoeur 2000, 108).

 While the veterans in my corpus write for the community of which they
were part and hope that they can reach a wider audience (Rostaing's "my
countrymen"), they also know that they have made debatable choices
and that their testimony won't be favorably received by all readers. Labat
seems to be aware of this liability when he titles his preface "In Guise of
a Warning," and then asserts defensively:

Who will dare to judge men who, without weakening, underwent cold, heat,
death, wounds, abandonment, the chiefs' betrayals, the firing squads, the penal
colony? Each of us faced all that. Any other offers? But the judgments that they
pass on one another matter to them, and it is for them that I wrote. May this
clumsy book be a memorial to their odyssey, and may they be the only ones to
forgive the shortcomings of the scribe. (12)

Labat's strong "warning" inscribes here another category of addressees.
While Labat claims that he is aiming his book at his comrades ("it is for
them that I wrote"), his mention of people who may "dare to judge"
shows that he also has another audience in mind: indifferent and even
hostile readers who will take up the book out of curiosity or – knowing

about its content – to confirm their beliefs about the evils of having sided with the Germans during the war. Likewise, Sajer introduces individuals who "read quietly about Verdun or Stalingrad in an armchair or in bed, their asses warm," instructing them to read war books "in discomfort, being forced to do so, and feeling lucky not to have to write to their family from the bottom of a trench, their asses in mud" (1967, 266). Sajer also posits an unfriendly reader, one to whom he aggressively declares, upon describing how the Grossdeutschland Division lost 50 percent of its roster between Konotop and Kiev: "You, who will perhaps one day read these lines, remember. One evening in the fall of 1943, communiqués must have reported that German troops surrounded in the pocket of Kronotop had thrust through the Bolshevik encirclement. It was true. But the price probably was never mentioned. For you, it did not matter: deliverance was on its way" (1967, 301). Less angrily, Degrelle concludes his "Preface" with a celebration of the Belgian volunteers and an address to an audience that he regards as potentially split: "Reader, whether friend or enemy, watch them live again; for we are in an era when one has to look for a long time in order to find real men, and those were real men to the marrow of their bones, as you will see" (16).[14]

The group that my memoirists intend to "represent" for different categories of readers obviously is most particular. It does not have many members left, and although it admits a few rabid supporters, it does not include a legion of active, highly visible sympathizers. What is the

[14] Identifying the actual readership of the volunteers' memoirs would take a sociological investigation I am not qualified to undertake. From looking at Internet sites and talking to book dealers, I can infer that (most of) these readers are male, amateurs of militaria, and admirers of the German army (especially of the Waffen-SS); some of them openly claim membership in a neo-Nazi or neo-fascist group. As far as size is concerned, however, that audience cannot compare with the "broad subculture of general readers, German military enthusiasts, wargame aficionados, military paraphernalia collectors, and reenactors" that Smelser and Davies identify in their study of the representations of the Eastern Front in American popular culture (3). As mentioned earlier, the volunteers' memoirs are now issued (or reissued) by small publishing houses and they have limited runs: 2,000 copies, according to the one publisher who agreed to talk to me, though he preferred not to be quoted by name. Joining the restricted circle that buys such book as the veterans' memoirs is not without risk for academics, however. One of the book dealers from whom I bought materials for this study addressed me immediately as *Kamerad* and used the informal "tu," thus placing me in a community modeled after military organizations, in which "tu" is automatic among soldiers of the same rank. *Kamerad* (instead of the French *camarade*) also gave that organization a German flavor, showing that scholars such as Kühne are not the only people to make the association "comradery-armies of the Third Reich."

specificity of that group? How does it compare with other groups that underwent similar ordeals during and after the war? In short, how can we characterize it from our own perspective, knowing what we know not just about World War II but about ensuing events, such as the Cold War, the fall of the Soviet regime, and, in France, the continuing debates about the Vichy regime? It is to those questions that I shall now turn.

7

From the Outcasts' Point of View

Robert Frank, in his essay "La mémoire empoisonnée [Poisoned Memory]," distinguishes five types of "group memory" among the French who have been affected by World War II: the memory of the Resistance members; of the prisoners of war; of the camp survivors; of the people who were sent to forced labor; and finally, of the collaborationists. Out of thirty-two pages, Frank devotes only nine lines to that last category, insisting that its members never constituted a unified community (554–5). Frank does not stipulate how many people it takes for their recollections to form a genuine "group memory." It can only be pointed out that dozens of individuals branded as collaborationists have written books to account for their activities during the Occupation, whether as ministers in the Vichy government (e.g., Yves Bouthillier, Jacques Benoist-Méchin, Jérome Carcopino); as political activists (e.g., Raymond Abellio, Pierre Andreu, Henri Charbonneau); as journalists (e.g., Lucien Rebatet, Lucien Combelle, Pierre-Antoine Cousteau); or as literary and show business personalities (e.g., Sacha Guitry, Arletty, Henri Béraud). The question, therefore, is not to know whether there is a memory of the collaboration or not; it is to determine whether those many testimonies are homogeneous enough to comprise a "collaborationist memory," which in turn would be a subset of what Frank describes as France's "collective memory" (546).

Restricting the issue to the texts written by the volunteers, I would submit that they have enough common features to constitute a community of reminiscence that might be called "outcast memory." As a community, it could have been granted a chapter in the "Contre-mémoire" section of Nora's *Les Lieux de mémoire*, next to, for example, Jean-Clément

Martin's study of the Vendée. Indeed, its members' reminiscences contrast both with official historiography, for which the volunteers are traitors (as the Vendéens were "rebels" to be "pacified"), and with "good," "worthy" testimonies, such as those of camp survivors and members of the Resistance. The volunteers would probably not use the academic term "counter-memory" to describe the nature of their recollections. However, the idea that their experiences do not fit into France's collective memory permeates the texts they are writing, making readers ask the question that, according to the specialist Helen Buss, must be asked about any author of a life narrative: "What is the place of this writer in the culture represented?" (595). Given the French context, that question could be rephrased as: What is the place that the former volunteers think is assigned to them, and what is the place to which they wish they were assigned, in the postwar French culture?

VANQUISHED

Answering this question in implicit manner, the veterans first define themselves as "outcasts" (*maudits, exclus*), and they trace this condition to the fact that they are on the side of the vanquished – which, in this instance, also happens to be the "wrong" side. Because they were defeated, they insist, they are viewed as guilty of all kinds of evils and unfairly prosecuted by the justice system of the victors. In this respect, their recollections fall under the type of memory that Rousso (2001, 359) calls "memory of resentment"; as many former collaborationists do in their reminiscences, the volunteers "ruminate over their grievances and their rancors" (365), returning again and again to the subject of the treatment they underwent at the time of the Liberation. Laurier, making bold historical connections, asserts that the volunteers after the war resemble the French who throughout history were pursued by "hate, fanaticism, injustice, and stupidity": "the members of the Paris Commune under Thiers, the monarchists under the Terror, the protestants at the time of the wars of religion, the Templars who survived torture..." (57). Going one step further, Saint-Loup affirms that he and his comrades are victims of the "most fearsome persecution that the world has ever known," but that, just as the "last Cathars escaped from the Inquisition," he is ready to "face the false prophets" and "win the night battles," without alienating "a scrap of [his] convictions, a drop of [his] blood, a day of [his] freedom" (1986b, 226–7). Saint-Loup's hyperboles notwithstanding (the "most fearsome" persecution?), the fact remains that the purge in France was severe. According to Rousso (2001, 543–4), who sums up the known data on this subject, 8,000 to 9,000 people were executed during the extrajudicial purge of 1944; 1,500 to 1,600 executed after a regular trial; over 44,000 sentenced to time in jail; and over 50,000 sentenced to "national indignity," that is, deprived of their civil rights. The volunteers obviously had to account to the courts for their involvement, and their testimonies in this regard have significant documentary interest. Complementing the memoirs of better-known French personalities who were also arrested and tried for "intelligence with the enemy," (e.g., Rebatet, Benoist-Méchin, Brasillach), they help answer such questions as: What happened after the war to the surviving members of the LVF and the French SS? How were they treated by the victors, whether in camps, in court, or later in penitentiaries? And do they really qualify as "vanquished," as they maintain that they do?

Not all the authors in my corpus were equally victims of the abuses that Laurier and Saint-Loup denounce with so much vehemence. Bayle and Sajer, as mentioned earlier, were freed, provided that they enroll in the French army as evidence of their professed patriotism. Degrelle, Laurier, Saint-Loup, Malbosse, and the author of *Vae Victis* went into exile. Rusco, with the help of family and friends, escaped arrest and lived for five years without papers. Dupont came back to France under a false identity, and Mit ended the war as a translator in the American army, but neither provides any detail about his activities after 1945. Taken prisoner on the battlefield and handed over to the justice system of their own country or arrested upon their return, Auvray, Emmanuelli, Gaultier, Gilles, Labat, La Mazière, Levast, Marotel, Rostaing, Philippet, Terlin, and Lobsiger were tried and given prison terms of various lengths. The only memoirist sentenced to death was Bassompierre, although his execution, according to historians of the period (e.g., Brissaud 227), had little to do with his enrollment in the LVF and the Charlemagne. The main charge against Bassompierre was his membership in the Milice, more precisely his role in the repression of an uprising at the Santé jail in July 1944, a repression that resulted in twenty-eight inmates being summarily tried and shot. Bassompierre, for his defense, argued in vain that the Germans had initially asked for many more executions, and that thanks to his intervention, no political prisoner (i.e., nobody jailed because of Resistance activities) had been among the victims.

Whether the treatment their authors underwent qualifies as persecution or not, the texts left by the volunteers tell what it was like to be both on the side of the defeated and on the guilty side in the years following the war. Some of my memoirists testify that they lived for some time on the run, their writings adding in this regard to the testimony provided in such works as *Je Suis Partout* editor Pierre-Antoine Cousteau's *Les Lois de l'hospitalité* and Radio-Paris editorialist Jean Hérold-Paquis's *Illusions … Désillusions*. Saint-Loup, Lobsiger, and Bassompierre tell that they headed for Italy, hoping to settle there under a new identity or to embark from an Italian harbor for South America. Lobsiger claims that he lived in the spring and summer of 1945 in southern Tyrol, where one of his jobs was to "dispose" of the valuables that the French Intelligence Service had seized from collaborationists who had been arrested in the area (229); finally exposed as a former Waffen-SS, he elected to cross into Switzerland and surrender. Saint-Loup reports that he witnessed partisan activities in Milan, which he describes, using a Biblical metaphor, as his "encounter with the Beast" (1986b, 187). Specifically, he recounts his and his three companions' successive arrests and releases, the Italians finally believing (or pretending to believe) that this strange French party was comprised of former deportees and allowing them to go home. Bassompierre was less lucky. Taken prisoner in Pomerania, he escaped from the train that was taking him back to France and reached Naples. But he was caught by the Italian police on a boat for Argentina he had boarded, handed over to the British, and finally extradited to France after being identified as a major collaborationist.

The adventures that Philippet and Malbosse recount, because of their length and incongruity, best illustrate the Collaboration's life on the run during the last months of the war and even the years that followed. Philippet was at the SS Junkerschule of Bad Tölz, in Bavaria, when he and his comrades learned of Germany's capitulation. He returned to Belgium, only to discover that his family, known for its collaborationist sympathies, had moved to Germany. Joining his mother and siblings in Lühnde, near Hanover, he spent some time with them until British Occupation officials informed them that "all foreigners had to go home" (II, 206). While his family was taken to a camp for displaced persons, Philippet ran off to Cologne and then to Münster. He worked in the Münster area as a farmhand and then as a mason, before being turned in, arrested by the American military police, and handed over to the Belgian authorities in October 1946. Malbosse also remained in Germany after the war, staying there until 1948. After being moved from camp to camp alongside former POWs and forced laborers, he settled in a wooded region south of Cologne. Working on farms, he also contributed to his guest families' food supply by poaching. Arrested because of these activities, he did time in jail and was supposed to be returned to France. He escaped during his transfer and went to Belgium, where he was arrested again and sentenced for illegal border crossing. His family, upon his release, helped him move to Spain, where he joined his brother, who had also run into trouble and taken refuge there.

Like most narratives of this type, Saint-Loup's, Philippet's, Bassompierre's, and Malbosse's accounts of their life on the run raise issues of credibility; written several years after the facts, they may mis-identify places, misdate events, and even originate in the imagination of authors anxious to embellish their lives. Possibly aware of the doubts that readers may have about his story, Malbosse includes two maps whose function is to attest that he really did what he claims that he did: one representing the area near Cologne where he lived as a farmhand and a hunter (heads of deer and wild boars indicate the territories rich in game) (83), the other reconstructing his whole journey from Schwerin to Cologne to Brussels to Paris to Madrid. Whether those maps suffice or not to legitimize the text is debatable. But readers familiar with postwar testimonies such as Primo Levi's *The Reawakening* will know that odys-seys resembling Philippet's and Malbosse's were not uncommon; deport-ees, POWs, and foreigners working in Germany often spent months and even years on the road before being allowed to go home – or wherever they were able to settle.

Because several of the volunteers were taken prisoner by the Russians in Pomerania and Berlin, their testimonies constitute "captivity narra-tives" (Smith and Watson 2001, 192) that supply firsthand information about conditions in the camps run by the Soviets. Bayle and Auvray, for example, were sent from Germany to Tambow, southeast of Moscow. Both bitterly complain about the cruelty of the Russians, who whipped the hands of prisoners about to take bread (Auvray 109), obliged wounded men to walk (Auvray 121), and failed to provide enough food, causing many deaths among the POWs (Bayle 2008, 221). Charging the Allies with double standards, Bayle argues that the pictures of deportees he saw in British and American magazines when he was transferred from the Soviet to the American zone were not worse than those of prisoners in Soviet camps. He includes in his book the picture of prisoners in Tambow (2008, 218), asking why suffering is treated in "discriminatory manner," as the press indicts the German concentrations camps while ignoring that "the same conditions were prevailing in the USSR" (224). Auvray is more nuanced. Echoing Bartov's theme of the "barbarisation of warfare," he traces his and his comrades' poor treatment at the hand of the Soviets to the nature of the war on the Eastern Front:

This inexpiable war has produced, for mankind's misfortune, the idea that the enemy is in no case worthy of respect. The instinctive contempt inflicted upon the soldier who has laid down his arms is augmented by the contempt that he himself had for the opponent. Supposing that we reverse the roles, we obtain the same degree of visceral hate spread over a world that is on the brink of cannibalism. (108)

Auvray's and Bayle's pages about their lives as prisoners also contain suggestive details pertaining to the Soviet system, the heterogeneity of the prisoner population, and the hazards of the return. Bayle reports that in Moscow, he and other members of the Charlemagne who no longer had identification papers were given a French examination by young female students, because the Russians wanted to make sure that the prisoners who claimed to be French really were from France (215). Some forcibly enrolled Alsatians who spoke only German did not make it, causing between them and the volunteers of the Charlemagne a conflict that, according to Auvray, exacerbated in Tambow, where "victims and executioners" were grouped in the same camp, in front of "laughing or indifferent Russians" (148).

Journeys home could also take unexpected turns, and Bayle's title *De Marseille à Nowossibirsk* was coined to describe the author's extravagant tour. Bayle was carried by train from Tambow to Siberia before being returned to France, a 10,500 kilometer trip, according to the author's calculations (228). What Bayle fails to point out is that his journey, admittedly long in terms of distance, was short in terms of time and by the standards of the period, as his and Auvray's sojourns in Russian camps were also short. Whereas thousands of German POWs did not return to their home country before the 1950s, Auvray was back in France in October 1945 (186), and Bayle, in January 1946 (232). To be sure, not all the French volunteers who were taken prisoner by the Russians spent so little time in camps. Malardier was in the USSR for almost three years, and Cisay for eighteen months. Cisay devotes his whole memoir to this experience, describing his life as a laborer in factories, a farmhand in kolkhozes, and a cartoonist in charge of decorating the walls of workshops. Because of its focus, this account is most valuable; it is the only one in my corpus that portrays at length the USSR in the months that followed the war, and does so in a balanced way. Cisay finds many things to praise in the USSR, from the healthcare system to the treatment of children to the apparent happiness of the households. Still, he remains true to his convictions and advances strange theories, arguing, for example, that the USSR had to be temporarily "colonized" (117) by the Germans in order to realize its full potential: a thesis that, to my knowledge, no historian has endorsed, and that in all likelihood would find very few supporters in the Russian population.

If most of the volunteers who were taken prisoner did not stay in camps for long, their transfer from the Soviet, British, and American authorities to representatives of the new French government was often marked by alleged acts of brutality. Bourdrel (2002, 77–8), in his study of the extrajudicial purge that took place in France at the time of the Liberation, points out that former volunteers were tortured by members of the Resistance in Paris, Brittany, Isère, and Dauphiné. None of my memoirists affirms that he was "tortured," properly speaking. Several complain, though, that they were mistreated upon their return, as the French police (or whoever was acting in that capacity) were confident that they could manhandle former collaborationists with impunity. Gaultier recounts that in a Paris police station he was "beaten with a flail" because he would not turn in his "accomplices" (309), then "knocked down and kicked" while being taken to his cell (310). Likewise, Rostaing attests that he was victim of abuse on the part of French officials in Berlin when he returned from Russian captivity in October 1945. Upon his arrival to the Tegel jail, he was "kicked, smacked, and punched" (220). The head of the French military police then visited him every night in his cell to whip him with a crop, adding voyeurism to sadism by frequently coming accompanied by "a young woman and a police dog" (221). Asking repeatedly "Why so much hate, why?" (222), Rostaing seems unaware that millions of POWs and deportees had undergone worse at the hands of the Nazis, and that he and his comrades were viewed at the time as people who had earned widespread contempt and deserved serious punishment. Neither Gaultier nor Rostaing, in other words, adopt the retrospective standpoint that would enable them to account for, if not to excuse, the treatment they endured at the end of the war. Writing more than thirty years after the events that they report, they still act as if they could plead ignorance and claim – as they were able to do with some degree of legitimacy in 1945 – that they did not know how the Nazis had treated the people they had arrested or taken as prisoners.

The historians who have studied the trials of the French collaborationists have granted little space to the proceedings against the volunteers. Whereas whole books are devoted to the cases against such figures as

Pétain (Garçon 2007), Laval (Jaffré 1995), Pucheu (Kupferman 1980), and Brasillach (Kaplan 2000); most of the works about the purge (e.g., Novick 1968, Bourdrel 2002, Baruch 2003) do not even bring up that former members of the LVF, the Frankreich, and the Charlemagne were also brought to court. Only Herbert Lottman shows some interest in the fate of the military collaborationists, as he mentions that Bassompierre and Mayol de Luppé (the French units' chaplain) were arrested, and that the repatriated were "encouraged" to turn in the "false" POWs and deportees (read: the former volunteers) who might have joined their ranks (285). Still, several among my memoirists were tried, and they account in different ways for their court appearances. Some deal with the matter in a few words. Gilles records curtly that "on December 7, 1945 [he] was sentenced to 10 years of forced labor," adding that "at a time when one could no longer keep count of death sentences and executions," this punishment "was regarded as light" (II, 369). Others tell selectively about their trial, focusing on some moments and deemphasizing others. Labat reproduces verbatim the long statement he was allowed to make in his defense (584–7), but then reports via a single sentence that he was given "eight years of forced labor," adding the terse comment "for the time, it was little" and the information that "after three years, [he] was pardoned" (587). Yet some memoirists dedicate whole chapters to the proceedings, first to the *instruction* (the investigation of the case in the French system), and then to the trial proper. Gaultier, for instance, revels in sarcastic descriptions of the justice system and its representatives: his *juge d'instruction* is "of average height, podgy, has a soft voice, and from the start of the hearing shows commendable restraint" (328); his lawyer has little understanding for his client's "allergy to pronounce a few historic words in front of a firing squad" (331); the physician assigned to his case "seems to be perfectly annoyed by these commissions that oblige him to deal too often with rascals of my kind" (336); and members of the jury "seem ready to provide the Republic with all the uncompromising help it is entitled to hope for" (341), that is, ready to give a guilty verdict. La Mazière also grants a whole chapter ("The Hour of Truth") to his *instruction* and trial, focusing on moments of embarrassment and incongruity. Thus, he recounts over four pages the testimony of the Jewish tailor whom the La Mazière family claimed they had saved by moving him from Paris to their village in the Touraine area, but who at the trial proved uncooperative, insisting that although the people in the village were friendly, they "did not like the suits he was making" (256). That deposition, La Mazière observes with amusement, led to an awkward situation, as the defendant had to rescue his witness by explaining that clothes that were fashionable in Paris probably were less suited to the taste of the provincial middle class that formed the tailor's customer base in Touraine. La Maziére eventually was sentenced to five years in jail (of which he served three) and ten years of "national indignity" (266), a penalty – frequently inflicted at the time – that involved losing one's civil rights.

As the volunteers acknowledge, the sentences they received were short by the standards of the period. The courts apparently were more sympathetic to military collaborators, who had taken physical risks on the battlefield, than to writers and journalists, who had advocated the collaboration from the comfort of their homes and offices. Pierre Assouline has documented this aspect of the purge, which saw "intellectuals" such as Paul Chack, Jean Luchaire, Jean Hérold-Paquis, and Robert Brasillach to be executed, while others, such as Jacques Benoist-Méchin, Lucien Rebatet, and Pierre-Antoine Cousteau were pardoned after spending months and even years in jail, waiting for the sentence to be carried out. Still, my memoirists all object to what they feel was the unfairness of the procedures against them. Their main problem concerns the use the courts were making of Articles 75 and 86 of the Penal Code, which punished acts "harmful to national defense," "secret dealings with the enemy," and "breaches of the exterior security of the State." Indeed, these articles had been modified on June 26, 1944 to include "acts of informing" and "acts committed against the allies of France at war," the latter modification enabling the courts, since France had then become allied with the USSR, to indict the French volunteers who had fought on the Eastern Front (Rousso 2001, 509). Both Gaultier and Labat point to the retroactive provision of Articles 75 and 86 in their new versions. Gaultier sarcastically observes that even de Gaulle's governments in London and Algiers had not been able "to pride themselves on the touching alliance" with the USSR (343), and Labat argues that diplomatic relations between France and the USSR, which "had been broken at the time of the Russian invasion of Finland in 1939," had not been reestablished "when [he and his comrades] joined the LVF" in 1942 (585). Labat also contends that French law allows French citizens to wear a foreign uniform "provided that they have fulfilled their military obligations and received the authorization from their government." This, according to Labat, was the case for the volunteers, as most of them had been members of the French army in 1939–40, and the constitution of the LVF, the Frankreich, and the Charlemagne had been sanctioned by Vichy, then the only "legal" government of France (585).

Commenting on this situation from the Belgian side, Philippet asserts that he fell victim to a similar retroactive application of the law, as Articles 113 and 117 of the Belgian Penal Code were modified by the government in exile. Belgian citizens could then be indicted not just for bearing arms against allies of Belgium but against "any country that, independently from a treaty of alliance with Belgium, was fighting the common enemy" (II, 247), a measure obviously directed at the Walloon and Flemish volunteers. Less legalistic than his comrades, Gilles sees in the prosecution of the volunteers a "communist plot." Most of the French courts immediately after the war, according to him, were infiltrated by the communists (*cocos* in French slang), who, anxious to "appease their thirst for vengeance," were ready to have anybody suspected of collaboration "sentenced to death and shot" (II, 368). Portraying oneself as a victim of the communists, for that matter, was at the time a widespread strategy among the people who had endorsed the cause of the Axis during the war. Luc Van Dongen, in his study of Switzerland as a "discreet purgatory" after 1945, explains that the German Nazis, Italian fascists, and French collaborationists who were seeking asylum in the Confederation often employed their anticommunism as a "convenient excuse," alleging that they were prospective targets in their own countries because of their political beliefs (94). Gilles gloats that he successfully used that scheme to have his case transferred from the "communist infiltrated" civilian court to a military tribunal, where, judged by "peers," he received what he acknowledges was a "light" sentence (II, 369).

While the volunteers benefited from the indulgence of the courts, they also spent little time in penitentiaries. Whether they were sentenced to five (e.g., La Mazière) or ten (e.g., Gilles) years behind bars, they had been freed by 1950, that is, before the official French amnesties of 1951 and 1953. As they allocate from a few lines to whole chapters to their trial, they write at different lengths about their sojourns in penitentiaries. Labat, using what narratologists call "unnarration," that is, "foregrounding his refusal to narrate" (Warhol 2005, 222), treats this period in his life in one sentence. He writes: "I will not talk about these three years," a decision he justifies by adding: "People who bemoan their hardships have always repulsed me" (587). Auvray, Gilles, Lobsiger, Rostaing, and Terlin are hardly more loquacious. They grant a few lines or pages to their time in jail, briefly describing their activities (e.g., Rostaing was employed as a weaver, Lobsiger as a cowherd), or focusing on one revealing event (e.g., Terlin recounts a Belgian minister's visit to his jail). In contrast, La Mazière and Philippet dedicate whole chapters to their imprisonment: La Mazière possibly because he spent just a few weeks in Pomerania and does not have much to report in the way of military feats, Philippet because he wants to provide a detailed account of his experiences in four different camps, where he lived in the most liberal as well as in the most repressive conditions. Whether they focus or not on their prison term, the volunteers claim that this period in their lives did not change their attitudes toward their past involvement on the side of the military collaboration. As Philippet puts it while reporting his dealings with the military judge and former member of the Belgian resistance who was in charge of his case: "We had chosen to serve our country in different camps, which only the outcome of the war had labeled as good and bad" (II, 253). In short, my memoirists refuse to consider the idea that they were wrong; they trace the guilty verdict pronounced against them to the fact that their side was defeated, not to any fault they might have committed when they made the "choice" to which Philippet is referring here.

The volunteers' account of their tribulations at the end of the war, as well as their self-definition as defeated, raises several questions bearing on storytelling and the concept of "defeat." Readers interested in the pragmatics of life writing may first ask why some of the memoirists leave their reports open, passing over in silence what happened to them at the end of the war or when they were released from jail. Bayle, Costamagna, Gilles, Laurier, and Rostaing offer glimpses of their lives "after"; Emmanuelli continues his story up to the moment of writing; and La Mazière, in *Le Rêveur blessé*, provides a sequel to *Le Rêveur casqué*. But Auvray, Gaultier, Labat, Levast, Leverrier, Marotel, Lobsiger, Philippet, and Terlin do not tell how they adjusted to civilian life when their prison term was over; Dupont does not explain what he did after returning to France in possession of a false ID; Mit ends with a description of his activities as an auxiliary in the American army; and Rusco, with the item that he lived for five years underground, helped by family and friends. In this respect, several of the volunteers' recollections constitute instances of the memoir as I defined it in my Introduction: a narrative that bears on one, limited period in the author's life and does not necessarily provide information about earlier and later moments in that life. While readers are probably familiar with memoirs that match this definition, they nevertheless may feel frustrated when they reach the conclusion of such accounts as those of Leverrier and Mit; having become acquainted with the authors, they would like to know how the latter – whose biographies do not figure in the public record – fared in postwar society.

The case of Saint-Loup is especially vexing in this regard. As mentioned above, Saint-Loup concludes *Götterdämmerung* with the scene of himself and his three comrades leaving Milan in May 1945. Giving himself the pseudonym "Gévaudan" and writing in the third person, he resumes his narrative in *Les Nostalgiques* with the account of his encounter in Paris with another former SS member and of his embarkation for Argentina in December 1946 (1967, 18). Thus, inquisitive readers may ask what Saint-Loup did during these nineteen months, specifically, whether he hid in the mountain area (Savoy? Tyrol? Aosta Valley?) that he knew well, and to which he later devoted some of his books, such as *La vallée d'Aoste* and *La République du Mont-Blanc*. Likewise, Saint-Loup writes in *Les Nostalgiques*: "Three months after his arrival in Buenos Aires, the former political officer of the SS Division Charlemagne obtained a position with the Peron government as 'technical advisor' in the Ministry of Labor and Social Welfare, run by Eva Peron" (1967, 19). He does not reveal, however, how "Gévaudan" was introduced to the Perons, nor how he convinced the dictator that he was qualified to become a "technical advisor" to his government and later "to the mountain troops of the Republic of Argentina" – the title that Saint-Loup proudly displays below his name on the title page of *Monts Pacifique*, the book about some of his expeditions to the islands and mountains of South America that he published in France in 1951, two years before his return from exile. Incomplete, Saint-Loup's narrative of his life after 1945 also raises obvious issues of credibility. A scholarly biography of this intriguing though admittedly minor figure of the collaboration would certainly be welcome, as attested by the reception of works on lesser known personalities of the Vichy regime, such as Assouline's biography of Jean Jardin, Laval's chief-of-staff.

Although the volunteers define themselves as vanquished, hold the purge as the revenge of the victors, and contribute in this respect to Rousso's "memory of resentment," their attitudes toward the idea of "defeat" is more complex. Indeed, some of the memoirists affirm that they actually were the victors, as in the context of an election or an athletic competition a loser sometimes claims to be the "moral victor." Terlin, whose right arm and left hand were torn off during the struggles of the Wallonie in Estonia, writes that on April 2, 1949 he left the Merxplas jail "without arms, but with the spirit of a victor" (1972, 286). Likewise, Bayle states that although he is officially among the vanquished, there is for him "only one victor": the vanquished who, "in the smoking ruins, has remained faithful to his dreams and to the ideal 'My honor is loyalty'" (240). Saint-Loup, not unexpectedly, is the most verbal on the topic "moral victor."

Quoting *Revelations* at the end of *Götterdämmerung*, he proclaims confidently: "The true victor according to the spirit was the survivor of the LVF who was walking through Milan, where the riots were ending. Better than his Lordship Schuster [Milan's bishop], I represented 'those who had been beheaded for Jesus's testimony and God's word, who had not worshiped the Beast, nor its image, and who had not received its mark on their foreheads' (*Rev.* XX-4)" (1986b, 226). In short, the volunteers acknowledge their defeat on the battlefield, complain about their banishment (which they trace to that defeat), but declare victory in the area of the "spirit." That strategy allows them to back both horses, as they can participate in what Jean-Michel Chaumon calls "the competition of the victims," while asserting that because they have remained faithful to their ideal, they actually must be counted among the "victors."

Such a scheme could of course be dismissed, as people who fought alongside the Axis, by today's ethical standards, are in no position to affirm any kind of moral superiority over anybody else. But the volunteers, more interestingly perhaps, could also be challenged on their own turf, namely on the assertion that their victory is not military but "of the spirit." Pierre Vidal-Naquet, in one of his essays on negationism, has denounced the propensity of some intellectuals to always "fall in with the vanquished," or "with those who happen to be on the wrong side" (1987, 57). The Germans, Vidal-Naquet argues, "are certainly the vanquished" and "they have dreadfully suffered"; but the Jews "have not been vanquished, they have been destroyed," and the Nazis, by successfully murdering most of the Jewish population of Central Europe, "have won the battle of the genocide" (62). Extending Vidal-Naquet, it could be contended that the volunteers, insofar as they participated in the enterprises of the Third Reich, contributed to winning that very battle. Their victory, therefore, is not just "moral." It is "actual," because they cannot maintain, as they have done, that they were, so to speak, part-timers who were involved in some of the operations undertaken by the Nazis but not in others. Thus, the volunteers' claim that they won a "victory of the spirit" must be assessed with respect to the issue of their co-responsibility in the crimes committed by the Nazis – an issue to which I shall return later. That same claim also points to more general questions that can be raised about World War II, such as: Who were the victors in that war, and who were the losers? According to what criteria can we determine that one side prevailed and the other was defeated? Under what conditions it is legitimate to redescribe the positions "victors" and "vanquished," as Terlin does when he insists that the volunteers won a "moral" victory, and Vidal-Naquet, that the Nazis must be viewed as having "won" the war, at least in the area of the Judeocide?

ESTRANGED

According to historians of the collaboration, the volunteers of the LVF, the Brigade Frankreich, and the Division Charlemagne were never popular with their countrymen. Jacques Delarue reports that when recruiting offices of the LVF opened in Paris on July 8, 1941, they were immediately stoned and vandalized; they had to be guarded day and night, which did not keep them from being attacked again and again (191). Brunet, in his biography of Doriot, mentions similar incidents, as members of the LVF on leave "insulted and hit" policemen whom they held to be "Gaullist, communist, or at least unworthy of their trust" (439). Delarue and Brunet also emphasize that the volunteers were exploited by their own administration. The latter had grown "to the point of obesity" (Brunet 411), having no less than three "centers" and 120 employees in Paris, a "delegation" in each department, and a whole network of "inspectors" whose main function was to provide family and friends with steady jobs (Delarue 211). Worse, that administration did not only use for salaries and expenses a large part of the money designated for the volunteers; it also appropriated most of the gifts intended for the soldiers, diverting them to its members and the black market. Among other incidents, none of the food collected on the occasion of Christmas 1941 and 1942 reached the troops, and a railroad car loaded with tobacco and cigarettes vanished in a similar manner. Out of patience, the volunteers sent representatives to defend their interests in Paris. Complaints, however, kept coming, suggesting that the abuses had not stopped (Delarue 224–5).[1]

The volunteers do not dwell on the story of the missing Christmas parcels, but they remember their feeling of estrangement when they first had to deal with officials of their organization. Labat recounts that when he went to the LVF office in Versailles, the recruiting sub-lieutenant hardly had military business in mind; he first asked the prospective

---

[1] While the volunteers blame their administration for not being up to its tasks, the reverse is also true. De Brinon, appointed president of the LVF in February 1943, writes in his memoir that the enterprise was a "failure from the start" (75), as most men and officers were "mediocre," making for "lamentable contingents" (76). A visit to the troops in their camp near Smolensk in June 1943 did not change de Brinon's opinion; his "impression," which he states in the form of a euphemism, was "not extraordinary" (90). Yet this judgment is retrospective, and it may not coincide with declarations that de Brinon made upon his return from the USSR.

enlistee whether he knew "how to sing," then whether he would sell him his "suit," his "shoes," his "food card," or "whatever he wanted to get rid of" (25–6). Labat admits that he was stunned by this encounter with a "recruiter turned flea market merchant," as he was stunned, more generally, by a scene that evoked less a recruitment office than "the court of King Pétaud" (27), that is, the court of the head of the corporation of beggars in the Middle Ages, by metaphorical extension, a site of extreme disorder and confusion.[2] The author of *Vae Victis* had a similar experience during his days in Versailles. His clothes "disappeared" while he was showering before the medical examination, stolen by another recruit or by a member of the LVF staff (9). That same volunteer also points out that for many "clever patriots" in Versailles, "enlistment was a valuable industry," as watches, clothes, jewels, and even identities were sold or bartered (9). Such commercial activities exasperated the few "stubborn" people who were there to enroll and nothing else, making them even more anxious to go to "other, more glorious heavens" (9).

My memoirists have even worse recollections of their rare returns to the homeland, as the population had little understanding and sympathy for the cause that they represented. Labat "unnarrates" his first leave in 1943 as he will later unnarrate his time in jail, stating tersely: "About this leave, I will say only one thing: it is with relief that I appeared at the barracks 21 days later, ready to go back to Russia" (172). Labat is wordier about his second leave in 1944, but it is to make explicit the reasons for his disaffection. In this instance, he found no pleasure in the nights he spent on the town. The "fragile, chatty women" in night clubs were too different from the "beautiful females, smelling a warm perfume of pure animality" he had met in Russia (364), and none of the men had the "craggy wrinkles, in which [he] liked to read the memory of overcome pains and strains" (365). Reflecting retrospectively on his identity at the time, Labat states that while he was "a foreigner" in the Wehrmacht he had become "stateless" in France (365), as his countrymen could only feel "ironic contempt" for him, and he, "hate" for them (366). The author of *Vae Victis* went through similarly difficult moments during his sojourns in the homeland, as he was the object of verbal violence. During his first leave in 1943, a night club hostess in Montmartre "showered abuse" at him, confessing provocatively that she was "a communist" (85). Another unpleasant incident occurred during his second leave in 1944, when a

---

[2] Always eager to flaunt his knowledge of literature, Labat probably alludes here to *La Cour du Roi Pétaud* [King Pétaud's Court], a play in which Alexandre Dumas parodies his own *Henri III et sa cour*.

café owner, "an attractive woman," told him upon learning that he was a member of the LVF coming back from Russia: "With such a pretty face, it's really unfortunate" (226). Saint-Loup, for that matter, had already described in 1942 the feeling of abandonment and alienation that the volunteers experienced when they returned to France, writing on one of the last pages of *Les Partisans*: "The legionary is alone. He has excluded himself from the community (how this word has been depreciated by those who churn out texts for money!), because his gesture did not agree with the disposition of the people and the elite, who talk about greatness, but only play the comedy of greatness" (1986a, 185). "Between satisfaction and greatness," Saint-Loup concludes using one of the alpine metaphors in which he revels, "the legionary has chosen greatness"; for "it is better to sit on the pure snow of the summit, fight against the cold, the night, and the tempest, while waiting for the return of the light" (191).[3]

If we believe their memoirs, the Belgian volunteers had a better time than the French when they occasionally returned to the homeland. Degrelle affirms that the Wallonie was "cheered" by "tens of thousands of people" when it marched through Charleroi and Brussels in April 1944, between its campaign in the Ukraine and its struggles in Estonia (333). "The crowd," Degrelle writes, "was throwing thousands of roses," having launched a "marvelous celebration" and genuinely "sharing with the troops" (333). Degrelle adds sadly that "five months later, through the same route, Anglo-American tanks entered Brussels" (333), but he does not indicate whether those units were cheered as the Wallonie supposedly had been.[4] Philippet also had a positive experience when he came home for Christmas 1942, as he and his comrades were greeted by a crowd shouting "long live the Legion" (I, 138). He then went to midnight mass and served as witness at a wedding without incident, only aware that

---

[3] Neither Labat nor Saint-Loup mention that the LVF had a few devoted supporters among hardcore collaborationists. Brasillach, for instance, who had accompanied de Brinon on his visit to the troops (see note 1), wrote at least two enthusiastic articles about the LVF in *Je Suis Partout* in July and August 1943. Far from being the "lost children of the collaboration," Brasillach ensures readers of this collaborationist magazine, the men of the LVF are "extraordinarily likeable"; they also understand "French needs," which means that they are determined to "do the Revolution" when they come back to the homeland after "pacifying" Belorussia (260). Brasillach's visit to the LVF is evoked by Leverrier, who states that the writer seemed "embarrassed" among the soldiers and only found "few words" to say (129–30).

[4] Two pictures of the Wallonie's triumphal march in Brussels are included in Littell's study of Degrelle (98). Littell, however, specifies that the "hundreds of tanks" making up the "seventeen kilometer long column" that rode through Belgium had actually been borrowed from the SS Division Hitlerjugend – a detail that Degrelle suppresses in his narrative of the event.

people were "watching and judging" him, even though they did not make "the least gesture nor the least remark" to show some kind of disapproval (I, 140). The discrepancy between the volunteers' homecoming in France and in Belgium is difficult to account for. One can only surmise that Degrelle's personality, perceived at the time as charismatic, played a role, as well as the fact that the Wallonie fought as a homogeneous unit in places that became identified as sites of major battles, such as Cherkassy. On the contrary, the LVF was split into two or three battalions and chased the partisans throughout Belorussia, in spots whose names were never publicized in the media and were difficult to pronounce and remember to begin with, such as Klimowitschi, Tscherikow, and Ordchonikidze-Grad (to take three names mentioned by Leverrier, 139).

Whether they are from France or Belgium, the volunteers complain that they faced not just estrangement but outright rejection after the war. Auvray concludes his reminiscences by observing that "we" who "were dreaming of another France and another Europe" are now "physically excluded and civically disenfranchised" (193), a reference to the fact that people held as collaborationists were both imprisoned and deprived of many of their rights when sentenced to "national indignity." Marotel observes bitterly that the "hate" that surrounded him and his comrades after the war "never abated" and "is still there, forty years later" (139). Sajer interrupts his narrative for a prolepsis in which he makes a similar case, lamenting that after the war he was often held as a "fanatic and unlikable character," who had "joined the wrong army," had better "not bug people with his boring war stories," and should "learn how to live, since he had not known how to die" (1967, 175). As for Mit, who wants to discourage his German friend Hermine from fancying any future together, he explains what things will be like for him when he returns to France:

You know as I do that I won't be able to lead a normal life. Not because of my injuries. But in my country I will be pointed at as the lowest and most despicable of the patricides, while I only wanted to do good ... All the honors I can receive now won't heal the wound I have in my heart. The wound to be banished, because I dared to proclaim loudly that I had an idea and I was fighting for that idea. I won't be blamed for fighting, only for fighting on the wrong side ... For my countrymen, I am the Nazi marked with all kinds of stigmata, prey to all kinds of vices, and capable of all kinds of crimes. I am the Übermensch, the evil genius of destruction. (177)

Prospects were hardly better for the Belgians who, while welcomed as soldiers on leave, were now regarded as *inciviques*. Upon returning to

Liège on May 31, 1945, Philippet found out quickly that the purge had started; the front of the store owned by the parents of his fellow legionary Jean Charbonnier was painted with swastikas, and the store itself was watched as a possible haven for Wallonie veterans and other undesirable individuals. "I did not expect," Philippet writes, "to be received with open arms, but I believed that after a serious explanation I could prove my good faith and the purity of my intentions. Instead, I encountered a world of hatred and lack of understanding, in which the issue was never to explain, but to settle accounts ... I had come home to be spanked, perhaps deservedly, and then to take my place again in my country. But then I had no home, my country was rejecting me, I was an outcast" (II, 182–3). As mentioned earlier, Philippet then decided to return to Germany, where he worked for some time before being exposed, sent back to Belgium, and jailed for several years.

Some of the volunteers claim that they were rejected once again during their imprisonment, when they asked to enlist in the Foreign Legion and go fight in the Far East. Rostaing, for instance, affirms that he wrote "every week" to the Ministry of Justice; he was eager, instead of "rotting in a cell," to "go fight the communists in Indochina," that is, to "carry forward with [his] countrymen a combat [he had] started in a French uniform and continued in a German uniform" (237). Rostaing's letters were ignored, and it is not before 1948 that the French administration authorized former members of the LFV and the Charlemagne to bear arms again. Convicts, Labat signals in a footnote, were then invited "to enlist in the Indochina Army for the purpose of redeeming their errors," and some accepted, "if only to get out of jail" (579). La Mazière also tells about these dealings, but his version is notably different from Rostaing's and Labat's. According to him, the recruiters from the Foreign Legion who came to Clairvaux (one of the penitentiaries where collaborationists were jailed) had no success with the veterans. The latter laughed at the suggestion that they could go "defend the French flag in Indochina, keep this marvelous province for France," asking "what they would defend in Indochina's ricefields," since it was France's military courts that had sentenced them to years in jail (1972, 296). Marotel tells that recruiters also came to the Struthof (the camp where he was detained in Alsace), and that the response was the same as at Clairvaux; the veterans had no desire to become "cannon fodder" in Indochina, as the war in the Far East was for them strictly "the victors' business" (161). Neither La Mazière nor Marotel reports whether some of volunteers imprisoned at Clairvaux and at the Struthof eventually changed their minds, but some did elsewhere.

The unit that was constituted out of these individuals fought in Indochina and then in Algeria, assigned to the thankless tasks and treated in the indifferent manner that Raymond Muelle has described in his study *Le Bataillon des réprouvés* [The Battalion of the Banished].

Given the volunteers' extreme concern with estrangement and rejection, the accounts that they provide of the relations to their families are particularly noteworthy. In a few cases, the volunteers affirm that they had family support. Lobsiger includes a December 1944 picture of himself with his father, "expressly come from Switzerland to Bregenz" in order to visit with his son (n.p.). Lobsiger also asserts that his father was "saddened" at the prospect of the trial (236), had "tears in his eyes" after the verdict (238), and "wrote regularly without ever criticizing [him]" (238), although he "refused to cross the door of the penitentiary" (238). Lobsiger does not specify whether his father stood by him out of family spirit exclusively, or whether he shared his son's political beliefs – some of them at least.

While Lobsiger welcomed his family's help and understanding, other volunteers contend that they requested their relatives to refrain from offering any kind of assistance. La Mazière had asked his family not to come visit him in jail, as he wanted to "spare them the humiliation of seeing him behind bars," as well as to "spare himself the humiliation of being seen in this situation" (1972, 240). His father obliged, but his sister and her husband, a physician, devised a plan that would save the former Waffen-SS from going to jail: La Mazière would plead insanity, doctors would confirm that his mental state was disastrous, and he would be sent to an institution – only to leave it a few months later (242). La Mazière insists that he indignantly turned down his sister's scheme, as he preferred that people designate him by saying "here is the culprit" rather than "here is the madman" (243). Returning to the subject of the relations to his family in *Le Rêveur blessé*, La Mazière explains that he did not see his father again before 1949, one year after his release from jail. He then spent a few days with him, though there was little exchange between the two men. "The dialogue between father and son," La Mazière observes, generalizing his experience, "is always almost impossible. It is made up of too much silence, the unsaid, discretion. There are words that refuse to come out, that choke you, and one takes refuge in statements that are just screens, just decoys. Our reunion alleviated wounds, without erasing them" (2003, 127).

Ruth Klüger, Primo Levi, and many other Holocaust survivors have testified that when they returned home (or at least to a peace environment) after their liberation, they often were discouraged from recounting what they had endured. People generally were anxious to resume life as usual after the war, and narratives about camps, ghettos, and displacements could only interfere with this want. Klüger reports that upon her family's arrival in New York, her aunt told her: "You have to erase from your memory everything that happened in Europe. You have to make a new beginning. You have to forget what they did to you. Wipe it off like chalk from a blackboard" (177).[5] However incomparable the journeys of the two groups might have been, several of the returning volunteers state that they were kept from "telling" in similar fashion. That is, they could not even talk to their own relatives, for whom the subject of a soldier's ordeals in the USSR, Galicia, or Pomerania was definitely off limits. Evoking the moment when he was reunited with his family, Sajer writes:

Hours go by. I remain motionless and silent in front of my family that observes me, as though they had forgotten that the earth is turning. On the fireplace, I notice a picture of me, just younger. Beside it, in a small glass, a few flowers are fading. Minutes go by, time goes by, a monumental silence remains, the story is coming to an end. Those who had waited, and I who had hoped, will need just as much time to accept the evidence. (1967, 544)

His family's initial reticence, Sajer continues, hardly changed over time; he never had with his parents the conversation about the war that might have "relieved" him – a conversation in which he could have explained to them that his involvement was "neither a sign of greed, nor a reprehensible crime" (545). Bayle, too, claims that he was silenced by his family, especially by his mother: "My mother hardly talked to me, and then only about meaningless things. Even when she visited me in jail, she did not ask me any question about my life during the past three years, making me feel that the subject was taboo" (2008, 237). Yet Bayle does not take offence at this lack of curiosity, which he traces, in the manner of a sociolinguist, to family communication habits in the mid 1940s: "I didn't lend much importance to this, since parents at the time hardly talked with their children. Quite the opposite of current behavior!" (238).

Deprived of the opportunity of telling their stories to nonparticipants after the war, the volunteers deplored that they could not rely on

---

[5] Against the position that Klüger's testimony exemplifies, Hasia Diner (2009) has argued that in the late 1940s and 1950s, American Jews were aware of the Holocaust and ready to discuss its horrors. Yet Diner's investigation focuses on the United States exclusively; it does not take up the subject "awareness and discussion of the Holocaust" in France, nor more generally in Europe. I owe the reference to Diner's study to Marion Kaplan.

any support group, either. Andreas Rinke, in his study of the return of French POWs, deportees, and forced laborers between 1944 and 1951, lists no less than thirty-seven organizations linked to these diverse categories of displaced persons, from the *Amicale de Ravensbrück*, to the *Association des Déportées et Internées de la Résistance*, to the *Comité Central d'Assistance aux Prisonniers de Guerre*, to the *Fédération Nationale des Déportés du Travail*, to the *Union Nationale des Evadés de Guerre* (467–71). Not unexpectedly, volunteers coming back from the front or later getting out of jail could not count on any organization of this type. Bayle signals the existence and provides the address of a *Société des anciens de Tambow* (2008, 424), that is, of an association made of former prisoners who had spent time in this Russian camp, which Bayle describes earlier as a "death camp" (219). Bayle also mentions informal reunions of veterans from the LVF and the Charlemagne, which unfortunately have to take place "in private" because of "official pressures" (300); he even provides a picture of one of those reunions, held in Nice in 1990, showing himself, Rostaing, and Costamagna having wine and what looks like a good time (390).[6]

Taking up the subject of such reunions, La Mazière points out that the dinners he and former members of the Charlemagne shared in Paris soon caused serious problems. As the restaurant where the veterans met was well known, it was soon "packed with police informants"; and as the words spoken by the participants were often "unorthodox," the authorities were confirmed in their belief that they were dealing with a dangerous, right-wing or even neo-Nazi organization (2003, 214). Intervening into the debate, familiar to Holocaust scholars, about the role of the "second generation," La Mazière argues that the veterans made another mistake when they planned their reunions: they agreed to include spouses, children, and even grandchildren. Such inclusion, according to La Mazière, created for the children a "duty to remember," whereas there was "nothing to transmit" (2003, 215). "The fight had been over for a long time," La Mazière continues, "and we had lost it; our cause was not theirs, they did not have to take it over, and the idea that they could was absurd, without future, and even unhealthy" (215). Of course, La Mazière does not mean that what he and his comrades accomplished (or failed to accomplish)

---

[6] On its website, the *Association Française Buchenwald Dora et Kommandos* affirms that Bayle leads a "discreet association," *Histoire et Tradition*, which gathers former members of the LVF and the SS as well as young "admireors" (http://www.buchenwald-dora.fr. Accessed 2/14/2005). Bayle does not mention *Histoire et Tradition* by name in his memoir, but it might be the group whose meetings have to be held "in private."

on the Eastern Front should remain unreported; his own activities as a writer, a lecturer, and an interviewee testify to his desire to call attention to what he obviously regards as a suppressed aspect of World War II. Rather, his dismissal of the volunteers' dinners must probably be understood as a polemical gesture directed at the diverse organizations of displaced persons studied by Rinke: organizations whose objective has been, among other things, to make the next generations aware that they have the "duty" to remember (and recount) what happened to their elders. For La Mazière, such duty is incumbent on the participants themselves and should not be imposed upon other people, especially not upon the participants' offspring. Thus, La Mazière is pleased that the dinners he scorns were eventually discontinued, and that the veterans eager to meet have since done so in more "informal," "discreet" manner (2003, 215).

La Mazière's injunctions notwithstanding, some of the veterans' children and grandchildren, apparently anxious to keep the flame burning, have started a *Cercle des descendants des vétérans français du Front de l'Est* [Circle of the Descendants of the French Veterans of the Eastern Front]. I have not found any trace of a meeting held by this organization, but some of its members speak in its name when they contribute to Internet sites. The CDVFFE thus joins other groups that "meet" online to discuss subjects related to the role of the foreign volunteers in the German army on such sites as axishistory.com, feldgrau.com, history-quiz.com, and division-charlemagne.com. The Internet also reveals the existence of a group that calls itself *Les amis de Saint-Loup* [Saint-Loup's Friends], on the model of other groups constituted to carry forward the memory of a famous (or less famous) writer, painter, or musician. *Les amis de Saint-Loup* do not seem to be very active. The only information I have found about them is in a post on the right-wing American Patriot Friend Network, which signals an article in the daily newspaper *Libération* that reports an incident involving those "amis": on May 8, 1988, one of their meetings was disrupted by fifty people claiming to be members of the "Groupe d'Action Juive," who attacked the attendees with iron bars and baseball bats, injuring several elderly people (http://www.apfn.net/messageboard. Access 2/19/2004). While mostly invisible, such organizations as the *Cercle des descendants français des vétérans du Front de l'Est* and *Les Amis de Saint-Loup* nevertheless have what Pierre Milza, in his work on French fascism, calls a "virtual" presence (437). That is, they do not have a major voice in the debates concerning the period of the Occupation and its memory. But the Internet enables them to spread the word easily and broadly, as "Division Charlemagne" can now be found on the popular site Facebook, and songs related to that Division are on the no less popular site YouTube. A quick Google search, moreover, takes us from "Saint-Loup" or "Division Charlemagne" to a whole network of small publishing houses, specialized bookstores, blogs, online journals, Ebay auctions, and Abebooks listings, all devoted to the subject "World War II and the foreign volunteers in the service of Germany." It is too soon, of course, to determine whether this virtual countermemory will at some point make France's military collaboration the matter of heated public exchanges. Thus far, at any rate, none of the posts on the "Division Charlemagne" site, nor any of the books brought out by publishing companies such as Lore and L'Homme Libre, have produced polemics as acrimonious as those that surrounded in the 1990s the indictment of René Bousquet and Marcel Papon, exposing the role of the French administration in the deportation of Jews.[7]

In whatever manner the subject of France's contribution to Germany's war effort is treated in the future, the volunteers' self-definition as "defeated" and "estranged" raises a problem that today is still widely debated: that of the "victims," and of who should be counted as such. Examining the many associations that were born in France after the war, Rousso has argued that one of their goals was to establish a "hierarchy of suffering": The Resistance fighters did not want to be confused with the "racial" deportees, the POWs with the forced laborers; as for the victims of the purge, they were "in all memories, but in no association" (1987a, 34). For these diverse groups, according to Rousso, the task has been to ensure for themselves a place in the national memory community, more precisely to convince that community that their professed right to victimhood is indeed legitimate. For historians and cultural critics, however, the matter is not simply to record the claims made by the "sufferers." It is to interrogate those claims, asking whether the group that is making them is entitled to complain, and whether the fate of its members is representative of other fates or is theirs exclusively. As Dagmar Barnouw (56) has argued in her study of postwar Germany, neither "victims" nor, for that matter, "perpetrators" are stable, homogeneous labels that would apply to "the Germans"; many Germans became victims when their cities were bombed, but many others – and some of the same – had

---

[7] "Fascist," "neo-Nazi," and "negationist" organizations do not have the exclusivity on the Internet. The *Fédération nationale des déportés et internés*, for example, runs *Le Patriote résistant*, an active site warning against the "rehabilitation of Nazism" and the role of the "means of communication and distribution" in that rehabilitation. (http://www.fndirp. asso.fr. Accessed 2/4/2005)

been perpetrators in the countries conquered by the Nazis. Devised to account for the debates surrounding the claims to victimhood made in Germany after the war, Barnouw's description is certainly relevant to the volunteers' assertions that they were mistreated after their arrest, unfairly sentenced in the courts, and rejected by a society that had conveniently forgotten how it had accommodated itself to the German occupation. Indeed, even if we concede that they are right (or at least that they deserve to be heard), the volunteers cannot be characterized as "being" victims, in the sense of "having acquired the permanent status of victimhood." They became victims at a specific moment, which lasted for a certain length of time. In addition, and more importantly, many of them at some point had also become perpetrators. The LVF, as its veterans recount (see Chapter 3), participated in the ruthless occupation of Belorussia, plundering the land, burning villages, and terrorizing the local populations. While the volunteers acknowledge that they carried out activities of this type, that very acknowledgment makes us pose several questions about the ethical dimension of their reminiscences. What is, at the time of writing, their attitude toward what they did when they were in the USSR? Do they set out to explain their actions? Do they show some kind of remorse? Does the way they address these issues account for their still being outcast, specifically for our reluctance to support the kind of memory whose legitimacy they are striving to establish?

UNREPENTANT

Answering that last question first, we can only observe that while the volunteers maintain that they have been ostracized because they were among the defeated, they should lay part of the blame on themselves. Indeed, they have refused to make the gesture that could have led to their reintegration, namely to express regret, to indicate that they felt implicated, however indirectly, in the atrocities committed by the Third Reich. Renaud Dulong and Jean-Marie Marandin, in their account of the diverse ways in which the defendant may admit his or her offense during the judicial process, draw on a dichotomy that is available in French, though not in English: between the *confession* (the defendant's spontaneous admission of his or her offense), and the *aveu* (the defendant's admission of that offense as the outcome of an interrogation) (135–6). Placed by the courts and by public opinion in the position of defendants, the volunteers have turned neither to *confession* nor to *aveu* to help their case. To be sure, they have admitted to killing prisoners and civilians.

Some of them have also disclosed that they were disappointed with the Nazis; told that they were fighting for a new, National-Socialist Europe, they found out that they were actually serving the worst form of Pan-Germanism.[8] Addressing his friend Hermine, Mit thus proclaims: "Please believe that I'm not interested at all in your war; I was interested in the idea for which you were fighting. This idea was a con designed to fill the ranks of an anemic army. The quality of the goods was misrepresented to us" (174). Still, the awareness of that breach of trust does not lead Mit or his companions to exhibit any misgivings. As Shaw notices in his review of the American translation of *Le Rêveur casqué*, La Mazière has "no second thoughts about the nature of the SS" (85), and he does not seem to be concerned about "the horrors with which he associated himself" (86). That is, he does not tell whether he feels somehow answerable for those "horrors," and neither do most of the volunteers who have written their reminiscences.

Such an attitude must of course be contextualized, as it does not characterize the veterans' recollections exclusively. Jeannelle, in his study of the development of the genre "memoir" in France after World War II, emphasizes that the "denial of responsibilities" is an essential feature of the life narratives that collaborationists have published (141). Jeannelle quotes the milicien Henry Charbonneau's statement: "My comrades and I only acted the way we did because we thought it was our duty" (141), but declarations of this type abound in the defensive, self-justifying memoirs written after the war by people who in diverse ways had collaborated. The fierce *Je suis partout* editorialist Pierre-Antoine Cousteau, for example, writes at the end of his ironically titled *Les Lois de l'hospitalité*: "We did not commit an error of judgment. There were just too many tanks and too many planes against us" (210).[9] Likewise, the former Vichy minister Benoist-Méchin affirms that his several journeys to Germany only had one purpose: He wanted to "accelerate the liberation of our prisoners, to defend the integrity of our territory, to encourage our recovery, to ensure the future of our youth, to improve the fate of our working people and of those who overseas had remained faithful to us" (1989 II, 431–2). As for

---

[8] Whether right-wing (Venner) or professionally neutral (Gordon), historians have pointed to the "illusions of a fasciste internationale" (Venner 423) and a "European army" (Gordon 272), arguing that Hitler "never deviated from his idea of a German-dominated Europe ruled from Berlin" (Gordon 272). According to Gordon, the realization of this deceit led some French SS volunteers like Philippe Merlin to suicide (273).

[9] Cousteau's title refers to the fact that no country, not even Switzerland, wanted to grant political asylum to Cousteau after the war, thus breaking what the *Je Suis Partout* editorialist takes to be "the laws of hospitality."

Maurice Papon, who as General Secretary of the Préfecture of Gironde had signed the order deporting hundreds of Jews from the Bordeaux area, he declared in an interview to the magazine *Le Point* in 2003: "Remorse can only occur if it finds a stock. And if, as I am confident, I have never been in the position to generate an event that was likely to cause remorse, I do not see why I would express any ... In order to express remorse, the conscience must feel guilty" (quoted in Stern, 325).

In the volunteers' memoirs, the refusal to acknowledge responsibility is particularly conspicuous in the passages where the authors do not seek to reconstruct their state of mind "at the time," but – as Mit does in the above quotation – assess their endeavor from the retrospective standpoint of what Jeannelle calls the "remembering subject" (363). Echoing Edith Piaf's hit song *Je ne regrette rien*, the author of *Vae Victis* strews his text with the formula "I don't regret anything" (e.g., 19, 25, 94, 228). Labat, observing that the members of the LVF were called "mercenaries in German uniform," firmly replies: "I was one of those mercenaries, I'm still proud of it today, and I don't care about those who speak ill of us" (268). Also striking up the theme of unshaken self-esteem, Lobsiger states long after the end of the war (his book was published in 1985): "Today, I'm still proud of the fact that I was the head of a unit in a mountain division of the Waffen-SS, proud, too, of the friendship of my subordinates and my superiors" (218). And Levast, no more concession-minded than his comrades, affirms that whenever he makes a "final assessment of his journey," "the balance sheet is positive": Being a member of the Charlemagne gave him "a sense of responsibilities and a discipline of life," as well as the "indelible memory" of the comrades "who died during this epic, aware that the combat was basically unequal" (165). The most explicit of the memoirists is Philippet, who, upon recounting a meeting with his pardon board during which he has mocked their question "Do you regret what you have done?", comments on his decision (and addresses silently the board) in a most provocative manner:

No, I do not regret what I did! I will never regret it. First, because it would be useless and sterile, like all regrets. And then, what you did not understand is that such a fantastic adventure made me get out of myself, forced me dozens of times to surpass myself, to always push back limits that I thought were insurmountable. It doesn't matter whether I was right or wrong. What counts is what I did, the fact that I always and in all circumstances took sides, instead of vegetating in the bourgeois comfort of which you are the bloated example. (II, 320)

I have pointed several times to the parallels between the testimonies of the volunteers and those of the deportees, but it is clear that the similarities stop in such areas as "expression of regret" and "acknowledgment of error." Unlike the volunteers, the deportees have everything to regret; they can only wish they never had to live through the ordeal that was forced upon them, and they have no longing for the past. In contrast, several of the veterans openly confess to a nostalgia for what Philippet describes as their "fantastic adventure." The last sentences in some of the memoirs are, in this respect, especially revealing. Speaking "for" his fellow French SS in a POW camp, Auvray writes: "And we ..., who had dreamed of a different France in a different Europe, we were beginning to think that a dream was gone, a dream whose traces would be difficult to erase" (193). Gaultier uses the same words to evoke the moment of his release from prison: "Strangely, on that day, during that first hour of freedom, I had the feeling that the big dream had just ended" (379). Yet it is Leverrier who makes the most qualified assessment when he contrasts the original dream with the bloody and mistaken attempt to realize it:

Nostalgia of what was? Impossible, after the horrors of the war and the errors of History. But nostalgia of my youth, yes. (248)[10]

The "horrors" to which Leverrier refers here likely include the geno-cide. But as they claim that they only had glimpses of labor camps and deportees, the volunteers also affirm that they were not apprised of the existence of extermination camps before 1945. Leverrier contends that he learned about the "final solution" after his arrest (225), and he denies any co-responsibility for it. Similarly, Rostaing asserts during his trial that he "was not aware of the camps," and that if he had been, he "would have acted differently" (230). In the same context, La Mazière declares to the court that if he "knew about arrests," it is not before his captivity as a POW in Hanover that he had "discovered the genocide" (1972, 250). None of the memoirists is openly negationist, though Bayle is skeptical about the number of the Jews actually murdered. Relying on the widely diverging statistics published in books and magazines, released by agencies, or used

---

[10] The volunteers' stubborn refusal to express any regret is also found in the individual dedications that the authors have sometimes given on the title page of their books. The used copy of *Stoï* I acquired is thus inscribed by Rusco in the following way: "To ..., whom this book will remind of the sacrifice of thousands of young Europeans of French origin, who died for the defense of Europe and for the construction of a new world of order, honor, and loyalty. The fight goes on!"

during trials, he argues that the figure of 6 million Jews killed is at best an "estimate" (2008, 424). Not unpredictably, he also asks why the focus has been on the Jews exclusively, whereas the genocides that have taken place in such places as Cambodia, Vietnam, and Kurdistan have been "passed over in silence" (425). The only one among the memoirists who expressly flaunts antisemitic attitudes is Laurier. According to him, the Jews in 1939 "have their war" (39); France at the Liberation is run by a "judeo-communist coalition" (39); collaborationists should avoid going to Uruguay, because it is a "judeo-masonic" stronghold (53); the shops in Caracas are held by "servile and arrogant Jews" (92), and the like. Laurier does not take up the subject of the genocide, possibly because he writes in the 1950s, when it was not widely discussed. His antisemitism, however, is most blatant, and it does not seem to cross his mind that the ideas he professes could have led not just to discriminatory measures against the Jews, such as the laws passed by the Vichy government in October 1940 and June 1941, but eventually to the Jews' deportation and killing.[11]

Several reasons may account for the volunteers' refusal to make amends and take responsibility for the crimes with which they were connected. Some are plainly stated in the texts by the volunteers themselves, who plead their case by turning to arguments of an ethical and ideological nature. The memoirists first seek to establish what Dulong and Marandin call their "moral identity," that is, the "social type that will be projected to understand [their] behaviors and guess [their] motivations" (153). To counter the charges against them, they assert that they are and have always been patriots, and that such an essential virtue has preserved them from ever doing anything reprehensible. This position is best exemplified by Bassompierre, who righteously maintains that soldiers fighting on the Eastern Front with the Germans and in Africa with de Gaulle served, in fact, the same cause – that of France. Upon learning that his younger brother, who was a pilot in the Royal Air Force, had been killed in action over "our" Alsace, Bassompierre writes:

My pain is deep, and I cannot accept the idea that I will never again see the man who was the loyal and cheerful companion of my childhood, during the happiest youth one can imagine, within a family that was affectionately close. Superficial minds will think: "Enemy brothers." What a mistake! We both obeyed the French government, which in France encouraged the anti-Bolshevik struggle, while its representatives in North Africa ordered the resumption of fighting against the

---

[11] On the subject of the "statut des Juifs" of October 1940 and the "loi Vallat" of June 1941, see Kaspi, 53–86.

Germans. The same sense of duty and the same love of country have guided us. He knows that I am not insulting his memory when I state that I wanted to serve the same cause as he did, that of French greatness. (173)[12]

Bassompierre's views are of course debatable from a historical standpoint. Did Vichy "order" its representatives in Africa to resume fighting, or did some (though not all) of them decide to do so on their own? Ceding this question to Vichy specialists, I will only point out that Bassompierre's argument in this passage is most representative of the volunteers' strategies of justification. To begin with, he establishes his "moral identity": like his brother, he is a dedicated patriot. Then, switching from the ethical to the ideological sphere, he asserts the correctness of his political choice: As his brother fought the Germans, he fought the Bolsheviks, that is, the other evil. Expounding once again these views toward the end of his book, and apparently unaware that his description of the Soviet system could apply to the Nazi regime to which he was a party, Bassompierre writes:

If Bolshevism triumphed, concentrations camps, massive deportations, and "katynisations" would multiply on the surface of the earth.[13] In the name of the deified Revolution, the world would be nothing but a vast penal colony, where every individual, after losing all personality, would be exploited by his wardens and the party comrades. The latter alone would be entitled to think, to lead, to show initiative, and especially, as High Priests of Mankind's new Religion, to enjoy the misery of their slaves. (230)

Several of the memoirists argue along the same lines as Bassompierre to explain why they do not question their prior activities. Writing mostly during the Cold War, they put forth that the events that followed World War II, especially the rupture of the anti-Axis alliance, vindicate their earlier choice retrospectively: The real enemy was the USSR, and the men who took arms against Soviet Communism were not traitors, but pioneers. Defending this stand on the last page of his testimony, the author of *Vae Victis* observes dryly: "I admit to being guilty only of a mistake in timing. A few years later, we would have been the forerunners.

---

[12] In his book about the purge of French intellectuals after the war, Assouline points out that several writers and journalists who were charged with acts of collaboration argued along the same lines as Bassompierre during their trial, putting forward their patriotism. Brasillach, for example, addressed the district attorney with the words: "I am not angry with you, I know that you believe you did your duty. But I must tell you that I, too, only thought of serving my country. I know that you are a Christian, as I am. Only God will judge us" (Assouline 1990, 62).

[13] Bassompierre coins "katynisation" after Katyn, the place near Smolensk where many thousand Polish officers were killed by the Russians in spring 1940.

Instinctively, we went to the real problem" (226). Likewise, Bayle affirms that he and his comrades "were wrong to be right too soon" (2008, 19), and he gleefully quotes Churchill's alleged pronouncement "We killed the wrong pig" (2008, 40) – a pronouncement by which the British statesman surmised that the Allies had hit the wrong target, more precisely that at some point, a reversal of the alliances would have been advisable in order to contain the advance of the USSR in Central Europe.

The volunteers mostly conduct their narratives from this ideologically retrospective standpoint, a scheme that allows them to describe the collaboration with Germany as a sign of good things to come. Saint-Loup celebrates the Pétain-Hitler meeting in Montoire, often decried as a shameless attempt on the part of the French to ingratiate themselves with the Germans, as an occasion when "the two heads of the West sought to christianize politics, to introduce the forgetting of insults and the forgiving of them into the relations between countries" (1986b, 148). Similarly, denying that the volunteers were betrayed by the Nazis, Bayle insists that the community formed by the thousands of men who came from different countries to help Germany and fight the Soviets constituted an early version of the European Union. According to Bayle, who writes after the collapse of the USSR, it is time to return to the ideal that occupied those men; that is, it is time to transform the current "supermarket," "potatoes and prunes" European Union into a genuine Europe, which would stretch "from the Atlantic to the Volga" (Bayle generously includes "Christian Russia" in his Europe), and have a common army, diplomacy, and government (2008, 241–2). In this respect, Bayle agrees with right-wing, procollaboration historians such as Saint-Paulien, who contend that "the glorious battles of the volunteers inaugurated the current collaboration between France and Germany," as they contend that if the Allies had accepted "a compromise in the West," the Germans would have been able to "push the Russians back beyond the Dniepr River," thus preventing the states of Central Europe from becoming satellites of the USSR (Saint-Paulien 519–20).[14]

Bayle's and Saint-Paulien's argument that history proved them right could certainly be challenged for not being historical enough. Bartov (1991, 140), in a discussion of Hillgruber's views about the last months of the war, has insisted that the "heroic" resistance of the retreating Wehrmacht could not be (re)interpreted as a defense of "Europe" against a Soviet

---

[14] "Saint-Paulien" is the pen-name of Maurice-Yvan Sicard, the general press and propaganda secretary of Doriot's Parti Populaire Français, who during the war ran the PPF's newspaper *L'Emancipation Nationale*. Saint-Paulien escaped to Spain in 1945 then returned to France in 1957 after an amnesty.

takeover; the past cannot be "distorted in the name of the future," and the Nazis did not have Central Europe in mind when they were seeking to contain the Russians' advance from Vienna to Königsberg. Likewise, if we follow Bartov, the "glorious battles" of the French volunteers cannot be viewed as announcing the later reconciliation between France and Germany. More precisely, Bayle and the other memoirists who describe themselves as forerunners in their fight against Communism and their dedication to the idea of a Franco-German alliance commit the sin of anachronism; they dehistorize their involvement, as they do not consider the nature of the regime for which they were fighting or the nature of the collaboration in which their country (its government at least) was involved during the war.

Ideological reasons that the volunteers provide in order to demonstrate that they were (and still are) right also have psychological facets. However, those facets, unlike the justifying rationales I have just described, remain implicit, and they come to light only when we adopt perspectives that are different from those of the texts' authors. The volunteers' testimonies could thus be viewed with respect to attitudes toward change. Marc Augé, in his book on forgetting, submits that left- and right-wing memories do not follow the same patterns. Several communists, according to Augé, have recounted their journeys from left to center or from left to right, tracing, for instance, "the past of their illusion" (an obvious reference to the historian François Furet's memoir *Le Passé d'une illusion*). By contrast, for Augé, fascists are "without memory"; they "learn nothing," "forget nothing," and "live in the perpetual present of their obsession" (74). Augé links up on this point with Vidal-Naquet who, surveying the debates about negationism, observes that for several years. the negationists' theses "have not moved"; they are "the words of a sect, of people wholly incapable of discussing arguments, and even of beginning the discussion that they demand so loudly" (1987, 181). Measured by Augé's and Vidal-Naquet's yardstick, the volunteers' memoirs certainly do not trace any significant evolution. But if their authors have not "moved," say, from their faith in a National-Socialist Europe to an acknowledgment of the merits of the European Union, they are not averse to expounding the reasons for their choices. In this respect, the question that Augé asks about fascists, or more generally about right-wingers, "Will we ever hear their voices" (74), is answered in part in the volunteers' memoirs. For those memoirs make the voices of the collaboration heard, even though they do not organize their data along the lines of the plot model "John was wrong, he realized it, and then he changed" that Augé has in mind.

The dichotomy that Augé establishes between modes of reminiscing could be reframed from an even more strictly psychological standpoint. In her survey of current research about trauma, Suleiman, following Janet, Van der Kolk, and Van der Hart, distinguishes between two types of memory: "traumatic memory," characterized by "compulsive repetition and inflexibility," and "narrative memory," characterized by "fluidity and variability" (2006, 139). The subject of traumatic memory, in Suleiman's words, is "essentially passive, locked into a repetition that abolishes the difference between past and present," whereas the subject of narrative memory is "essentially active, able to situate the traumatic memory in the past and therefore to gain some emotional distance from it" (139). If we accept the idea that perpetrators (and not just their victims) may be subjects to trauma, the volunteers' testimonies can be seen as originating in "traumatic" memory. Indeed, their authors appear unable to emerge from a trauma, or rather from a double trauma, caused first by their experiences at the front and then extended by their ostracism at the end of the war. Such experiences, and not their ideological rigidity exclusively, may keep them from changing, in this instance, from reckoning with the reasons why the side that they endorsed is generally regarded as the guilty side. To put it otherwise (though still in the vocabulary of psychology), the memoirists have never fully "worked through" the traumatic events that marked their past; they have merely "acted them out," returning again and again to the same episodes in their lives and rehearsing the same arguments. LaCapra has frequently relied on this opposition to account for how survivors from the Holocaust deal with their past; that is, for how they can be "possessed by the past and performatively caught up in the compulsive repetition of traumatic scenes," or in contrast be "able to distinguish between past and present and to recall in memory that something happened to one (or one's people) back then, while realizing that one is living here and now with opening to the future" (2001 21, 22). Provided that we do not lose sight of the obvious differences between Holocaust survivors and soldiers who might have been involved in criminal activities, LaCapra's distinction is applicable to the memoirists in my corpus. For the latter return compulsively to such topics as their defeat and outcasting without apparently being able to distinguish between past and present, and thus to do the work of mourning that would allow them to come to terms with the losses they have suffered.

While my memoirists tend to act out their troubles, the texts they have produced can hardly be regarded as typical instances of traumatic discourse. Régine Waintrater, in her analysis of interviews with French Holocaust survivors conducted for the Yale Fortunoff Video Archives, has shown that the posttraumatic narratives presenting a "fixation on the trauma" involve a "rhetoric" (45). Specifically, witnesses who suffer from that fixation do not tell their stories to the interviewers according to the principles of "cooperation" and "relevance" (48); they do not establish a "hierarchy" among the events that they report (49); they frequently "digress," interrupting the flow of their narrative (50); they let traumatic contents "erupt," often in the form of "flashes" that disturb the coherence of the story (50); and they "idealize" certain moments of their pasts (55), such as the "before" that preceded their rejection from the national community, their arrest, and their deportation (55). In brief, according to Waintrater, witnesses who have not overcome their traumas do not, or rather cannot, organize their discourse according to the "implicit rules of testimonial narrative" (58). The interviews, as a result, resemble analytic sessions, during which it is up to the interviewer to give shape to the subject's "private associations" (59).

Reading the volunteers' memoirs through the lens of Waintrater's "rhetoric" hardly reveals the presence of the figures that Waintrater deems to be typical of traumatic narratives. True, the volunteers do not always "hierarchize" the events they recount; they accumulate details, confusing readers with extended descriptions of marches and battles; their chronologies are sometimes vague, making it difficult to figure out when what happened actually happened; and they "idealize" the time that they spent as soldiers, transforming ordeals into objects of nostalgia. Yet most of these shortcomings seem to be traceable to a lack of literary skills rather than to psychological troubles. The volunteers' memoirs remain generally unified and coherent, as they do not include the "digressions" and "flashes" that for Waintrater characterize the structure of traumatic testimonies. It could even be argued that those memoirs are overly coherent, more precisely that they expunge perhaps too conveniently the losses that have brought them about to begin with. Because of this excessive homogeneity, the volunteers' testimonies could be viewed as displaying what Eric Santner calls "narrative fetishism." Their authors, by frequently pointing out that they have no regrets to express and no mistakes to acknowledge, would simulate a "condition of intactness," undo "in fantasy" the "need for mourning" that their denials specifically reveal (144). Such a need, therefore, would be "indefinitely postponed," together with the need of having to reconstruct one's identity "under posttraumatic conditions" (144).

From my formalist corner, however, diagnostics of psychological problems in texts cannot be made without taking conventions of writing into account. In this instance, one should not forget that the volunteers compose life narratives, and that they are obviously striving to observe the very rules whose flouting Waintrater identifies in her analysis of deportees' testimonies. Wanting to be "cooperative," they select "relevant" events in their lives, then employ them in a way that will make their narratives reader-friendly; and they do so from the standpoint of a homogeneous subject who is not inclined to penitence and self-condemnation. Since the subgenre that they practice is the soldier's memoir, the constraints to which they submit are even more stringent. As Smith (90) has noticed in his study of testimonies from the Great War, soldiers are not prone to admitting their wrongs, especially when they are placed – as the volunteers are – in the position of defendants who have to plead their case; nor are they likely to offer the viewpoint of a fragmented, decentered subject, given to confessing scruples and hesitations. The memoirs of German generals such as Guderian and von Manstein are most characteristic in this respect, as none of these high-ranking soldiers seems ready to acknowledge what Smelser and Davies describe as their "relationship with National Socialism" and participation in a war of "racial enslavement and annihilation" (95).[15] I do not know whether the volunteers have read these or similar recollections (the literary references I identified in Chapter 5 are to literature and history rather than to memoirs), but their attitudes are comparable to those exhibited in the writings of these high-ranking soldiers. In other words, the volunteers' reluctance to express regrets may very well originate in "narrative fetishism"; but it may also be traced to a conscious or unconscious application of generic rules, in this instance, of the conventions of the military memoir. It could even be argued that if the volunteers had doubts about the value of their

---

[15] The titles of the books written by Guderian: *Erinnerungen eines Soldaten* [Memories of a Soldier] and von Manstein: *Verlorene Siege* (published in English as *Lost Victories*], are, in this respect, already revealing: they make the authors into individuals whose business is soldiery exclusively, and whose achievements at some point were undermined ("lost victories") by the decisions of incompetent nonprofessionals (read: by the interventions of Hitler and his circle). Smelser and Davies do not mention the memoirs of the SS generals Felix Steiner and Paul Hausser, but the titles of these books are equally indicative of the authors' unwillingness to mourn. Steiner's *Die Armee des Geächteten* [The Army of the Outlawed] refers to the necessity to defend the members of the SS against their ostracization, Hausser's *Soldaten wie andere auch* [Soldiers Like Any Other Soldiers], to the need of viewing the Waffen-SS corps as made, just as the Wehrmacht was, of "German soldiers." That latter issue had financial implications, since only soldiers were entitled to a veterans' pension from the German government.

involvement, the nature of the text they were writing forced them to elide passages in which they would express their misgivings, as it forced them to multiply phrases such as "I do not regret anything" and "today, I am still proud of what I did."

Along the same lines, the fact that the volunteers did not produce oral but rather written testimonies should also be taken into consideration. While the Holocaust survivors interviewed by Waintrater had to answer questions on the spot, a situation that made them particularly vulnerable, the volunteers could select the time when they would "tell." That is, even when they, in fact, wrote their book with a journalist, an editor, or a ghostwriter, they were never in the position of Waintrater's interviewees; the people with whom they worked were collaborators intent on helping them produce the best version of their lives, which could mean rewording some statements and eliding others – an option not available to Waintrater's interviewees. The volunteers who jotted down their recollections without professional assistance enjoyed the same advantage. Having written a first draft, they could rewrite it (and rewrite that second draft, etc.), in order to make their text better conform to the conventions of the genre, to the demands of the publisher, and to the image of themselves that they intended to project. In short, generic requirements and conditions of production must always be considered while assessing texts in general and life narratives in particular. For such requirements and conditions shape the works to be analyzed, or at least provide a framework from which writers, whatever their literary talent and psychological makeup might be, can hardly escape.

Conclusion

In his book *La Vision des vaincus* (published in English as *The Vision of the Vanquished*], the historian and anthropologist Nathan Wachtel examines how the inhabitants of Peru underwent the invasion of their land by the Spaniards. That is, he reverses the usual Eurocentric standpoint; describing the Conquest as it was seen not by the victors but by the vanquished, he asks how the Native Americans "experienced their defeat," how they "interpreted it," and how they "remembered it in their collective memory" (22). Such a reversal seems unproblematic when the vanquished have come to be perceived as representing a worthy cause, as have Native Americans, who fought to preserve their land and their culture. Taking a leftist perspective, the same thing could be said of other noble vanquished, such as the members of the Paris Commune and the Republicans in the Spanish Civil War, who lost to reactionary forces while defending the values of social change and democracy. By contrast, offering the viewpoint of the losing side raises several difficulties when that side is also regarded as the wrong side – as the side that endorsed untenable positions. Such is the case with the volunteers, whose memoirs present the outlook of a group that might be called the unlikable vanquished. Indeed, whether they belonged to the LVF, the Brigade Frankreich, or the Division Charlemagne, the volunteers remain associated in public opinion with the Nazi regime. They, therefore, are not likely to attract the compassion often granted to the defeated, all the more so since, taking the position of the unrepentant, they have refused to acknowledge any (co)responsibility for the crimes that the Nazis have committed.

The position of "unlikeable vanquished" has evident drawbacks. To begin with, the difficulty of summoning much sympathy and even understanding for this type of the defeated may explain why so few scholarly works have been devoted to the volunteers. More precisely, it may explain why most of the books about them have been written by such people as Mabire, Forbes, and Landwehr – that is, by unconditional admirers of the German army in general and the Waffen-SS in particular. That same difficulty may also account, in another area of discourse, for the low number of fictional texts in which the French military collaboration is treated as a theme and military collaborators appear as characters. There are certainly numerous novels about the time of the Occupation. But Nicholas Hewitt, Gérard Loiseaux, Alan Morris, Pascal Ory, Paul Sérant, and Jeannine Verdès-Leroux, in their studies of the literature of and about this period, do not signal any novel in which military collaborators play a central role. My own admittedly limited research has yielded few results. A member of the LVF, Malinier, has a minor part in Marcel Aymé's *Le Chemin des écoliers* [The Schoolboys' Path]; in *Le Diable en rit encore* [The Devil is Still Laughing about It], volume III in Régine Deforges's saga *La Bicyclette bleue*, Mathias, a teenage love of the central character Léa, joins the Charlemagne and is killed in Berlin; Max Aue, the SS member who narrates Littell's *Les Bienveillantes* [published in English as *The Kindly Ones*], runs into French volunteers in Pomerania, then witnesses the scene when Krukenberg decorates some of them in a Berlin subway station; François Ponthier, in *Plaidoyer pour personne* [A Plea for Nobody], tells about the trials of a few collaborationists after the Libération, notably of Paul Muller, a former member of the LVF who is sentenced to death; Jacques Laurent, in *Le petit canard* [The Little Duck], recounts the story of Antoine, an adolescent who joins the LVF and is executed for treason upon his return to France, but none of the chapters describes the young man's activities on the battlefield; Michel Mohrt, in *Mon royaume pour un cheval* [My Kingdom for a Horse], stages Bassompierre as "Bergemont," but the narrative takes place in 1939–40, when Bassompierre was an officer in the French army, not a volunteer in the service of the Germans;[1] and Frédéric Vitoux, in another *roman à clé*, *L'Ami de mon père* [My Father's Friend], tells about his encounters with a "Bernard du Perray" who stands for Christian de La Mazière – encounters that occurred, however, in the 1960s, when the prestige of La Mazière, then a show business agent, was due to his driving

---

[1] Mohrt and Bassompierre became friends when they were both stationed with the French army in the mountains above Nice in 1939–40. Designating Bassompierre by his own name, Mohrt evokes this period in his memoir, *Vers l'ouest*.

a Triumph convertible and dating Hollywood actresses, not to his past as a member of the Waffen-SS.[2]

The only novels exclusively devoted to the military collaboration I have found are Saint-Loup's *Sergent Karacho*, Saint-Paulien's *Les Lions morts: La bataille de Berlin* [Dead Lions: The Battle of Berlin], and Philippe Randa's *Le Rêve éclaté* [The Dream Exploded]. All are works of writers with sympathies for right-wing causes, who take sides without ambiguity for the collaborationists whom they stage in their narratives.[3] Saint-Loup's only book about the volunteers explicitly presented as fictional, *Sergent Karacho*, recounts the journey of a few members of the French Communist Party who enroll in the LFV (renamed here "Phalange anti-komintern") in order to sabotage it. The main character, Roger Auclair, is called "Sergent Karacho" by his comrades, after a Russian word meaning that everything is going well. Once in the USSR, however, the young men are soon disappointed by the realities of the communist regime; abandoning their plan, they elect to fight earnestly on the side of the Phalange, as it is the best way of serving France. The novel ends with Auclair's/Karacho's return to Belorussia after a frustrating leave in France. Anxious to resume the struggle, Auclair learns with enthusiasm that the Phalange will in the future use aggressive tactics against the partisans – tactics that resemble those of the "Section de chasse," of which Rusco and Rostaing were members, and whose operations they describe in their memoirs. As its title indicates, Saint-Paulien's book evokes the struggles that took place in Berlin in late April and early May 1945. The main character, Hauptsturmführer Christian Gauvin, participates in the combat in Neukölln and the Wilhelmstrasse, then manages to escape through the sewer system. After hiding for a few years in the mountains of Tyrol, he moves to Spain. A sequel to *La Bataille de Berlin*, *Le Rameau vert* [The Green Branch], finds him in a South-American republic, where he helps to crush a communist takeover. Randa's *Le Rêve*

---

[2] The American writer Rachel Kushner also stages La Mazière in her novel *Telex from Cuba*, imagining that he comes to Havana and gets enmeshed in the political scene that preceded Castro's coming to power. In an interview, Kushner stated that she saw *Le Chagrin et la pitié*, found La Mazière "strangely, seductively sympathetic ... in spite of his fascist background," and decided to give him a part as a French agitator in her novel. (http://search.barnesandnoble/Telex-from-Cuba/Rachel-Kushner. Accessed 5/15/2009.

[3] About Saint-Paulien, see Chapter 7, note 12. A prolific novelist, publisher, and blogger, Randa has edited a *Dictionnaire commenté de la Collaboration française* that is most favorable to the collaboration. Less an extremist than Saint-Paulien and Randa, Ponthier has written several war novels and an essay on the condition of the soldier: *L'Homme de guerre* [The Man of War].

éclaté has a "change-of-heart" plot that recalls *Sergent Karacho*'s. Two young people, François Delamare and René Taraz, want to join the Free French in London. Prevented from doing so through Spain, they devise the odd scheme of enrolling in the LVF, deserting, and flying to England from Moscow. Once on the battlefield, however, they soon realize that their plan is difficult to carry out, and they find themselves convinced by the arguments of those who want to "liberate" Russia from the communist yoke. The novel is open-ended. René has died, but François, who has crossed the Soviet lines on a special mission, will stay in the USSR with the attractive Russian woman he has met during this operation. Randa does not reveal whether the couple will join the partisans, keep fighting on the German side with the LVF, or just make a life for themselves.

This list makes no claim to exhaustivity. More novels about the volunteers may be out there, brought out by presses that have a large "popular war literature" department, such as Presses de la Cité and Editions du Gerfaut. The fact that no volunteer should figure as a major character in the mainstream literature of the Occupation is most telling, however. Collaborationists abound in that literature, appearing as blackmarketeers, supporters of the Vichy regime, and members of the German police in such important works as Albert Camus's *La Peste* [published in English as *The Plague*], Marguerite Duras's *La Douleur* [published in English as *The War: A Memoir*],[4] Jean Dutourd's *Au Bon Beurre* [At the Good Butter – the name of a dairy business], Roger Vaillant's *Drôle de jeu* [Strange Game], and several of Patrick Modiano's novels. Collaborationists are even portrayed at times in a positive manner, as in Pierre Benoît's *Fabrice*, which focuses on a pro-Pétain officer who at the end of the war is executed for his beliefs, and Roger Nimier *Les Epées* [The Swords], which recounts the journey of a member of the Resistance who eventually joins the Milice. Yet none of these novels, nor any of the works analyzed by specialists as constituting the "literature of the Occupation," includes the figure of a volunteer, not even as a villain.[5] This exclusion, to my knowledge, has not been discussed in literary scholarship, and it may tentatively be traced to two main kinds of reluctance. First, to paraphrase

[4] The title of the English-language translation, *The War: A Memoir*, is misleading, since several passages in Duras's text can only be fictional.
[5] I am restricting my inquiry to literature, but the same observation could be made about film. Sylvie Lindeperg, in her exhaustive investigation of the way World War II is represented in 133 French films released between 1944 and 1969, does not mention a single work that deals with the military collaboration or stages one of its representatives. Her only inclusion of the subject comes via La Mazière's appearance in *Le Chagrin et la pitié* (378).

a distinction made by Warhol about "the unnarratable" (222), novelists may think that stories about the volunteers "cannot be told," because the cause for which the protagonists are fighting is so discredited that no audience could relate to the narrative in minimal fashion. Second, agreeing with several historians, authors may deem that such stories are not "worth telling," because the events that they report are little known and had an insignificant influence on the course of World War II. No major French novelist was bold enough to risk taking up this kind of untellable material, a compliance with content-related narrative conventions that possibly explains the success of Littell's *Les Bienveillantes*. While Littell's narrator and main protagonist is not French, he is a volunteer as a member of the SS. Giving center stage to such a character, who confesses to many more wrongs than the French volunteers do in their memoirs, was certainly "new," and that newness may account for the sales figures that *Les Bienveillantes* generated and the polemics that it produced: The audience perceived that a taboo had been violated.[6]

While the label "unlikeable vanquished" entails a certain number of liabilities, the fact that it applies to my memoirists also makes it possible to raise several issues pertaining to testimonies in general and the implications of formal choices in this type of text in particular. The first such issue concerns the relations between text and reader in a first-person narrative. Literary theorists (e.g., Booth, Cohn) have asked whether readers necessarily follow the narrator in this textual situation, more precisely, to what extent they can keep themselves distant from the value system the narrator-protagonist is representing. This question is particularly sensitive when the narrator stands for activities and ideas that are generally regarded as ethically or politically debatable, or even as plainly wrong. Critics have long explored this matter in such novels as Choderos de Laclos's *Les Liaisons dangereuses*. Jean-Luc Seylaz, for example, has argued that we tend to read "with" the sexual predators Valmont and Madame de Merteuil and "against" the virtuous Cécile and Madame de

---

[6] To be accurate, Littell's novel was not really a "first" in French literature, though it was received that way by most readers and critics. Robert Merle, in 1952, published under the title *La Mort est mon métier* [Death is my Trade] a fictional autobiography of Rudolf Hoess, the infamous head of the Auschwitz concentration camp. Grounded in documents coming from the Nuremberg trials and the notes of the American psychologist G. M. Gilbert (who had interviewed the defendants in their cells), *La Mort est mon métier* went almost unnoticed. Merle observes in the preface to a 1972 reissue of his book that this failure did not surprise him; he was conscious that he was writing a text that in the early 1950s "went against the tide," and thus was "out-of-date before it was written" (1972, I).

Tourvel. The problem here is not merely one of narration; *Les Liaisons dangereuses* is an epistolary novel, which means that Cécile and Madame de Tourvel get to tell their side of the story. It is also one of ethics, as one might ask, as Seylaz does, why readers in some cases are "fascinated by the evil" (97), that is, why they are drawn to behaviors to which they would not want to be subjected, and which they themselves would be unable to carry out.

"Fascination for the evil" is also the term that Ory (1991, 47) uses to characterize France's lasting obsession with the Occupation and more specifically with the collaboration. Ory's study bears on the 1970s and 1980s, but the obsession that he describes has continued into the 1990s and the 2000s. During this period, the French became fixated on such events as the arrest and subsequent trial of the *milicien* Paul Touvier, charged with anti-Resistance activities and the killing of Jews in Lyon; the indictment for crimes against humanity of Vichy's police chief René Bousquet (who was assassinated before being brought to justice); the indictment and trial of former General Secretary of the Préfecture of Gironde Maurice Papon, held responsible for the deportation of hundreds of Jews in Bordeaux; and the publication of Pierre Péan's biography *Une Jeunesse française: François Mitterand, 1934–1947*, which provided details about Mitterand's involvement with Vichy before he joined the Resistance. Ory's (1991) diagnostic thus still applies, as the French have never ceased being "fascinated" by the disturbing subjects of the Occupation and the collaboration.[7]

As far as texts are concerned, this unsettling attraction for "evil" topics and characters poses a double problem of reception, which could be formulated as follows: Do we read first-person factual texts as we read fictional ones, in this instance, do we read "with" the volunteers, as – according to Seylaz – we read "with" Valmont and Madame de Merteuil? And if we do, do we become accomplices only because memoirs are first-person narratives, or also because we are seduced by the feats of the volunteers, as we are seduced by the feats of Laclos's cynical protagonists? Published in such journals as *Commentary*, *Worldview*, and the *New York Times*, the articles about Sajer's *Le Soldat oublié* and La Mazière's *Le Rêveur casqué* I quoted earlier show that reviewers were, to some extent, "taken" by the books they were assigned to discuss; that is, in spite of their obvious dislike for the positions defended in those texts,

---

[7] On the subject of the Touvier and Bousquet affairs, see Richard Golsan, ed., *Memory, the Holocaust, and French Justice* (1996).

they felt the need to acknowledge the appeal exercised by the authors' personalities and the way they accounted for their choices, however mistaken such choices might have been.

The same observation can be made about the reactions to La Mazière's appearance in *Le Chagrin et la pitié*. Critics have generally portrayed La Mazière favorably, for example, as a "youngish middle-aged penitent, languorous of manner and attractive in a classically Gallic way," characterized by his "nervous articulateness, touches of arrogance, and look of someone haunted" (Hux 52). In other words, they have recognized that they were somehow "fascinated by the evil" – captivated by a man whose ideas they certainly did not share, but who was handsome, elegantly dressed, and able to present his case in a convincing manner. The reviewers do not seem to notice that Ophuls and Harris here evidently load the dice, as they do in several other places in the film. By selecting a good-looking and articulate member of the French SS, they clearly seek to dissipate the image of the vile collaborationist who betrays his country out of greed or blind faith in National Socialism; they make a "wrong" cause alluring, an effect that would have been more difficult to achieve if they had picked a less engaging character, such as the haughty, self-righteous Saint-Loup (to take as example a well-known veteran who would have been available). Ophuls and Harris also conveniently pass over in silence the fact that La Mazière was hardly a typical representative of the volunteers' movement; having enlisted in summer 1944 and spent the fall and most of the winter in training, he had hardly been for one month at the front when he was taken prisoner. But he was a member of the SS and the Division Charlemagne (a name more likely to be familiar to the audience than the LVF), thus the "bad but attractive" character whose testimony could add to the critical overview of the Occupation that the two filmmakers provide in *Le Chagrin et la pitié*.

If the memoirs written by the volunteers partake of the evil and may in this capacity produce a specific fascination, one might then ask whether that fascination represents an actual danger, and for whom. Ory, in the essay quoted previously in this chapter, maintains that French memory still has to "catch up" on the subject of the Occupation. According to him, researchers are thus entitled to "stubbornly dig into" the most "embarrassing" aspects of the period, and audiences are entitled to take up the works that these inquiries have produced; the fact that exposure to such materials may draw people to unpleasant characters and endeavors clearly poses a problem, but it is "the price to pay" (1991, 47). Conversely, Chombart de Lauwe denounces the perils of what she calls the "counter-myth" challenging the "myth of the Resistance" (50). Nostalgics of Vichy and Nazism, she contends, have sought to reconstruct an image of the "pure Nazi hero" in order to rehabilitate National Socialism, justify their involvement in the collaboration, or even help reintroduce fascist movements in France. Chombart de Lauwe, as discussed in Chapter 6, does not mention books that would be representative of the "brown tide" that she views as having "filled kiosks with cheap works" celebrating war as an opportunity for "big, heroic adventures" (51).[8] She, however, designates the audience that she regards as especially vulnerable to this kind of publication: "young people" and a "popular public," who according to her are grossly deceived when members of the SS are portrayed as "heroic," and their opponents, as "rather vile" (51). Neither Ory nor Chombart de Lauwe mentions the volunteers' memoirs, although citing these texts could certainly have bolstered their arguments. The military collaboration constitutes one of the "embarrassing" subjects that Ory has in mind, and professional historians willing to research it would find a large amount of materials in the volunteers' testimonies. Those testimonies, however, could also be viewed as belonging to the "brown tide" that Chombart de Lauwe denounces. A few of them, specifically La Mazière's, Malbosse's, and Sajer's, were also published in paperback, which in Chombart de Lauwe's logic made them even more dangerous, since they then became available to a public likely to shop for cultural goods in such places as "kiosks." To my knowledge, no social scientist has gathered statistical data showing that readers have joined, say, Le Pen's Front National or some neo-fascist movement after taking up Sajer's, Malbosse's, or La Mazière's memoirs. Nevertheless, the problem remains of determining whether texts can affect behavior, and of how that influence can be measured: a problem frequently debated about fictional works, literary, televised, or filmic, but which could also be raised about texts that claim to represent real events, beginning with memoirs. [9]

Whether or not the volunteers' recollections exercise an unhealthy fascination with evil, they also participate in the conversation bearing on what Ricoeur (2000), following Mark Osiel, calls a "dissensus." Under

---

[8] Chombart de Lauwe may have in mind Mabire's trilogy *La Brigade Frankreich*, *La Division Charlemagne*, and *Mourir à Berlin*, which falls under "popular history"; or she may be thinking of such authors as Kurt Gerwitz's, Sven Hassel's, and Heinz Konsalik's war novels, which indeed stage German soldiers and often celebrate those soldiers' exploits against the Soviets.

[9] The subject "fascination for Nazism" has been treated by several scholars, notably by Peter Reichel. Reichel's study, however, is restricted to Germany and does not account for the phenomenon that Ory and Chombart de Lauwe are discussing here.

this term, Ricoeur refers to the possibility for professional historians to return to cases such as the Holocaust, that is, cases that have already been decided, both "at the level of national and international public opinion" and "at the legal and penal level" (427). Ricoeur concedes that new versions of the past can always be offered, and history can always be rewritten. The problem, according to him, is to know how historians can take up the Holocaust once again and come up with a new version that is not perceived as an exculpation. That is, it is to know whether any "margin" is left to a "dissensus" when there is a "consensus," and one that has long been established in the courts, in public opinion, and among most scholars (Ricoeur 427). Considering the works of German historians who have proposed novel interpretations of the Nazi period, provoking the *Historikerstreit* of the 1980s, Ricoeur points to places in those works where the argument breaks down. He singles out Ernst Nolte's contribution to *Devant l'histoire*, specifically the passage in which Nolte shifts from "comparing" the Holocaust with the Gulag to "establishing a relation of causality" between "the original and the copy" (429). Whereas it is legitimate, Ricoeur argues, to situate the Holocaust within a frame as wide as possible, no historical evidence shows that the Nazi crime originates in an "Asiatic crime," of which Germany could have become the "real or potential victim" (430), and against which that country would have sought to preserve itself by exterminating the Jews. Nolte's move here makes an explanation into an exoneration, disculpating the Nazis as well as doing away with the problem of the possible uniqueness of the Holocaust.

The memoirs of the volunteers raise similar issues, bearing, however, upon "personal" rather than "historical" texts. The distinction is important. The volunteers' "dissensus," unlike that of the scholars involved in the *Historikerstreit*, does not constitute a reinterpretation of the available evidence; it resides in the particular perspective that the volunteers provide. Thus, questions regarding a "dissensus" cannot be posed about Rusco's or Malardier's memoirs as Ricoeur poses them about historical research. In the case of the volunteers' testimonies, one might ask rather whether it is still legitimate to seek justifying an involvement that the courts have found criminal, public opinion found despicable, and historians found hardly worth investigating. Yet the convictions in which those testimonies are grounded cannot be debated the way scholars debate their colleagues' arguments. It would be difficult to demonstrate, say, that the volunteers' refusal to express any regret originates in faulty reasoning, as Ricoeur demonstrates that Nolte is mistaken when he traces the

Holocaust to the Gulag. The memoirists' affirmation of their blameless-
ness is a matter of belief – a belief that may be viewed as wrong, but that
cannot be proven wrong on the basis of documentary evidence or with
the help of logical argumentation.

One might ask, moreover, whether the volunteers' recollections constitute a "dissensus" with respect to a "consensus" that other memoirs
written about World War II have attained. When it comes to soldiers' testimonies, the very idea of a "consensus" seems most problematic, as members of the same group can assess a specific operation in different ways,
depending on personal circumstances; while soldier X was wounded and
then taken prisoner during battle Z, soldier Y participated in the last,
successful assault, and was later decorated. This observation applies to
the memoirs of the volunteers. Bayle and Rostaing, for example, claim
that the Charlemagne's engagement in Pomerania contributed to slowing
down the Russian advance, and Labat argues that it only led to pointless carnage. By their very nature, memoirs are thus less likely to reach a
"consensus" than the scholarly works examined by Ricoeur in his discussion of the *Historikerstreit*. The volunteers' recollections, therefore, can
only be said to reflect a "dissensus" insofar as they inscribe the standpoint I have been seeking to characterize: that of outsiders who willingly
fought on the side that turned out to be the wrong side, and who after
the war, by refusing to show remorse, became members in the category
"unlikeable vanquished."

While the volunteers' memoirs cannot constitute a "dissensus" in the
sense Ricoeur gives to the term, the fact that their authors have participated in the Nazi endeavor but reject any co-responsibility for Nazi
crimes nevertheless begs the following question: Is there such a thing as
"bad" or "unsound" memory? Some critics, as seen earlier, deem books
that stage German soldiers as heroes to be dangerous, because they could
be read by an uninformed and vulnerable public who would see them as
heroes. Yet those critics focus on problems of reception, and they take
for granted the dangerousness of the texts that they incriminate. In short,
and to limit the discussion to testimonies, they posit the existence of an
objectionable type of memory, but they do not describe this type, nor do
they ask why some types might be better than others. Taking up those
issues in her work about memory as a "repository for group affinities,
loyalties, and identity formation," Aleida Assmann calls for "critical vigi-
lance." The current memory boom, she contends, makes it necessary to
distinguish between "use" and "abuse" of memory, as well as between different kinds of reminiscences. According to her, "beneficial [wohltätig]"

memory is one that can deal with "historical truth," "opposite views," "neighbors," and "guilt"; and "dangerous [gefährlich]" memory, one that is "blind to truth," cannot accept "contradiction," is hostile to "other groups," and rejects any kind of "culpability" (2006, 276–7). Do the volunteers' recollections fall under "dangerous" memory because they represent the standpoint of a bitter minority and celebrate the deeds of despicable mercenaries? Or could they be included in "beneficial" memory because some of them call for a reconciliation among the French, arguing, as Bassompierre's *Frères ennemis* does, that volunteers fighting in the USSR with Germany and in North Africa with the Allies served, in fact, the same cause – that of "French honor"? However we answer these questions, Bassompierre and the other veterans' testimonies have the merit of raising them, and to do so in a provocative manner. Moreover, they show that the thesis, defended, for instance, by Jean Peyrot (338), according to which collective memory is highly selective as it preserves "pleasant" reminiscences and discards "unpleasant" ones, is hardly tenable. Whether the texts under consideration fall under "beneficial" or "dangerous" memory, reminding French society that some of its members actually fought on the German side during World War II can only be "unpleasant."

As the volunteers' memoirs make it possible to pose diverse problems bearing on the ethics of memory, they also have the virtue of pointing to a risk that is always present when we discuss the past and more particularly Vichy France: the risk of anachronism. Rousso and Conan warn against this danger in one of their many essays about the Occupation, alerting, for instance, to the "temptation of Judeocentrism," that is, to the temptation of "looking at the whole period through the prism of antisemitism," thus producing a confusion between "the ethics of posterity and the reality of the past" (398). Burrin had expressed similar concerns, pointing out that focusing on Vichy's policies of repression and persecution erases the "utopian dimension" of the regime: the fact that Vichy originated not only in the "shock of the 1940 defeat" but also in the "crisis of democratic values in the 1930s," to which it sought to provide an answer (1997, 2485). Rousso, Conan, and Burrin do not take condemnations of France's military collaboration as further instances of this loss of perspective, though an analysis of possible attitudes toward the volunteers' involvement certainly supports their argument. On the one hand, it would be mistaken to buy into the memoirists' claim, typical of the Cold War period, that they were wrong to be right too soon. Yet it would be equally erroneous to dismiss the volunteers' endeavor because it originated in "bad" choices – choices that landed the people who made them on the guilty side after the war. Things were not as clear between 1941 and 1944 as they are now, and judging the past in the light of present knowledge without taking into account the privilege of distance constitutes precisely a case of "anachronism." To be sure, as Ory and Ricoeur insist, to "place in context" is not necessarily synonymous with to "exonerate." In this instance, to let the volunteers account for the circumstances in which they made what we now hold to be unacceptable decisions does not mean that we endorse those decisions. But it is necessary to listen to their side of the story if we want to avoid anachronism, that is, if we want to avoid assessing past courses of action ignorant of the conditions that were prevailing at the time.

The attractiveness of the evil, the possibility of a dissensus, and the danger of anachronism obviously are not the only issues that the volunteers' memoirs raise. As works of people whose actions have been condemned in the judgment of History, these memoirs pose several additional questions that I cannot answer but will try to articulate to bring my discussion to a term, if not to a close. Some of those questions concern the duty to remember, generally speaking, as it has been discussed by such specialists as Suleiman and Coquio. To put it somewhat simplistically: Are all testimonies fit to be given and preserved? If some are not, by what criteria should we decide which ones deserve airing in the public realm and which ones do not? And who has the competence, or should be granted the power, to make such rulings? Other questions pertain to the memoirs in my corpus specifically: If all testimonies are allowed to be presented to the public, how should we treat the ones that uphold attitudes and positions that we now view as unacceptable? How should we deal with texts whose authors refuse to be contrite, insisting that they were right all along? Should we discard them, because – as Assmann argues – works that perpetuate "resentment, separatism, and violence" have no place in our culture? Should we preserve them because they have historical value, because their authors are sincere, and because rejecting them would replicate the inequities we are attempting to banish? If we keep them, however, how can we "unveil the repressed without rehabilitating it?" (Ory 1981, 113) That is, how can we investigate the testimonies of the volunteers without appearing to support the values for which their authors were standing? Finally, should we teachers, after showing *Le Chagrin et la pitié* to our students, make them read Rostaing and La Mazière, as we probably make them read Duras and Delbo, as part of a course about France and World War II? If so, how should we handle their possible expressions of sympathy or confessions of seduction? Last but not least, how should we acknowledge what LaCapra (1992, 110) calls the "trans-ferential relations" that we ourselves might have developed, as most – if not all – scholars do, to the "object" that we have researched and then brought into the classroom?

Appendix A

Biographical Notices

With a few exceptions, the authors in my corpus were ordinary soldiers who did not have public lives before or after the war. Information about them is thus difficult to obtain. The brief biographies included below are based on data found in studies of France's military collaboration, the World Biographical Index, different websites, and the memoirs themselves. Those biographies are tentative and sometimes duplicate information already available in the book; they should function as stopgaps for readers who, at some point, want to be reminded of "who was who" and "who did what."

ANONYMOUS. 1922–. The anonymous author of *Vae Victis* joined the LVF in spring 1942, left it in summer 1944, and apparently went into exile (he claims to be writing "from abroad"). Lefèvre and Mabire (2003, 58) introduce a "caporal de Saint-Allaire" as the author of *Vae Victis* and even include a picture of him (295). They specify, however, that de Saint-Allaire is a "pseudonym" (58), presumably used to protect the identity of someone who was still alive (and living in France) in the early 2000s. With Bassompierre's *Frères ennemis*, *Vae Victis* [Woe to the Vanquished, 1948) is the first testimony published by a volunteer after the war.

AUVRAY, JACQUES. 1926–. Joined the Milice in summer 1944, the Charlemagne in the fall of the same year. Fought in Pomerania. Taken prisoner by the Russians, handed over to the French. Tried and sentenced to a short jail term. *Les derniers grognards* (published in 1999, but written in the early 1970s). "Grognards" (grumblers) was the name given to Napoléon's soldiers. "Auvray" is probably a pseudonym: The author's *Soldbuch* is reproduced in a photograph on the first pages of *Les derniers grognards*, but the name of its owner is blotted out.

BASSOMPIERRE, JEAN. 1914–1948. While studying law and political science in Paris, was active in far-right organizations, such as Pierre Taittinger's Jeunesses Patriotes and Eugène Deloncle's Comité Secret d'Action Révolutionnaire (Cagoule). An officer in the French army, was stationed in the Alpes Maritimes in 1939–40. After the ceasefire, joined Vichy's Service d'ordre légionnaire. Enlisted in the LVF in September 1942 and fought in Belorussia. Called back to France in February 1944 to become General Inspector of the Milice. Left Paris in August 1944 with thousands of other miliciens, reaching the Charlemagne training camp in Wildflecken in October. Fought in Pomerania. Taken prisoner by the Russians in March 1945, escaped during his transfer to France. Arrested in Naples and handed over to the French as he was about to embark for South America in November 1946. Tried for his activities with the Milice, mainly for his role in the repression of an uprising at the La Santé jail in Paris in July 1944. Sentenced to death and executed in April 1948. *Frères ennemis* (1948). This title refers to the fact that Bassompierre and his brother Henri were not "enemy brothers," even though Henri had chosen the side of the Allies, enrolling in the RAF (he was killed during a mission over Alsace in 1944).

BAYLE, ANDRE. 1924–. Born and raised in Marseilles. In his teens, traveled with his parents as part of an acrobats' circus act. Attended the 1936 Olympics in Berlin with his family. Attracted by the discipline and athleticism of the Waffen-SS, joined that corps in 1943. Fought in Galicia and Pomerania. Taken prisoner by the Russians, then handed over to the French after a journey that took him to Siberia. Tried in 1946, but acquitted by the court because of his youth. After two years in the French army (1946–48), worked for different businesses, travelling to Canada, Germany, and the United States. Married, five children. A keeper of the flame, was still running – as of November 2009 – the group "Histoire et tradition," whose purpose, "far from any kind of political consideration," was "to share the adventures of the French volunteers who had been members of the elite corps of the Waffen-SS" (*www.histoire-tradition.com*). Has also written and been interviewed under the name "André Bailly." *Des Jeux Olympiques à la Waffen-SS* (2008); includes *De Marseille à Novossibirsk* and *San et Persante*, self-published in 1994.

CISAY, MICHEL (GUY HANRO?). 1917–. Before the war, involved in the Camelots du Roi (the youth movement of the royalist Action Française), then in Doriot's Parti Populaire Français. Drafted into the French army, took part in the 1939–40 campaign. Joined the LVF in 1943. Transferred to the Charlemagne in 1944. Taken prisoner in Pomerania in

March 1945. Spent eighteen months in the USSR as a POW, working as a laborer in factories and kolkhozes, but also employed as a cartoonist in charge of enlarging Soviet satirical drawings and decorating the walls of workshops. This latter job may indicate that "Cisay" is, in fact, Guy Hanro, a collaborationist cartoonist who enrolled in the LVF in late 1943. *Prisonniers en URSS* (1955).

COSTABRAVA, FERNAND (FERNAND COSTAMAGNA). 1926–. Born and raised in Nice. At age fifteen, became a member of the Union Populaire de la Jeunesse Française, the youth branch of Doriot's proto-fascist Parti Populaire Français (PPF). In May 1943, enrolled in the Nationalsozialistische Kraftfahrkorps (NSKK), which employed drivers, mechanics, and motorcyclists. Transferred in September 1943 to the Waffen-SS, sent to the training camp in Sennheim (Alsace). Fought in Galicia in August 1944. Taken prisoner, was in Soviet captivity from September 1944 to November 1945. Tried in Nice in January 1946 and given a six-month sentence. After spending time in the French army, worked in Nice for a yogurt-making company, of which he became the owner. Remained active in extremist organizations, such as the populist, antitax Movement Poujade (which defended the interests of shopkeepers and small businessmen), and the terrorist OAS (Organisation Armée Secrète, which opposed granting independence to Algeria). Married to the owner of a small supermarket, one child. *Le Soldat Baraka* (2007).

DEGRELLE, LEON. 1906–1994. Best-known Belgian volunteer. After studying in a Jesuit college, worked as a journalist for conservative Roman Catholic periodicals. Founded the Editions de Rex in 1934, the nationalist, proto-fascist Parti Rexiste in 1935. Met Hitler and Mussolini in 1936. Joined the Légion Wallonie in 1941. Fought in the Ukraine, Estonia, and Pomerania, becoming head of the Wallonie by the end of the war. Reached Norway in early May 1945, then flew to Spain. Remained in Spain until his death, acquiring Spanish citizenship in 1954. In Spain, ran different businesses with mitigated success, while continuing to publish, give interviews, and promote extremist causes. In Belgium, married, three children. His wife did not follow him to Spain, and he later married a sister of Joseph Darnand, the head of the French Milice (executed at the Liberation). *La Campagne de Russie* (1949). Speeches and interviews of Degrelle are available on YouTube.

DUPONT, PIERRE HENRI. 1923–. Born and raised in Bordeaux. Joined the LVF in July 1941, a few weeks after passing his baccalauréat. Fought in Belorussia with the LVF, then in Galicia with the Frankreich and in Pomerania with the Charlemagne. Got engaged to a young German woman who was killed during the bombing of Dresden. Wounded in Pomerania, returned to France using a false ID provided by his fiancée's father. *Au temps des choix héroïques* [At the Time of Heroic Choices, 2002]. This memoir is problematic both because of its narrative situation and its thematic content: Written in the third person, it stages a "Henri Duval" who – readers must assume – stands for the author Pierre Henri Dupont; Duval also goes from the LVF to the Frankreich to the Charlemagne, a journey taken by no other of the memoirists in my corpus.

EMMANUELLI, JEAN-BAPTISTE. 1917–. Born and raised in Toulon in a Corsican family. Member of the French army in 1939–40. Joined the LVF in early 1942, at the request of Simon Fabiani, an important member of Doriot's PPF and the head of Vichy's "Délégation" in Marseilles. Instructed by the Fabianis to retrieve their son, François, who had enlisted in the LVF. Returned to France in late 1942, upon learning that François had been killed. Without a job, volunteered to go to Berlin as a foreign worker. Jailed in Germany from 1943 to 1945 for conducting illegal traffic, then in France from 1946 to 1950 for his membership in the LVF. Enlisted in the Foreign Legion in 1950, fought in Indochina. Led a few failed business ventures upon his return to France in 1954. Twice married, two children. Indicates that he wrote his memoir in Costa Rica in 1973–74, but does not account for the circumstances that made him move to Central America. *Et j'ai cassé mon fusil* [And I Broke My Gun, 1974]. Although brought out by a major French publisher (Laffont), this memoir contains several episodes that challenge credibility.

GAULTIER, LEON. 1915–1997. The holder of a degree in Classics, worked in the 1930s as a history professor. Joined Doriot's PPF in 1936. During the Occupation, became a member of Paul Marion's Ministry of Information in 1941, of the Milice in 1943. Enlisted in the French Waffen-SS in 1943. Trained in Sennheim, fought in Galicia. Wounded on the first day of combat, spent the rest of the war in German hospitals. Tried upon his return to France and sentenced to ten years in jail. After his release in 1948, had positions with different companies, such as the news and advertising agency Havas and the Union of Foodstuffs Wholesalers. Close to the Front National, founded a publishing house with Jean-Marie Le Pen and contributed to the right-wing magazine *Rivarol*. Participated, in 1965, in the presidential campaign of the far-right candidate Jean-Louis Tixier-Vignancour, who was running against de Gaulle and Mitterand. Authored biographies of the seventeenth-century Spanish nun-turned-soldier Catalina de Erauso and of the fiftenth-century Breton ship owner and pirate Jean Coëtanlem. Married. *Siegfried et le Berrichon* (1991). Gaultier is from the province of Berrichon and he plays here with the title of Jean Giraudoux's well-known novel *Siegfried et le Limousin* (Limousin is another French province). Interview on YouTube, April 6, 2009.

GILLES, GILBERT. 1922–2010. A soldier in the French army, was taken prisoner by the Germans in 1940. Left his stalag to join the Waffen-SS in 1942, or more likely in 1944. Fought in Pomerania in February and March 1945. Upon his return to France, tried and sentenced to ten years of hard labor. Freed in 1948, moved to Algeria, and worked in the oil business. Jailed again in the early 1960s for his activities with the OAS. Joined Le Pen's Front National in the 1970s. Self-published several books about the Eastern Front (e.g., *SS Kommando, Bielgorod, Citadelle*), which must be classified as "historical novels" rather than as memoirs. Married to a French Algerian, six children. *Un ancien Waffen-SS français raconte* [A Former French Member of the Waffen-SS Reports, 1989]. Gilles's biography is especially difficult to establish, because Gilles is both an activist and a mythomaniac whose claims to have participated in the events that he describes remain, in many cases, unattested.

GRUBER, FERNAND. 1923–. Belgian volunteer. Born and raised in Brussels. As a teenager, was a supporter of Degrelle's Parti Rexiste. Volunteered to go work in Germany in April 1941, then – against his parents' will – joined the Légion Wallonie in April 1942. Fought in the Ukraine until February 1944, when he was wounded during the Wallonie's breakout from Cherkassy. After spending time in German hospitals, rejoined the Wallonie in March 1945. Fought in Pomerania, then returned to Belgium. Arrested upon his arrival in May 1945, tried, and sentenced to twenty years in jail. Freed in 1950. Remained active in Belgian veterans' organizations, whose members, among other activities, always meet in January in order to celebrate the Wallonie's successful breakout from the pocket in Cherkassy. *Nous n'irons pas à Touapse* [We Won't Go to Tuapse, 1991]. Tuapse is a town on the northeast coast of the Black Sea, which the Wallonie was supposed to occupy but never reached.

LABAT, ERIC. 1920–1964. Son of a French diplomat and an Austrian woman, spent part of his youth in Vienna. Proficient in German, a rarity among the French volunteers. A university graduate in literature, before the war was a member of Doriot's PPF, then of Pierre Clémenti's Parti Français National Collectiviste. Joined the LVF in August 1942. Transferred to the Charlemagne in late 1944 but refused to go to

Pomerania and was assigned to propaganda services. Spent time in Berlin in March-April 1945, though not as a combatant. Arrested upon his return to France, tried, and sentenced to eight years of hard labor. Freed in 1949. After his release, participated in different business ventures and worked for publishers, translating books about economics and medicine from German into French. Married. *Les Places étaient chères* [The Seats Were Expensive, 1969]. A first, shorter edition of this text had been published in 1951. Labat is sometimes described in other memoirs (e.g. as "Balat" in *Vae Victis* and in Leverrier's *C'était pendant l'horreur d'une profonde nuit*) as a difficult, undisciplined character, as well as someone who at the front was already thinking of writing a book about the LVF and was taking notes to this effect.

LA MAZIERE, CHRISTIAN DE (CHRISTIAN LA MAZIERE, the particle is apparently usurped). 1922–2006. The best-known of the French volunteers because of his interview in Ophuls's documentary film *Le Chagrin et la pitié*. Son of a career officer, grew up in an antisemitic, anticommunist family, though one with royalist ("Action Française") rather than fascist convictions. Enlisted in the French army in 1939, had no activities at the front. After the ceasefire, worked as a journalist for *Le Pays Libre*, Pierre Clémenti's collaborationist paper. Enrolled in August 1944 in the Waffen-SS, trained at Wildflecken, fought with the Charlemagne in Pomerania in February-March 1945. Taken prisoner by the Poles, handed over to the Russians and then to the French. Tried in 1946, sentenced to five years in jail. Freed in 1948. After his release, worked in journalism and as an agent in the entertainment business. Founded his own company, International Relations Press. Lost his clients after the revelations about his past brought about by *Le Chagrin et la pitié*. Returned to journalism, first to the conservative, Roman Catholic news agency *Beta Press*, then to *Figaro Magazine*. In the late 1980s, served briefly as "personal advisor" to the ruler of Togo, General Eyadéma. Back in France, resumed his activities as a journalist, contributing to the right-wing magazine *Révolution Européenne*. Never married but supposedly had affairs with show business personalities, such as the French pop singers Dalida and Juliette Gréco. *Le Rêveur casqué* (published in English as *The Captive Deamer*, 1972); *Le Rêveur blessé* [The Wounded Dreamer, 2003]. The interview in *Le Chagrin et la pitié* is available on YouTube.

LARFOUX, CHARLES (CHARLES FOULARD). 1923–1980. Before the war, member of Deloncle's Comité Secret d'Action Révolutionnaire. Enlisted in the first contingent of the LVF in summer 1941. Participated in the march toward Moscow in fall 1941, the combat at Djukovo in early

December, the retreat to a training camp in Poland in January–February 1942. Returned to France in summer 1942, disappointed by the lack of concrete involvement on the part of the politicians who had called for the constitution of the LVF. Married. *Carnets de campagne d'un agent de liaison* [Logbook of a Communication Officer, 2008]. The book comes with a preface written in 1943 by one of Larfoux's superiors, but apparently was not published before 2008; France's National Library has no trace of a 1943 edition.

LAURIER, MATHIEU (PIERRE VIGOUROUX). 1919–1980. Grew up in an anticommunist, xenophobic family of merchants. In the 1930s, became a member of several extremist organizations, such as Deloncle's Comité Secret d'Action Révolutionnaire, Pierre Taittinger's Jeunesses Patriotes, and Pierre Clémenti's Parti Français National Communiste. Drafted, spent the first part of the war with colonial troops in Casablanca, Morocco. Demobilized, enrolled in the LVF in summer 1941 and participated in the march toward Moscow. Wounded, was evacuated to France. Worked as an editor of the antisemitic, antimasonic journal *Au Pilori* in 1943, also joining the Milice. Fled to northeastern France with the Milice in August 1944, but refused to continue to Germany. Under a false identity, reached Tangier and then Spain, finally going into exile in Venezuela in 1947. Lived in Venezuela up to his death, first working as a taxicab driver. Married. *Il reste le drapeau noir et les copains* [The Black Flag and the Buddies Remain, 2002 (1953)]. The title is a quote from the collaborationist writer Robert Brasillach who meant that after the failure of fascism, the only option was an anarchistic, individualistic lifestyle of the type that Laurier deemed was available in South America.

LEVAST, LOUIS (LOUIS LAVEST). 1925–200?. Born in Central France, son of a career soldier. As a lycée student, member of several Vichy youth organizations. Moved to Lyons in April 1944 and became part of the Franc-Garde, the Milice's armed unit. Left France for Germany with the Franc-Garde in August 1944, reaching Ulm in October. Transferred to the Waffen-SS in early November. Trained in Wildflecken, fought in Pomerania and Berlin. Arrested upon his return to France, tried, and sentenced to eight months in jail. Freed after three months because of his youth. Married, children. *Le Soleil se couchai à l'est* [The Sun Set in the East, 2008]. Levast's daughter, in an acknowledgment, states that her father wanted his memoir to be published, but she does not indicate when her father died, or when the memoir was written.

LEVERRIER, ALFRED (ALFRED CATON). 1912–1998. A journalist, was an admitted "fascist" in the 1930s and knew extremists such as Céline, Drieu La Rochelle, and Alphonse de Châteaubriant. Drafted, was in the French army in 1939–40, but had no activities at the front. Enlisted in the LVF in August 1941. Participated in combat near Moscow, then in the retreat to Poland. Fought in Belorussia from early 1942 to summer 1944. Transferred to the Charlemagne in fall 1944, trained at Wildflecken. Identified as a journalist, sent to Berlin in late 1944 as a war correspondent for the Waffen-SS. In April 1945, dispatched to Doriot's headquarters in Mainau, a small island in Lake Constance. Upon learning that Doriot had been killed, crossed over to Austria. Taken prisoner by the Americans, handed over to the French. Tried in 1946 and sentenced to life of hard labor. Freed after four years. Successfully managed his return to civilian life, working for companies such as publishing houses . Married, children. *C'était pendant l'horreur d'une profonde nuit* [It Was during the Horror of a Dark Night, 2007]. This title quotes the first line of the main character's "dream monologue" in Racine's *Athalie*. Published in 2007, Leverrier's memoir was written before 1989: The author mentions that "today ... there is a wall in Berlin" (29).

LOBSIGER, FRANCOIS. 1915–. Swiss volunteer. Son of a farmer who turned to running a coffee-roasting business. Raised in a bilingual part of Switzerland, then in French-speaking Lausanne. In his teens, joined the Swiss proto-fascist movement Front National and was briefly jailed for his activities. Anxious to live in a regime that agreed with his beliefs, left for Germany in 1937. During his stay, was contacted by the Security Services and invited to take, in Tübingen, courses designed for foreign supporters of National Socialism. Returned to Switzerland in September 1939 and rejoined his unit with the Swiss army. In June 1941, elected to go fight for Hitler's "new Europe" and crossed over to Germany. After training near Prague, became a member of the SS division Leibstandarte Adolf Hitler. Fought in the Ukraine from summer 1941 to July 1942 and from January to July 1943, participating in the battle of Kharkov. Transferred to Italy in July 1943, became a member of the unit in charge of protecting Mussolini after his rescue from captivity by a German commando raid in September 1943. Sent in March 1944 to the SS officer school in Bad Tölz, in Bavaria. Stationed in Southern Tyrol at the end of the war, put on civilian clothes and remained in this area for a few months. Returned to Switzerland and gave himself up in September 1945. Tried and sentenced to two years in jail. After his release, settled in the Basel area and had a career in business. Married, children. *Un Suisse au service d'Hitler* [A Swiss in Hitler's Service, 1985]. In his study about the Swiss volunteers, Oertle states that he knows the author and "Lobsiger" is a pseudonym.

MALARDIER, JEAN. 1919–. Fought with the LVF in Belorussia, then transferred to the Charlemagne. Trained in Wildflecken. Sent to the SS officer school in Neweklau, did not participate in the struggles in Pomerania. Rejoined the Charlemagne in Berlin. Taken prisoner by the Russians, spent three years in captivity. Does not indicate whether he was tried and sentenced upon his return to France. In the 1950s, became a member of far-right organizations, such as Jeune Nation and the Parti Nationaliste. Married. *Combats pour l'honneur* [Fighting for the Honor of It, 2008]. Though 698 pages long, Malardier's memoir contains no information about the author's activities before and after the war; focusing on the battle of Berlin, it also includes detailed accounts of the activities of the LVF and the Brigade Frankreich, as well as lengthy personal ruminations.

MALBOSSE, CHRISTIAN. c1925–. Enrolled in the LVF on religious grounds (to defend Christianity against Bolshevism). Fought in Belorussia and Pomerania. Stayed for three years in Germany after the end of the war, doing odd jobs for farmers and poaching in the woods in the Cologne area. Moved to Belgium in 1948. Arrested for illegal border crossing and briefly jailed. Returned to France after his release, then moved to Spain with the help of his family, joining his similarly compromised brother. *Le Soldat traqué* [The Stalked Soldier, 1971]. The author was supposedly an aristocrat: "Malbosse" is a pseudonym, probably coined after the phrase "rouler sa bosse" (to knock about). Focussing on Malbosse's wandering in Germany after the war, the memoir says little about the author's experiences with the LVF and the Charlemagne.

MAROTEL, EMIL (a germanophile, Marotel insisted on the German spelling of his first name). 1925–1996. Son of a career soldier, raised in Chambéry (Savoy). Joined different Vichy youth organizations, then the Milice in 1943. As a member of the armed Franc-Garde, participated in operations against the Resistance in Savoy. Left for Germany with other miliciens in August 1944, spending some time in Ulm. With most of the Franc-Garde, joined the Charlemagne. Fought in Pomerania in early 1945, but did not go to Berlin. Fled west with a small group of French and German soldiers, reaching Schwerin in early May. Repatriated to France as a deportee, but identified as a member of the SS because of his tattoo. Tried and sentenced to ten years of hard labor. With many other collaborationists, imprisoned in Alsace at the Struthof camp, which had served as a concentration camp for racial and political deportees during the war. Freed in 1950. Worked for some time as a traveling salesman. Married, children. *La longue marche* [The Long March, 2007]. Marotel indicates at the end of his manuscript that it was written in April-May 1989 (174).

MIT, SERGE. 1926–. Joined the Waffen-SS in 1943 out of admiration for Germany. Wounded in Galicia, evacuated to a hospital near Salzburg, in Austria. In December 1944, wearing an American uniform, participated in the German counterattack in the Ardennes as a member of an intelligence unit sent across Allied lines. Upon his return to Central Europe, sent to work in an armaments factory near Pilsen, in Czechoslovakia. Back in Salzburg at the end of the war, hired by the American army as an interpreter. *Carcasse* à *vendre* [Carcass for Sale, 2001 (1950)]. Authentic (according to its publisher) but of sometimes dubious veracity, this testimony was the first one (in 1950) to describe the activities of the Brigade Frankreich in Galicia.

PHILIPPET, HENRI. 1924–. Belgian volunteer. In his teens, a member of Gamins du Rex [Rex's Kids], the youth movement of Degrelle's Rexist Party. Enrolled in the Légion Wallonie, leaving Belgium with the first contingent in August 1941. Fought in the Ukraine and Estonia from 1942 to 1944. Sent to the SS officer school in Bad Tölz, Bavaria, in January 1945. Was in Bad Tölz at the end of the war. Returned to Belgium, only to find out that his family, compromised because of their political beliefs, had fled to Germany. Rejoined his family in Germany, then worked in the Münster area until August 1946. Turned in, arrested, and sent to Belgium. Sentenced in 1947 to twenty years of forced labor. Freed in 1950. Married (to a Belgian woman he met during a leave from the front). *Et mets ta robe de bal* [And Put Your Party Gown on, 1991]. Written in 1973, this memoir was first self-published in the 1980s. Its odd title refers to one of the marching songs of the Légion Wallonie, which Philippet quotes on the title page of his recollections: Nous mettrons les Russes en fuite/Bien loin jusqu'à l'Oural/Si j'y reste ma petite/Que ton coeur n'ait point de mal/Et mets ta robe de bal. (We will chase the Russians/As far as the Ural/If I die my sweetheart/Do not be sad/And put your party gown on.)

ROSTAING, PIERRE. 1909–1995. A career soldier, served before the war with France's colonial troops in Indochina, Morocco, Algeria, and Tunisia. Sent to Finland as a technical advisor during the Russo-Finnish war of 1939–40. Took part in the May-June 1940 campaign as a member of the French army. Joined the Légion Tricolore in October 1942, the LVF in January 1943. Fought in Belorussia, Pomerania, and Berlin. Taken prisoner by the Russians in May 1945, handed over to the French. Tried and sentenced to life in prison. Freed in 1949. Moved to Toulon and became a mason. The only author in my corpus who confesses that his involvement cost him his marriage: His wife left him after his departure for the USSR. Wed again in southern France after the war, one son. *Le Prix d'un serment* [the Price of an Oath, 1975]. The front cover signals that Rostaing was Hauptscharführer SS (First Sergeant) and "the most decorated French soldier in the German army."

RUSCO, PIERRE (PIERRE RUSKONÉ). 1922–2005. Raised in a family with far-right connections; his father was a member of Colonel de la Rocque's Croix de Feu, a movement that was banned in 1936, becoming the Parti Social Français. Enlisted in the LVF in January 1942. Fought in Belorussia, then transferred to the Charlemagne. Wounded in Pomerania, was evacuated to a military hospital in Ulm. After transiting through Lichtenstein and Switzerland, returned to France under a false identity as a forced laborer in May 1945. Lived for five years underground with the help of family and friends, then resumed normal activities and was professionally successful. Married, children. *Stoï!* [Stop (in Russian), 1988].

SAINT-LOUP (MARC AUGIER). 1908–1990. Studied law in Bordeaux, but soon turned to sports journalism. An avid climber, skier, and motorcyclist, was among the founders of the Auberges de la Jeunesse (a French version of the YMCA). A member of the Socialist Party in the 1930s, belonged in 1936 to Léo Lagrange's "Sports and Leisure" undersecretariat in the Front Populaire government. Turned to fascism in the late 1930s. At the beginning of the Occupation, contributed to Alphonse de Châteaubriant's collaborationist journal *La Gerbe* and founded Jeunes de l'Europe Nouvelle, a group promoting a "socialist and European revolution." Joined the LVF in July 1942. Wounded and repatriated, started in June 1943 *Le Combattant européen*, a magazine designed for the LVF. Back in Germany in 1944, edited *Devenir*, the journal of the French Waffen-SS. In this capacity, lived at the SS training school in Hildesheim, then in Berlin. Left for Italy in April 1945, witnessing the troubles in Milan and the arrival of the Americans. Lived for several months underground, then left for Argentina in 1947. Became an instructor with Argentina's mountain troops. Returned to France in 1953 after an amnesty. Resumed his activities with extremist organizations, such as the Comité France-Rhodésie, which supported maintaining a "white" government in Rhodesia. Married, children. A prolific author, Saint-Loup wrote novels (e.g., *La Nuit commence au Cap Horn*, which would have won the prestigious Prix Goncourt in 1953 if the identity of "Saint-Loup" had not been revealed); biographies (e.g., *Renaud de Billancourt*); travel narratives (e.g., *Solstice en Laponie*); and "historical studies" about the Waffen-SS, studies that should rather be labelled "docu-novels" (e.g., *Les Hérétiques*). Saint-Loup's memoirs as a volunteer include *Les Partisans* (1986a [1943]) and *Götterdämmerung* (1986b). Saint-Loup, in *Götterdämmerung*, traces his pen-name to Loup, the bishop of the city of Troye who in the fifth century negotiated with the invading Huns, saving the area from war and destruction. Charged with collaborating with the enemy and expelled from his diocese, Loup was later reinstated and canonized.

SAJER, GUY (GUY MOUMINOUX). 1926–. Alsatian volunteer. Regarded as German after Alsace's de facto annexation into the Third Reich in 1940, was sent to youth camps in Strasbourg and Kehl. Volunteered for the army in 1942, becoming a member of the Wehrmacht. Took part in the operations of the Grossdeutschland Division in the Ukraine in 1943 (battles of Kharkov and Kursk), then in East Prussia in 1944–45. Evacuated by boat from Gotenhafen in March 1945, surrendered to the British in April near Kiel. Taken for an Alsatian who had been forcibly enrolled in the Wehrmacht, escaped the French justice system. After the war, had a successful career as an author of cartoons, comic strips, and graphic novels, contributing to such popular youth magazines as *Tintin*, *Spirou*, and *Pilote*, as well as to the satirical weekly *Charlie Hebdo*. Some of his graphic novels (e.g., *Kursk*, *Kamikazes*, *Kaleunt*) are about World War II as seen from the perspective of the Axis. Married. *Le Soldat oublié* (published in English as *The Forgotten Soldier*, 1967). The best-seller of the volunteers' memoirs, this book was awarded the literary Prix des Deux Magots, has been translated into several languages, and is still one the most talked-about testimonies of World War II. Under "Dimitri," his pen-name as a graphic artist, Sajer wrote another memoir that tells about his activities after the war: *La BD* [The Comic Strip, 1999]. "Mouminoux" is his father's name, "Sajer" is his mother's maiden name.

TERLIN, PAUL. 1921–2008. Belgian volunteer. A supporter of Degrelle's Rexist Party before the war, joined the Wallonie in August 1941. Took part in the Wallonie's major operations in the Ukraine, including the breakout from Cherkassy in early 1944. Lost his right arm and left hand during the struggles in Estonia in August 1944. In an American POW camp in Bavaria from 1945 to 1947, was treated by orthopedists in Munich, receiving prosthetic arm and hand. Arrested upon his return to Belgium and sentenced to ten years in jail. Freed in 1949. *La Neige et le sang* [Snow and Blood, 1972]. This memoir was also published under the name "Henri Moreau," and it is not clear whether "Terlin" or "Moreau" is the author's actual surname.

Appendix B

Maps

229

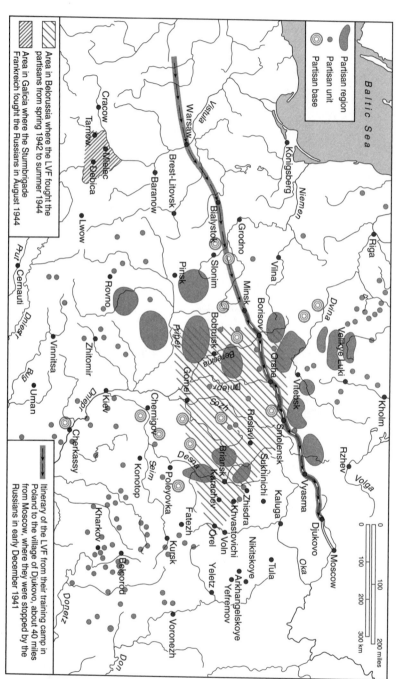

The French in Belorussia and in Galicia (1942–1944)

Baltic Sea

Partisan region
Partisan unit
Partisan base

Area in Belorussia where the LVF fought the
partisans from spring 1942 to summer 1944

Area in Galicia where the Sturmbrigade
Frankreich fought the Russians in August 1944

Itinerary of the LVF from their training camp in
Poland to the village of Djukovo, about 40 miles
from Moscow, where they were stopped by the
Russians in early December 1941

Cracow
Tarnow
Mielec
Debica
Lwow
Baranow
Brest-Litovsk
Warsaw
Vistula
Königsberg
Niemen
Riga
Kholm
Rzhev
Volga
Vilna
Dvina
Velikiye-Luki
Grodno
Bialystok
Slonim
Pinsk
Rovno
Cernauti
Prut
Dniester
Vinnitsa
Zhitomir
Bug
Uman
Dnieper
Kiev
Cherkassy
Chernigov
Seim
Konotop
Desna
Poleyovka
Fatezh
Kursk
Kharkov
Belgorod
Donetz
Don
Voronezh
Yeletz
Orel
Voln
Khvastovichi
Zhisdra
Briansk
Karachev
Sukhinichi
Roslavl
Sozh
Smolensk
Kaluga
Oka
Nikitskoye
Tula
Arkhangelskoye
Yefremov
Vyasma
Djukovo
Moscow
Gomel
Dnieper
Beresina
Pripet
Bobruisk
Minsk
Borisov
Orsha
Vitebsk

0   100   200   300 km
0   100   200 miles

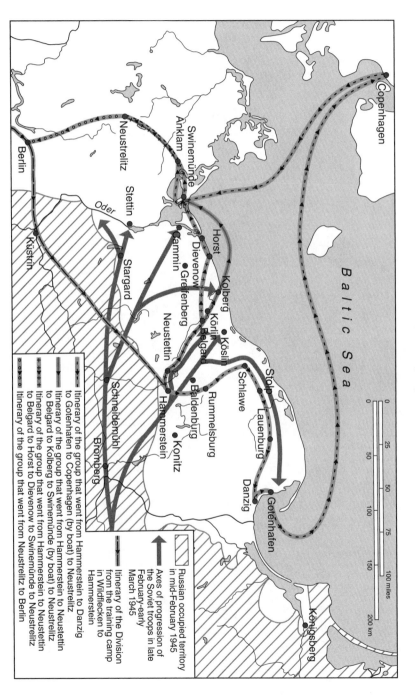

The French in Pomerania (February–April 1945)

Baltic Sea

Copenhagen

Neustrelitz
Anklam
Swinemünde
Berlin
Stettin
Oder
Küstrin
Stargard
Cammin
Greifenberg
Dievenow
Horst
Kolberg
Neustettin
Körlin
Belgard
Köslin
Schneidemühl
Hammerstein
Baldenburg
Rummelsburg
Bromberg
Konitz
Schlawe
Stolp
Lauenburg
Danzig
Gotenhafen
Königsberg

0   25   50   100   150   200 km
0   25   50   75   100 miles

Russian occupied territory
in mid-February 1945

Axes of progression of
the Soviet troops in late
February–early
March 1945

Itinerary of the Division
from the training camp
in Wildflecken to
Hammerstein

Itinerary of the group that went from Hammerstein to Danzig
to Gotenhafen to Copenhagen (by boat) to Neustrelitz
Itinerary of the group that went from Hammerstein to Neustettin
to Belgard to Kolberg to Swinemünde (by boat) to Neustrelitz
Itinerary of the group that went from Hammerstein to Neustettin
to Belgard to Horst to Dievenow to Swinemünde to Neustrelitz
Itinerary of the group that went from Neustrelitz to Berlin

The French in Berlin (April–May 1945)

Legend:
1 Belle-Alliance-Platz
2 Gestapo Headquarters
3 Air Ministry
4 Potsdamer Platz
5 Reich Chancellery
6 Kaiserhof subway station
7 Stadtmitte subway station
+++ Position on April 28 and 29, 1945
●●● Position on April 30, 1945
■■■ Position on May 1 and 2, 1945

Map labels:
FRANZÖSISCHE STR.
WILHELM STR.
VOSSSTR.
TAUBENSTR.
MOHRENSTR.
FRIEDRICHSTR.
LEIPZIGER STR.
STR.
ZIMMERSTR.
PRINZ-ALBRECHT-STR.
KOCHSTR.
ANHALTER STR.
SAARLAND STR.
PUTTKAMER STR.
SCHÖNEBERGER STR.
HEDEMANNSTR.
HALLESCHES UFER
TEMPELHOFERUFER
LANDWEHRKANAL
MÖCKERNSTR.
HALLESCHE STR.
KLEINBEERENSTR.
LANDWEHRKANAL

Bibliography

Memoirs and Other Personal Texts by the Volunteers

Anonymous. 1948. *Vae Victis: ou deux ans dans la L.V.F.* Paris: La Jeune Parque.

Auvray, Jacques. 1999. *Les derniers grognards.* Lyon: Irminsul.

Bassompierre, Jean. 1948. "Frères ennemis." In Jean Ambroise Colin, *Sacrifice de Bassompierre.* Paris: Amiot-Dumont. 115–236.

Bailly, André (André Bayle). 1984. "SS français à 17 ans." *Historama* 1, 90–5.

Bayle, André. 2008. *Des Jeux olympiques à la Waffen-SS.* Paris: Lore.

—— 1994. *Von Marseille bis Nowossibirsk: Französische Freiwillige im Kampf für Europa.* Trans. Claude Michel. Rosenheim: Deutsche Verlagsgesellschaft.

Cisay, Michel. 1955. *Prisonniers en U.R.S.S.* Paris: André Martel.

Costabrava, Fernand. 2007. *Le Soldat Baraka.* Avec la collaboration de Frédéric Loeuillet. Nice: Faccopies Office Document.

Degrelle, Léon. 1949. *La Campagne de Russie.* Paris: La Diffusion du Livre.

Dimitri (Guy Sajer). 2008. "Interview de Dimitri." http://www.livresdeguerre.net. Access 2/20/2008.

—— 2003. "Interview BD: Dimitri." Interview with Stéphane L. http://www.brusselsbdtour.com. Access 12/16/2009.

—— 1999. *La BD: Un merveilleux métier de chien.* Paris: Gergovie.

Doriot, Jacques. 1942. *Réalités.* Paris: Les Editions de France.

Dupont, Pierre Henri. 2002. *Au temps des choix héroïques.* Paris: L'Homme Libre.

Emmanuelli, Jean-Baptiste. 1974. *Et j'ai cassé mon fusil.* Paris: Laffont.

Fernet (Fenet), Henri. 1973. "A Berlin jusqu'au bout." *Historia* 32, 156–71.

Gaultier, Léon. 1991. *Siegfried et le Berrichon: Le parcours d'un "collabo."* Paris: Perrin.

Gilles, Gilbert. 1989. *Un ancien Waffen-SS français raconte...* Clearwater, FL: Gold Mail International Publishing. 2 vols.

Gruber, Fernand K. 1991. *Nous n'irons pas à Touapse: Du Donetz au Caucase, de Tcherkassy à l'Oder.* Brussels: Bibliothèque Royale Albert Ier.

Labat, Eric. 1969. *Les Places étaient chères*. Paris: La Table Ronde.

La Mazière, Christian de. 2003. *Le Rêveur blessé*. Paris: Fallois.

    1974. *The Captive Dreamer*. Trans. Francis Stuart. New York: Dutton.

    1972. *Le Rêveur casqué*. Paris: Laffont.

Larfoux, Charles. 2008. *Carnet de campagne d'un agent de liaison: Russie Hiver 1941–1942*. Paris: Lore.

Laurier, Mathieu (Pierre Vigouroux). 2002 (1953). *Il reste le drapeau noir et les copains*. Paris: L'Homme Libre.

Levast, Louis. 2008. *Le Soleil se couchait à l'est*. Paris: L'Homme Libre.

Leverrier, Alfred. 2007. *C'était pendant l'horreur d'une profonde nuit...* Paris: Arctic.

Lobsiger, François. 1985. *Un Suisse au service d'Hitler*. Paris: Albatros.

Malardier, Jean. 2007. *Combats pour l'honneur: Bataillon d'assaut Charlemagne, 24 avril-2 mai 1945*. Paris: L'Homme Libre.

Malbosse, Christian. 1971. *Le Soldat traqué*. Paris: La Pensée Moderne.

Marotel, Emil. 2007. *La longue marche*. Paris: Arctic.

Mit, Serge. 2001 (1950). *Carcasse à vendre*. Paris: L'Homme Libre.

Philippet, Henri. 1999. *Et mets ta robe de bal*. Erpe, Belgium: De Krijger. 2 vols.

Rostaing, Pierre. 1975. *Le Prix d'un serment*. Souvenirs recueillis par Pierre Demaret. Paris: La Table Ronde.

Rusco, Pierre. 1988. *Stoï: Quarante mois de combat sur le front russe*. Avec la collaboration de Philippe Randa. Paris: Avalon.

Saint-Loup (Marc Augier). 1991 (1941). *J'ai vu l'Allemagne*. Paris: Editions du Flambeau.

    1986a (1943). *Les Partisans: Choses vues en Russie*. Paris: Art et Histoire d'Europe.

    1986b. *Götterdämmerung: ou Rencontre avec la Bête (Témoignage, 1944–1945)*. Paris: Art et Histoire d'Europe.

    1951. *Monts Pacifique: De l'Anaconcagua au Cap Horn*. Paris: Arthaud.

Sajer, Guy. 1993. "L'auteur du *Soldat oublié* juge *Stalingrad*, le dernier film de Joseph Wilsmaier." Interview with André Guignicourt. *39/45 Magazine* 90, 4–8.

    1971. *The Forgotten Soldier*. Trans. Lily Emmet. New York: Harper and Row.

    1967. *Le Soldat oublié*. Paris: Laffont.

Terlin, Paul. 1973. "La percée fantastique." *Historia* 32, 50–5.

    1972. *La Neige et le sang*. Paris: La Penséee Moderne.

Other Works Consulted

Abellio, Raymond. 1980. *Sol Invictus: 1939–1947*. Paris: Ramsay.

Abetz, Otto. 1953. *Histoire d'une politique franco-allemande, 1930–1950: Mémoires d'un ambassadeur*. Paris: Stock.

Agamben, Giorgio. 2002. *Remnants of Auschwitz: The Witness and the Archive*. Trans. Daniel Heller-Roazen. New York: Zone Books.

Ambroise-Colin, Charles. 1971. *Un Procès de l'Epuration: Robert Brasillach*. Paris: Mame.

Amossy, Ruth. 2005. "L'écriture littéraire dans le témoignage de guerre: Les récits des infirmières de 14-18." Dornier et Dulong. 19–37.

Amouroux, Henri. 1978. *La grande histoire des Français sous l'Occupation.* Paris: Laffont. 10 vols.

Andreu, Pierre. 1977. *Le Rouge et le blanc: 1928–1944.* Paris: La Table Ronde.

Anonymous. 2006 (1954). *A Woman in Berlin: Eight Weeks in the Conquered City: A Diary.* Trans. Philip Boehm. New York: Metropolitan Books.

Arad, Yitzhak, Shmuel Krakowski, and Shmuel Spector, eds. 1989. *The Einsatzgruppen Reports.* New York: Holocaust Library.

Arletty (Arlette-Léonie Bathiat). 1971. *La Défense.* Paris: La Table Ronde.

Armstrong, John A., ed. 1964. *Soviet Partisans in World War II.* Madison, WI: University of Wisconsin Press.

Aron, Robert. 1967–75. *Histoire de l'épuration.* Paris: Fayard. 4 vols.

Arzalier, Francis. 1990. *Les Perdants: La dérive fasciste des mouvements autonomistes et indépendantistes au XXe siècle.* Paris: La Découverte.

Assmann, Aleida. 2010. "Four Formats of Memory: From Individual to Collective Forms of Constructing the Past." *Performing the Past.* Ed. Karin Tilmans, Jay Winter, and F.P.I.M. van Vree. New Haven, CT: Yale University Press.

—— 2006. *Der lange Schatten der Vergangenheit: Erinnerungskultur und Geschichtspolitik.* Munich: C.H. Beck.

Assouline, Pierre. 1990. *L'Epuration des intellectuels.* Paris: Complexe.

—— 1986. *Une Eminence grise: Jean Jardin, 1904–1976.* Paris: Balland.

Aubrac, Lucie. 1984. *Ils partiront dans l'ivresse.* Paris: Seuil.

Aubrac, Raymond. 1996. *Où la mémoire s'attarde.* Paris: Odile Jacob.

Augé, Marc. 1998. *Les Formes de l'oubli.* Paris: Payot and Rivages.

Aymé, Marcel. 1946. *Le Chemin des écoliers.* Paris: Gallimard.

Azéma, Jean-Pierre. 1979. *De Munich à la Libération.* Nouvelle histoire de la France contemporaine, vol. 14. Paris: Seuil.

—— 1975. *La Collaboration.* Paris: PUF.

Azéma, Jean-Pierre, and François Bédarida, eds. 2000. *La France des années noires.* Paris: Seuil. 2 vols.

—— 1992. *Vichy et les Français.* Paris: Fayard.

Azéma, Jean-Pierre, and Olivier Wieviorka, eds. 1997. *Vichy: 1940–1944.* Paris: Perrin.

Bacot, Jean-Pierre, ed. 1999. *Travail de mémoire: Une nécessité dans un siècle de violence.* Paris: Autrement.

Bakhtin, Mikhail. 1981. "Forms of Time and the Chronotope of the Novel." *The Dialogic Imagination.* Ed. Michael Holquist. Trans. Caryl Emerson and Michael Holquist. Austin, TX: University of Texas Press. 84–258.

Barnouw, Dagmar. 2005. *The War in the Empty Air: Victims, Perpetrators, and Postwar Germans.* Bloomington, IN: Indiana University Press.

Baroni, Raphaël. 2007. *La Tension narrative.* Paris: Seuil.

Barthes, Roland. 1980. *La Chambre claire: Note sur la photographie.* Paris: Cahiers du Cinéma, Gallimard, Seuil.

Bartov, Omer. 2000. *Mirrors of Destruction: War, Genocide, and Modern Identity.* New York: Oxford University Press.

—— 1991. *Hitler's Army: Soldiers, Nazis, and War in the Third Reich.* New York: Oxford University Press.

1986. *The Eastern Front, 1941–45: German Troops and the Barbarisation of Warfare.* New York: St. Martin's Press.

Baruch, Marc Olivier, ed. 2003. *Une Poignée de misérables: L'épuration dans la société française après la Seconde Guerre mondiale.* Paris: Fayard.

Baynac, Jacques. 1998. *Les Secrets de l'affaire Jean Moulin: Contexte, causes et circonstances.* Paris: Seuil.

Beevor, Anthony. 2002. *The Fall of Berlin.* New York: Viking.

Belser, Christophe. 2005. *La Collaboration en Loire-Inférieure 1940–1944.* vol. 2: *Intelligence avec l'ennemi.* La Crèche: Geste Editions.

Benjamin, Walter. 1969. "Theses on the Philosophy of History." *Illuminations.* Trans. Harry Zohn. New York: Schocken Books. 253–64.

Benoist-Méchin, Jacques. 1989. *A l'épreuve du temps.* Paris: Julliard. 2 vols.
    1985. *De la défaite au désastre.* Paris: Albin Michel. 2 vols.

Benoît, Pierre. 1956. *Fabrice.* Paris: Albin Michel.

Béraud, Henri. 1951. *Quinze jours avec la mort: La chasse au lampiste.* Paris: Plon.

Billson, Marcus. 1977. "The Memoir: New Perspectives on a Forgotten Genre." *Genre* 10, 259–82.

Bishop, Chris. 2005. *Hitler's Foreign Divisions: Foreign Volunteers in the Waffen-SS, 1940–1945.* Staplehurst, Kent: Spellmount.

Blondin, Antoine. 1982. "Le Demi-solde du demi-siècle: Les éprouvés de la LVF." *Ma vie entre des lignes.* Paris: La Table Ronde. 115–17.

Bock, Ernst Ludwig. 1993. *Übergabe oder Vernichtung: Eine Dokumentation zur Befreiung der Stadt Halle im April 1945.* Halle: Fliegenkopf.

Booth, Wayne C. 1961. *The Rhetoric of Fiction.* Chicago: University of Chicago Press.

Bourdrel, Philippe. 2007. *La grande débâcle de la collaboration.* Paris: Le Cherche Midi.
    2002. *L'Epuration sauvage: 1944–1945.* Paris: Perrin.

Boursier, Jean-Yves, ed. 1997. *Résistance et résistants.* Paris: L'Harmattan.

Bouthillier, Yves. 1950–51. *Le Drame de Vichy.* Paris: Plon. 2 vols.

Brasillach, Robert. 2002 (1943). "Sur le front de l'Est avec la Légion française." *Articles à "Je Suis Partout" et "Révolution Nationale."* Lyon: Irminsul. 258–63.

Brinon, Fernand de. 1949. *Mémoires.* Paris: LLC.

Brissaud, André. 1967. *La dernière année de Vichy.* Paris: Culture, Art, Loisir.

Brown, Louis. 1992. "The Forgotten Soldier." http://www.warfarehq.com. Access 11/5/2004.

Browning, Christopher R. 1998. *Ordinary Men: Reserve Police Battalion 101 and the Final Solution in Poland.* New York: Harper.

Brunet, Jean-Paul. 1986. *Jacques Doriot: Du communisme au fascisme.* Paris: Balland.

Bruneteau, Bernard. 2003. *"L'Europe nouvelle" de Hitler: Une illusion des intellectuels de la France de Vichy.* Paris: Editions du Rocher.

Bruyne, Eddy de, and Marc Rikmenspoel. 2004. *For Rex and for Belgium: Léon Degrelle and Walloon Political and Military Collaboration, 1940–45.* Solihull, West Midlands: Helion.

Burrin, Philippe. 2000. *Fascisme, nazisme, autoritarisme*. Paris: Seuil.

    1997. "Vichy." *Les Lieux de mémoire* II. Pierre Nora, ed. Paris: Gallimard. 2467–87.

    1995. *La France à l'heure allemande: 1940–1944*. Paris: Seuil.

Buss, Helen M. 2001. "Memoirs." *Encyclopedia of Life Writing: Autobiographical and Biographical Forms*. Ed. Margaretta Joly. London and Chicago, IL: Fitzroy Dearborn Publishers. Vol. 2. 595–6.

Campclaux, Christophe. 1991. "La Seconde Guerre Mondiale dans l'édition." Kantin and Manceron. 200–12.

Camus, Albert. 1947. *La Peste*. Paris: Gallimard.

Capdevila, Luc. 2002. "L'identité masculine et les fatigues de la guerre." *Vingtième Siècle* 75, 97–110.

    2001. "The Quest for Masculinity in a Defeated France, 1940–1945." *Contemporary European History* 10, 423–45.

Capdevila, Luc, François Rouquet, Fabrice Virgili, and Danièle Voldman. 2003. *Hommes et femmes dans la France en guerre*. Paris: Payot.

Carcopino, Jérôme. 1953. *Souvenirs de sept ans: 1937–1944*. Paris: Flammarion.

Carrard, Philippe. 1992. *Poetics of the New History: French Historical Discourse from Braudel to Chartier*. Baltimore: Johns Hopkins University Press.

    1986. "Récit historique et fonction testimoniale: Les archives de Lavisse's *La Grande Guerre*." *Poétique* 65, 47–61.

Champclaux, Christophe. 1991. "La Seconde Guerre Mondiale dans l'édition." Kantin and Manceron. 200–12.

Charbonneau, Henri. 1969. *Le Roman noir de la droite française: Les mémoires de Porthos*. Paris: Robert Desroches. 2 vols.

Châteaubriant, Alphonse de. 1937. *La Gerbe des forces: Nouvelle Allemagne*. Paris: Grasset.

Chauvy, Gérard. 1997. *Aubrac: Lyon 1943*. Paris: Albin Michel.

Chéroux, Clément, ed. 2001. *Mémoire des camps: Photographies des camps de concentration et d'extermination nazis, 1933–1999*. Paris: Marval.

Chaumont, Jean-Michel. 1997. *La Concurrence des victimes*. Paris: La Découverte.

Chombart de Lauwe, Marie-José. 1991. "Les dangers d'un contre-mythe." Kantin and Manceron, 50–62.

Clemons, Walter. 1971. "A Young Man's Marriage to War." Review of Sajer's *The Forgotten Soldier*. *New York Times*, January 18, 37.

Cochet, François. 1992. *Les Exclus de la victoire: Histoire des prisonniers de guerre, déportés et STO, 1945–1985*. Paris: S.P.M.

Cohn, Dorrit. 1999. *The Distinction of Fiction*. Baltimore, MD: Johns Hopkins University Press.

Cointet, Jean-Paul. 1996. *Histoire de Vichy*. Paris: Plon.

Cointet, Michèle and Jean-Paul Cointet. 2000. *Dictionnaire historique de la France sous l'Occupation*. Paris: Tallandier.

Colignon, Alain. 2001. "Degrelle." *Nouvelle biographie nationale* VI. Brussels: Académie Royale de Belgique. 111–23.

Combelle, Lucien. 1978. *Péché d'orgueil*. Paris: Olivier Orban.

Conan, Eric, and Daniel Lindenberg. 1992. "Que faire de Vichy?" *Esprit* 5, 5–15.

Conway, Martin. 1993. *Collaboration in Belgium: Léon Degrelle and the Rexist Movement, 1940–1944.* New Haven, CT: Yale University Press.

Cooper, Matthew. 1979. *The Nazi War against Soviet Partisans: 1941–1944.* New York: Stein and Day.

Coquio, Catherine, ed. 2004. *L'Histoire trouée: Négation et témoignage.* Nantes: L'Atalante.

ed. 1999. *Parler des camps, penser les génocides.* Paris: Albin Michel.

Corbin, Alain. 2005. "History and Memory." *The Columbia History of Twentieth-Century French Thought.* Ed. Lawrence Kritzman. New York: Columbia University Press. 55–60.

Cordier, Daniel. 1995. "Histoire et mémoire." Guillou and Laborie. 299–311.

Cotillon, Jérôme. 2003. *Ce qu'il reste de Vichy.* Paris: Armand Colin.

Cotta, Michelle. 1964. *La Collaboration.* Paris: Armand Colin.

Couser, Thomas. 2004. *Vulnerable Subjects: Ethics and Life Writing.* Ithaca, NY: Cornell University Press.

Cousteau, Pierre-Antoine. 1957. *Les Lois de l'hospitalité.* Paris: La Diffusion du Livre.

Cru, Jean-Norton. 1929. *Témoins: Essai d'analyse et de critique des souvenirs de combattants édités en français de 1915 à 1928.* Paris: Les Etincelles.

1967 (1930). *Du témoignage.* Paris: Pauvert.

Dac, Pierre. 1972. *Un Français libre à Londre.* Paris: France-Empire.

Dallin, Alexander. 1981. *German Rule in Russia, 1941–1944: A Study in Occupation Policies.* Boulder, CO: Westview.

Dard, Olivier, ed. 2005. *Les Archives Keystone sur la LVF.* Paris: Grancher.

Davey Owen Anthony. 1971. "The Origins of the Légion des volontaires français contre le bolchevisme." *Journal of Contemporary History* 6, 29–45.

Dawidowicz, Lucy S. 1975. *The War Against the Jews.* New York: Bantam.

Deforges, Régine. 1985. *Le Diable en rit encore.* Paris: Fayard.

Delarue, Jacques. 1968. *Trafics et crimes sous l'Occupation.* Paris: Fayard.

Delbo, Charlotte. 1971. *Auschwitz et après.* Paris: Minuit. 3 vols.

Delatour, François. 1973. "SS et Français: Pourquoi?" *Historia* 32, 114–21.

Deloncle, Luc. 2004. *Trois jeunesses provençales dans la guerre.* Paris: Dualpha.

Delperrie de Bayac, Jacques. 1969. *Histoire de la Milice: 1918–1945.* Paris: Fayard.

Dereymez, Jean-William, ed. 2001. *Etre jeune en France: 1939–1945.* Paris: L'Harmattan.

Desforges, Régine. 1993. *Le Diable en rit encore.* Paris: Fayard.

Diner, Hasia. 2009. *We Remember with Reverence and Love: American Jews and the Myth of Silence after the Holocaust, 1945–1962.* New York: New York University Press.

Dobry, Michel, ed. 2003. *Le Mythe de l'allergie française au fascisme.* Paris: Albin Michel.

Dongen, Luc van. 2008. *Un Purgatoire très discret: La transition "helvétique" d'anciens nazis, fascistes et collaborateurs après 1945.* Paris: Perrin/ SHSR.

Dornier, Carole. 2003. "Le récit de témoin: La littérature du factuel." *L'Analyse du discours dans les études littéraires.* Ed. Ruth Amossy and Dominique Maingueneau. Toulouse: Presses Universitaires du Mirail. 405–16.

Dornier, Carole, and Renaud Dulong, eds. 2005. *Esthétique du témoignage.* Caen: Editions de la Maison des Sciences de l'Homme.

Douzou, Laurent. 2005. *La Résistance française: Une histoire périlleuse.* Paris: Seuil.

Dreyfus, Georges. 1990. *Histoire de Vichy.* Paris: Perrin.

Dulong, Renaud. 1998. *Le Témoin oculaire: Les conditions sociales de l'attestation personnelle.* Paris: Editions de l'Ecole des Hautes Etudes en Sciences Sociales.

Dulong, Renaud, ed. 2001. *L'Aveu: Histoire, sociologie, philosophie.* Paris: Presses Universitaires de France.

Durand, Yves. 1994. *Les Prisonniers de guerre dans les stalags, les oflags et les kommandos, 1939–1945.* Paris: Hachette.

1990. *Le nouvel ordre européen nazi: 1938–1945.* Brussels: Complexe.

1987. *La Vie quotidienne des prisonniers de guerre dans les stalags, les oflags et les kommandos, 1939–1945.* Paris: Hachette.

Duras, Marguerite. 1985. *La Douleur.* Paris: P.O.L.

Duroselle, Jean-Baptiste. 1982. *L'Abîme: 1939–1945.* Paris: Imprimerie Nationale.

Dutourd, Jean. 1952. *Au Bon Beurre ou dix ans de la vie d'un crémier.* Paris: Gallimard.

Eisenhower, Dwight. 1948. *Crusade in Europe.* Garden City, NJ: Double Day.

Estes, Kenneth William. 2003. *A European Anabasis: Western European Volunteers in the German Army and SS, 1940–1945.* New York: Columbia University Press. Electronic book. Access 1/24/2010.

Finell, Karin. 2006. *Good-Bye to the Mermaids: A Childhood Lost in Hitler's Berlin.* Columbia: University of Missouri Press.

Fishman, Sarah, ed. 2000. *France at War: Vichy and the Historians.* New York: Berg.

Forbes, Robert. 2000. *Pour l'Europe: The French Volunteers of the Waffen-SS.* Trowbridge, England: Redwood Books.

Förster, Jürgen. 1998a. "Operation Barbarossa as a War of Conquest and Annihilation." Militärgeschichtliches Forschungsamt IV. 481–521.

1998b. "Volunteers for the 'European Crusade against Bolshevism'." Militärgeschichtliches Forschungsamt IV. 1049–70.

Frank, Robert. 2000. "La mémoire empoisonnée." Azéma and Bédarida II. 541–76.

Friedlander, Saul, ed. 1992. *Probing the Limits of Representation: Nazism and the "Final Solution."* Cambridge, MA: Harvard University Press.

Friedrich, Jörg. 2003. *Brandstätten: Der Anblick des Bombenkriegs.* Berlin: Propyläen.

2002. *Der Brand: Deutschland im Bombenkrieg, 1940–1945.* Berlin: Propyläen.

Fritz, Stephen G. 1995. *Frontsoldaten: The German Soldier in World War II.* Lexington, KY: University of Kentucky Press.

Funkelstein, Amos. "History, Counterhistory, and Narrative." Friedlander. 66–81.

Furet, François. 1995. *Le Passé d'une illusion: Essai sur l'idée communiste au XXe siècle.* Paris: Laffont/Calmann-Lévy.

Fussell, Paul. 2003. *The Boys' Crusade: The American Infantry in Northwestern Europe, 1944–1945.* New York: The Modern Library.

1975. *The Great War and Modern Memory*. New York: Oxford University Press.

Galtier-Boissière, Jean. 1994. *Mémoires d'un Parisien*. Paris: Quai Voltaire.

Garçon, Maurice, ed. 2007. *Le Procès du Maréchal Pétain: Compte-rendu sténographique*. Paris: de Vecchi.

Garde, Paul. 1999. "Le témoin des traces de la guerre: A propos du conflit yougoslave." Bacot. 67–71.

Garrett, Stephen A. 1996. *Ethics and Airpower in World War II: The British Bombing of German Cities*. New York: St. Martin's Press.

Genette, Gérard. 1991. *Fiction et diction*. Paris: Seuil.

1987. *Seuils*. Paris: Seuil.

1983. *Nouveau discours du récit*. Paris: Seuil.

1972. *Figures III*. Paris: Seuil.

Geyer, Michael. 2003. "Katastrophischer Nationalismus." *Tagesspiegel*, September 4, B6.

Gilbert, Martin. 1988. *Atlas of the Holocaust*. New York: Pergamon.

Gildea, Robert. 2002. *Marianne in Chains: Everyday Life in the French Heartland Under the German Occupation*. New York: Henry Holt.

1996. *France since 1945*. New York: Oxford University Press.

Giolitto, Pierre. 1999. *Volontaires français sous l'uniforme allemand*. Paris: Perrin.

1997. *Histoire de la Milice*. Paris: Perrin.

Giquel, Bernard. 1974. "Illusions retrouvées." Review of La Mazière's *The Captive Dreamer*. *Harper's* 248 (1489), 93–4.

Glantz, David M., and Jonathan M. House. 1995. *When Titans Clashed: How the Red Army Stopped Hitler*. Lawrence: University Press of Kansas.

Golsan, Richard J., ed. 1996. *Memory, the Holocaust, and French Justice: The Bousquet and Touvier Affairs*. Hanover: University Press of New England.

Gordon, Bertram M. 1980. *Collaborationism in France during the Second World War*. Ithaca, NY: Cornell University Press.

Gray, Glenn J. 1971. "A Survivor Born to Die." Review of Sajer's *The Forgotten Soldier*. *The New York Times Book Review*, February 7, 4–5.

Grayling, A.C. 2006. *Among the Dead Cities: The History and Moral Legacy of the World War II Bombing of Civilians in Germany and Japan*. New York: Walker.

Grenkevich, Leonid D. 1999. *The Soviet Partisan Movement, 1941–1944: A Critical Historiographical Analysis*. Ed. David M. Glantz. Portland, OR: Frank Cass.

Grossmann, Atina. 2007. *Jews, Germans, and Allies: Close Encounters in Occupied Germany*. Princeton, NJ: Princeton University Press.

1997. "A Question of Silence." *West Germany under Construction: Politics, Society, and Culture in the Adenauer Area*. Ed. Robert G. Moeller. Ann Arbor, MI: University of Michigan Press. 33–52.

Guderian, Heinz. 1952. *Panzer Leader*. Trans. Constantine Fitzgibbon. New York: Dutton.

Guillou, Jean-Marie, and Pierre Laborie, eds. 1995. *Mémoire et histoire: La Résistance*. Toulouse: Privat.

Guitry, Sacha. 1947. *Quatre ans d'occupations [sic]*. Paris: L'Elan.

Hamburger Institute for Social Research, ed. 1999. *The German Army and Genocide: Crimes against War Prisoners, Jews, and Other Civilians, 1939–1944.* Trans. Scott Abbott with editorial oversight by Paula Bradish. New York: The New Press.

Harbulot, Jean-Pierre. 2003. *Le Service du travail obligatoire: La région de Nancy face aux exigences allemandes.* Nancy: Presses universitaires de Nancy.

Hausser, Paul. 1966. *Soldaten wie andere auch: Der Weg der Waffen-SS.* Osnabrück: Muning Verlag.

1953. *Waffen-SS im Einsatz.* Göttingen: Plesse Verlag K.W. Schütz.

Heesch, Johannes, and Ulrike Braun. 2006. *Orte Erinnern: Spuren des NS-Terrors in Berlin: Ein Wegweiser.* Berlin: Nicolai.

Hewitt, Nicholas. 1996. *Literature and the Right in Postwar France: The Story of the "Hussards."* New York: Berg.

Higgins, Ian, ed. 1987. *The Second World War in Literature.* Edinburgh: Scottish Academic Press.

Hilberg, Raul. 2001. *Sources for Holocaust Research: An Analysis.* Chicago, IL: Ivan R. Dee.

2003. *The Destruction of the European Jews.* 3 vols. New Haven, CT: Yale University Press.

Hill, Christopher. 2009. *The Great Patriotic War of the Soviet Union, 1941–45: A Documentary Reader.* New York: Routledge.

Hirsch, Marianne, and Irene Kacandes, eds. 2004. *Teaching the Representation of the Holocaust.* New York: MLA.

Hirschfeld, Gerhard, and Patrick Marsh, eds. 1989. *Collaboration in France: Politics and Culture during the Nazi Occupation, 1940–1944.* New York: Berg.

Historia 32. 1973. Special issue: "L'Internationale SS."

Hoffmann, Joachim. 1998. "The Conduct of the War through Soviet Eyes." Militärgechichtliches Forschungsamt IV. 832–940.

Hogan, David J. 2001. *The Holocaust Chronicle: A History in Words and Pictures.* Lincolnwood, IL: Publications International.

Hux, Samuel. 1975. "*The Captive Dreamer* by Christian de La Mazière." *Worldview* 18(10), 52–4.

Isorni, Jacques. 1946. *Le Procès de Robert Brasillach: 19 janvier 1945.* Paris: Flammarion.

Jäckel, Eberhard. 1968. *La France dans l'Europe de Hitler.* Trans. Denise Meunier. Paris: Fayard.

Jackson, Julian. 2001. *France: The Dark Years.* New York: Oxford University Press.

Jaffré, Yves-Frédéric. 1995. *Il y a cinquante ans, Pierre Laval: Le procès qui n'a pas eu lieu.* Paris: Albin Michel.

Jeanclos, Yves, ed. 2003. *La France et les soldats d'infortune au XXe siècle.* Paris: Economica.

Jeannelle, Jean-Louis. 2008. *Ecrire ses mémoires au XXe siècle: Déclin et renouveau.* Paris: Gallimard.

Joseph, Gilbert. 2002. *Fernand de Brinon, l'aristocrate de la collaboration.* Paris: Albin Michel.

Kahan, Claudine. 1999. "La honte du témoin." Coquio. 493–513.

Kantin, Georges, and Gilles Manceron, eds. 1991. *Les Echos de la mémoire: Tabous et enseignements de la Seconde Guerre Mondiale.* Paris: Le Monde-Editions.

Kaplan, Alice. 2000. *The Collaborator: The Trial and Execution of Robert Brasillach.* Chicago, IL: University of Chicago Press.

Kaspi, André. 1997. *Les Juifs sous l'Occupation.* Paris: Seuil.

Kennedy, Edward L. 1997. "*The Forgotten Soldier*: Authentic Fiction by a Real Guy." *Military Review* 77, 2–3.

1992. "*The Forgotten Soldier*: Fiction or Fact?" *Army History* 22, 23–5.

Kettenacker, Lothar, ed. 2003. *Ein Volk von Opfern? Die neue Debatte um den Bombenkrieg, 1940–1945.* Berlin: Rowohlt.

Klüger, Ruth. 2001. *Still Alive: A Holocaust Girlhood Remembered.* New York: Feminist Press.

Kopleck, Maik. 2006. *Pastfinder Berlin, 1933–1945: Traces of German History.* Trans. Adelheid Korpp. Berlin: Ch. Links.

Krukenberg, Gustav. 1980. *Probleme um die Division Charlemagne.* Typewritten manuscript.

1964. *Kampftage in Berlin: 24.4–2.5. 1945.* Typewritten manuscript.

Kühne, Thomas. 2006. *Kameradschaft: Die Soldaten des nazionalsozialistischen Krieges und das 20. Jahrhundert.* Göttingen: Vandenhoeck und Ruprecht.

Kupferman, Fred. 1980. *Les Procès de Vichy: Pucheu, Pétain, Laval.* Bruxelles: Complexe.

LaCapra, Dominick. 2001. *Writing History, Writing Trauma.* Baltimore, MD: Johns Hopkins University Press.

1992. "Representing the Holocaust: Reflection on the Historians' Debate." Friedlander. 108–27.

Ladd, Brian. 1997. *The Ghosts of Berlin: Confronting German History in the Urban Landscape.* Chicago, IL: University of Chicago Press.

Lambert, Pierre, and Gérard Le Marec. 2002. *Les Français sous le casque allemand.* Paris: Grancher.

Landwehr, Richard. 1989. *Charlemagne's Legionnaires: French Volunteers of the Waffen-SS, 1943–1945.* Silver Spring, MD: Legion Books.

Larguier de Bancels, Jacques. 1906. "La psychologie judiciaire: Le témoignage." *L'Année Psychologique* 12, 157–232.

Larson, Thomas. 2007. *The Memoir and the Memoirist: Reading and Writing Personal Narrative.* Athens, OH: Ohio University Press.

Last Letters from Stalingrad. 1955. Trans. John E. Vetter. McLean, VA: Coronet Press.

Laurent, Jacques. 1976. *L'Histoire égoïste.* Paris: La Table Ronde.

1954. *Le petit canard.* Paris: Grasset.

Lauritzen, Paul. 2004. "Arguing with Life Stories: The Case of Rigoberta Menchù." *The Ethics of Life Writing.* Paul John Eakin, ed. Ithaca, NY: Cornell University Press. 19–39.

Lefèvre, Eric, and Jean Mabire. 2003. *Sur les pistes de la Russie centrale: Les Français de la LVF, 1943.* Paris: Grancher.

1995. *La Légion perdue: Face aux partisans, 1942.* Paris: Grancher.

1988. *Léon Degrelle et la Légion Wallonie: 1941–1945*. Paris: Art et Histoire d'Europe.

1985. *La LVF 1941: Par -40°devant Moscou*. Paris: Fayard.

Lejeune, Philippe. 1980. *Je est un autre: L'autobiographie de la littérature aux médias*. Paris: Seuil.

1975. *Le Pacte autobiographique*. Paris: Seuil.

Le Roy Ladurie, Emmanuel. 1983. "Le système Sigmaringen." Review of Henry Rousso's *Un Château en Allemagne. Parmi les historiens*. Paris: Gallimard, 1983. 237–40.

Le Tissier, Tony. *The Battle of Berlin: 1945*. New York: St. Martin's Press.

Levi, Primo. 1965. *The Reawakening: A Prisoner's Long March Through East Europe*. Trans. Stuart Woolf. Boston, MA: Little Brown.

Lewin, Christophe. 1987. *Le Retour des prisonniers de guerre français: Naissance et développement de la F.N.P.G., 1944–1952*. Paris: Publications de la Sorbonne, 1995.

Lindeperg, Sylvie. 1997. *Les Ecrans de l'ombre: La seconde guerre mondiale dans le cinéma français (1944–1969)*. Paris: CNRS Editions.

Littell, Jonathan. 2008. *Le Sec et l'humide: Une brève incursion en territoire fasciste*. Paris: Gallimard.

2006. *Les Bienveillantes*. Paris: Gallimard.

Littlejohn, David. 1985. *Foreign Legions of the Third Reich*. San Jose, CA: James Bender. 4 vols.

Loftus, Elizabeth F. 2000. *Eyewitness Testimony*. Cambridge, MA: Harvard University Press.

Loiseaux, Gérard. 1995. *La Littérature de la défaite et de la collaboration*. Paris: Fayard.

Lottman, Herbert. 1986. *L'Epuration: 1943–1953*. Trans. Béatrice Vierne. Paris: Fayard.

Mabire, Jean. 2007. *Mourir pour Dantzig: Les SS français en Poméranie*. Paris: Dualpha.

2000. *Les jeunes fauves du Führer: La Division SS Hitlerjugend*. Paris: Grancher.

1997. *Division Nordland: Dans l'enfer glacé de Leningrad*. Paris: Grancher.

1995. *Brigade d'assaut Wallonie: La percée de Tcherkassy*. Paris: Grancher.

1994. *La Division "Tête de mort": Sur le Front de l'Est, 1941–1945*. Paris: Grancher.

1987. *Légion Wallonie: Au Front de l'Est, 1941–1944*. Paris: Presses de la Cité.

1975. *Mourir à Berlin: Les SS français derniers défenseurs du bunker d'Adolf Hitler*. Paris: Fayard.

1974. *La Division Charlemagne: Les combats des SS français en Poméranie*. Paris: Fayard.

1973. *La Brigade Frankreich: La tragique aventure des SS français*. Paris: Fayard.

Maechler, Stefan. 2002. *The Wilkomirski Affair: A Study in Biographical Truth*. Trans. John E. Woods. New York: Schocken.

Manstein, Erich von. 1955. *Verlorene Siege*. Bonn: Athenäum.

Martin, Jean-Clément. 1984. "La Vendée, région mémoire: Bleus et blancs." *Les Lieux de mémoire* I. Ed. Pierre Nora. Paris: Gallimard. 595–617.

Martin du Gard, Maurice. 1948. *La Chronique de Vichy: 1940–1944*. Paris: Flammarion.

McAdams, Dan. 2006. "The Role of Narrative in Personality Psychology Today." *Narrative Inquiry* 16(1), 11–18.

Merglen, Albert. 1977. "Soldats français sous l'uniforme allemand, 1941–1945: LVF et 'Waffen-SS' français." *Revue d'Histoire de la Deuxième Guerre Mondiale* 108, 71–84.

Merle, Robert. 1972 (1952). *La Mort est mon métier*. Paris: Gallimard.

Merriam-Webster's Collegiate Dictionary. Tenth Edition. Springfield, MA: Merriam-Webster, 1996.

Militärgeschichtliches Forschungsamt (Research Institute for Military History), ed. 1998. *Germany and the Second World War*. 9 vols. Trans. editor Ewald Osers. New York: Oxford University Press.

Milza, Pierre. 1987. *Fascisme français: Passé et présent*. Paris: Flammarion.

Mohrt, Michel. 1988. *Vers l'Ouest: Souvenirs de jeunesse*. Paris: Olivier Orban.

1949. *Mon royaume pour un cheval*. Paris: Albin Michel.

Morris, Alan. 1992. *Collaboration and Resistance Reviewed: Writers and the Mode Rétro in Post-Gaullist France*. New York: Berg.

Mosse, George. 1986a. "Rushing to the Colors: On the History of Volunteers in War." *Religion, Ideology, and Nationalism in Europe and America: Essays Presented in Honor of Yeshova Arieli*. Jerusalem: The Historical Society of Israel. 173–84.

1986b. "Two World Wars and the Myth of the War Experience." *Journal of Contemporary History* 21(4), 491–513.

Muelle, Raymond. 1989. *Le Bataillon des réprouvés: Indochine, 1949–1950*. Paris: Presses de la Cité.

Müller, Rolf-Dieter. 2007. *An der Seite der Wehrmacht: Hitlers ausländische Helfer beim "Kreuzzug gegen den Bolschewismus," 1941–1945*. Berlin: Ch. Links.

Müller, Rolf-Dieter, and Gerd R. Überschär, eds. 2009. *Hitler's War in the East, 1941–1945: A Critical Assessment*. Trans. Bruce Little. Providence, RI: Berghahn Books.

eds. 1995. *Kriegsende 1945: Die Zerstörung des Deutschen Reichs*. Frankfurt am Main: Fischer.

Musial, Bogdan. 2008. *Kampfplatz Deutschland: Stalins Kriegspläne gegen den Westen*. Berlin: Propyläen.

Naimark, Norman M. 1995. *The Russians in Germany: A History of the Soviet Zone of Occupation*. Cambridge, MA: Harvard University Press.

Nash, Douglas E. 1998. "Sajer: A Real 'Guy'." *Military Review* 78, 3.

1997. "*The Forgotten Soldier*: Unmasked." *Army History* 27, 12–20.

Naumann, Klaus. 1998. *Der Krieg als Text: Das Jahr 1945 im kulturellen Gedächtnis der Presse*. Hamburg: Hamburger Edition.

Nelson, Harold W. 1990. "From My Bookshelf." *Military Review* 40, 90.

Neulen, Hans. 1992. *An deutscher Seite: Internationale Freiwillige von Wehrmacht und SS*. Munich: Universitas.

Nimier, Roger. 1948. *Les Epées*. Paris: Gallimard.

Nora, Pierre. 1997. "Présentation." *Les Lieux de mémoire* I. Ed. Pierre Nora. Paris: Gallimard. 15–22.

Novick, Peter. 1968. *The Resistance Versus Vichy: The Purge of Collaborators in Liberated France.* New York: Columbia University Press.

Nünning, Ansgar F. 2006. "Reconceptualizing Unreliable Narration: Synthesizing Cognitive and Rhetorical Approaches." Phelan and Rabinowitz. 89–106.

Ophuls, Marcel. 1975. *The Sorrow and the Pity.* Film script translated by Mireille Johnston. New York: Berkeley Window Book.

Ory, Pascal. 1991. "Histoire et mémoire de la collaboration." Kantin and Manceron. 45–9.

——. 1981. "Comme de l'an quarante: Dix ans de 'rétro-satanas'." *Le Débat* 16, 109–17.

——. 1980. *Les Collaborateurs.* Paris: Seuil.

——. 1977. *La France allemande, 1933–1945: Paroles du collaborationisme français.* Paris: Gallimard/Julliard.

Overy, Richard J. 1996. *The Penguin Historical Atlas of the Third Reich.* London: Penguin Books.

Paxton, Robert O. 2000. "La collaboration d'Etat." Trans. Denis and Marianne Ranson. Azéma and Bédarida I. 349–83.

——. 1972. *Vichy France: Old Guard and New Order, 1940–1944.* New York: Columbia University Press.

Péan, Pierre. 1998. *Vies et morts de Jean Moulin: Eléments d'une biographie.* Paris: Fayard.

Peikert, Paul. 1966. *Festung Breslau.* Berlin: Union Verlag.

Perec, Georges. 1995. *W ou le souvenir d'enfance.* Paris: Denoël.

Peyrot, Jean, 1991. "Aux prises avec la mémoire." Kantin and Manceron. 337–41.

Phelan, James, and Peter Rabinowitz, eds. 2006. *A Companion to Narrative Theory.* Malden, MA: Blackwell.

Picaper, Jean-Paul. 2005. *Le Crime d'aimer: Les enfants du STO.* Paris: Syrtes.

Picaper, Jean-Paul, and Ludwig Norz. 2004. *Les Enfants maudits.* Paris: Syrtes.

Pinçon, Michel, and Monique Pinçon-Charlot. 1997. *Voyage en grande bourgeoisie: Journal d'enquête.* Paris: Presses Universitaires de France.

Piverd, Jean. 1973. "Le sauve-qui-peut des maudits." *Historia* 32, 172–81.

Plaît, Antoine. 2001. "Les jeunes Français volontaires sous l'uniforme allemand, 1941–1945." Dereymez. 119–27.

Ponthier, François. 1973. *Plaidoyer pour personne...* Paris: Presses de la Cité.

Prince, Gerald. 2003. *A Dictionary of Narratology.* Lincoln: University of Nebraska Press.

Randa, Philippe. 1997. *Dictionnaire commenté de la collaboration française.* Paris: Jean Picollec.

——. 1989. *Le Rêve éclaté.* Paris: Presses de la Cité.

Read, Anthony, and David Fisher. 1992. *The Fall of Berlin.* New York: Norton.

Ready, J. Lee. 1987. *The Forgotten Axis: Germany's Partners and Foreign Volunteers in World War II.* Jefferson, NC: McFarland.

Rebatet, Lucien. 1976. *Mémoires d'un fasciste* II. Paris: Pauvert.

Reichel, Peter. 1993. *La Fascination du nazisme.* Trans. Olivier Mannoni. Paris: Odile Jacob.

Richie, Alexandra. 1998. *Faust's Metropolis: A History of Berlin*. New York: Carroll and Graf.

Ricoeur, Paul. 2000. *La Mémoire, l'histoire, l'oubli*. Paris: Seuil.

1985. *Temps et récit III: Le temps raconté*. Paris: Seuil.

Riedweg, Eugène. 1995. *Les "Malgré nous": Histoire de l'incorporation de force des Alsaciens-Mosellans dans l'armée allemande*. Mulhouse: Editions du Rhin.

Rigoulot, Pierre. 1990. *La Tragédie des "malgré nous": Tambov, le camp des Français*. Paris: Denoël.

Rinke, Andreas. 2002. *Le grand retour: Die französische Displaced-Person-Politik (1944–1951)*. Frankfurt am Main: Peter Lang.

Robert, Paul, ed. 1996. *Le Petit Robert: Dictionnaire illustré des noms propres*. Paris: Robert.

Robin, Régine. 2003. *La Mémoire saturée*. Paris: Stock.

Rocolle, Pierre. 1992. *Le Sac de Berlin: Avril-mai 1945*. Paris: Armand Colin.

Röhr, Werner, ed. 1994. *Okkupation und Kollaboration (1938–1945): Beiträge zu Konzepten und Praxis der Kollaboration in der deutschen Okkupationspolitik*. Berlin: Hüthig.

Roth, Andrew, and Michael Frajman. 1998. *The Goldapple Guide to Jewish Berlin*. Berlin: Goldapple Publishing.

Rougemont, Denis de. 1968. *Journal d'une époque: 1926–1946*. Paris: Gallimard.

Rousso, Henry. 2007. *Le Régime de Vichy*. Paris: Presses Universitaires de France.

1992a. *Vichy: L'événement, la mémoire, l'histoire*. Paris: Gallimard.

1992b. *Les Années noires: Vivre sous l'Occupation*. Paris: Gallimard.

1987a. *Le Syndrome de Vichy (1944–198 ...)*. Paris: Seuil.

1987b. *La Collaboration: Les noms/les thèmes/les lieux*. Paris: M.A. Editions.

1980. *Un Château en Allemagne: La France de Pétain en exil: Sigmaringen, 1944–1945*. Paris: Ramsay.

Rousso, Henry, and Eric Conan. 1994. *Vichy: Un passé qui ne passe pas*. Paris: Fayard.

Rürup, Reinhard. 2000. *Topography of Terror: Gestapo, SS, and Reichssicherheitshauptamt on the "Prinz-Albert-Terrain:" A Documentation*. Trans. Werner T. Angress. Berlin: Willmuth Arenhövel.

Saint-Loup (Marc Augier). 1994 (1944). *Sergent Karacho*. Châtillon-sur-Chalaronne: Le Flambeau.

Saint-Loup (Marc Augier). 1991 (1941). *J'ai vu l'Allemagne*. Châtillon-sur-Chalaronne: Le Flambeau.

1986a (1943). *Les Partisans: Choses vues en Russie, 1941–1942*. Paris: Art et histoire d'Europe.

1986b. *Götterdämmerung: Rencontre avec la Bête*. Paris: Art et histoire d'Europe.

1982. *La République du Mont-Blanc*. Paris: La Table Ronde.

1978. *La Division Azul: Croisade espagnole de Leningrad au Goulag*. Paris: Presses de la Cité.

1976. "Une Europe des 'patries charnelles'?" *Défense de l'Occident* 136, 70–5.

1975. *Les SS de la Toison d'Or: Flamands et Wallons au combat, 1941–1945.* Paris: Presses de la Cité.

1971. *Plus de pardon pour les Bretons.* Paris: Presses de la Cité.

1969. *Nouveaux cathares pour Montségur.* Paris: Presses de la Cité.

1967. *Les Nostalgiques.* Paris: Presses de la Cité.

1965. *Les Hérétiques.* Paris: Presses de la Cité.

1963. *Les Volontaires.* Paris: Presses de la Cité.

Saint-Paulien (Maurice-Yvan Sicard). 1964. *Histoire de la collaboration.* Paris: L'Esprit Nouveau.

1958a. *Les Lions morts: La bataille de Berlin.* Paris: Plon.

1958b. *Le Rameau vert.* Paris: Plon.

Santner, Eric. 1992. "History beyond the Pleasure Principle: Some Thoughts on the Representation of Trauma." Friedlander. 143–54.

Schachter, Daniel. 2001. *The Seven Sins of Memory: How the Mind Forgets and Remembers.* Boston, MA and New York: Houghton Mifflin.

Schönhuber, Franz. 1981. *Ich war dabei.* München: Langen Müller.

Schöttler, Peter. 2003. "Eine Art 'Generalplan West': Die Stuckart-Denkschrift vom 14. Juni 1940 und die Planungen für eine deutsch-französische Grenze im Zweiten Weltkrieg." *Sozial.Geschichte* 18(3), 83–131.

Scott, Joan W. 1991. "The Evidence of Experience." *Critical Inquiry* 17(4), 773–97.

Sebald, W.G. 2004. *On the Natural History of Destruction.* Trans. Anthea Bell. New York: The Modern Library.

Seidler, Franz W. 1995. *Die Kollaboration, 1939–1945: Zeitgeschichtliche Dokumentation in Biographien.* München: Herbig.

Semprun, Jorge. 1994. *L'Ecriture ou la vie.* Paris: Gallimard.

Sérant, Paul. 1964. *Les Vaincus de la libération: L'épuration en Europe occidentale à la fin de la Seconde Guerre Mondiale.* Paris: Laffont.

Seylaz, Jean-Luc. 1958. *"Les Liaisons dangereuses" et la création romanesque chez Laclos.* Geneva: Droz.

Shaw, Peter. 1974. "Apologue." Review of La Mazière's *The Captive Dreamer. Commentary* 58(5), 84–8.

Shields, James G. 2007. "Charlemagne's Crusaders: French Collaboration in Arms 1941–1945." *French Cultural Studies* 18, 83–105.

Slaughterhouse: The Encyclopedia of the Eastern Front. 2002. Garden City, NY: The Military Book Club.

Slepyan, Kenneth. 2006. *Stalin's Guerrillas: Soviet Partisans in World War II.* Lawrence: University Press of Kansas.

Smelser, Ronald, and Edward J. Davies II. 2008. *The Myth of the Eastern Front: The Nazi-Soviet War in American Popular Culture.* New York: Cambridge University Press.

Smith, Leonard B. 2007. *The Embattled Self: French Soldiers' Testimony of the Great War.* Ithaca, NY: Cornell University Press.

Smith, Sidonie, and Julia Watson. 2006. "The Trouble with Autobiography: Cautionary Notes for Narrative Theorists." *A Companion to Narrative*

Theory. James Phelan and Peter Rabinowitz, eds. Malden, MA: Blackwell. 356–71.

2001. *Reading Autobiography: A Guide for Interpreting Life Narratives*. Minneapolis, MN: University of Minnesota Press.

Speer, Albert. 1970. *Inside the Third Reich: Memoirs*. Trans. Richard and Clara Winston. New York: Macmillan.

Spigelmire, Michael F. 1990. "From my Bookshelf." *Military Review* 40, 89–90.

Spivak, Gayatri Chakravorty. 1988. "Can the Subaltern Speak?" *Marxism and the Interpretation of Culture*. Cary Nelson and Lawrence Grossberg, eds. Urbana, IL: University of Illinois Press. 271–313.

Stark, Jared. "Broken Records: Holocaust Diaries, Memoirs, and Memorial Books." Hirsch and Kacandes. 191–204.

Stein, George H. 1966. *Waffen-SS: Hitler's Elite Guard at War*. Ithaca, NY: Cornell University Press.

Steiner, Felix. 1993 (1963). *Die Armee der Geächteten*. Rosenheim: Deutsche Verlagsgesellschaft.

1958. *Die Freiwilligen der Waffen-SS: Idee und Opfergang*. Göttingen: Plesse.

Stern, Anne-Lise. 2004. *Le Savoir déporté: Camps, histoire, psychanalyse*. Paris: Seuil.

Struk, Janina. 2004. *Photographing the Holocaust: Interpretations of the Evidence*. London: I.B. Tauris.

Suleiman, Susan. 2006. *Crises of Memory and the Second World War*. Cambridge, MA: Harvard University Press.

Theweleit, Klaus. 1987. *Male Fantasies: Women, Floods, Bodies, History*. Trans. Stephen Conway, with the collaboration of Erica Carter and Chris Turner. Cambridge: Polity. 2 vols.

Todorov, Tzvetan. 1995. *Les Abus de la mémoire*. Paris: Arléa.

Vaillant, Roger. 1946. *Drôle de jeu*. Paris: Corrêa.

Vallat, Xavier. 1952. *Le Nez de Cléopatre: Souvenirs d'un homme de droite*. Paris: Les Quatre Fils d'Aymon.

Veillon, Dominique. 1984. *La Collaboration*. Paris: Libraire Générale Française.

Venner, Dominique. 2000. *Histoire de la collaboration*. Paris: Pygmalion.

Verdès-Leroux, Jeannine. 1996. *Refus et violences: Politique et littérature à l'extrême droite des années trente aux retombées de la Libération*. Paris: Gallimard.

Veyne, Paul. 1983. *Les Grecs ont-ils cru à leurs mythes? Essai sur l'imagination constituante*. Paris: Seuil.

Vidal-Naquet, Pierre. 1987. *Les Assassins de la mémoire*. Paris: La Découverte.

Vinen, Richard. 2007. *The Unfree French: Life under the Occupation*. New York: Penguin.

Vitoux, Frédéric. 2000. *L'Ami de mon père*. Paris: Seuil.

Vittori, Jean-Pierre. 2007. *Eux, les STO*. Paris: Ramsay.

Wachtel, Nathan. 1971. *La Vision des vaincus: Les Indiens du Pérou devant la conquête espagnole, 1530–1570*. Paris: Gallimard.

Waintrater, Régine. 2005. "Peut-on parler d'une rhétorique du traumatisme?" Cornier and Dulong. 41–60.

2003. *Sortir du génocide: Témoigner pour réapprendre à vivre*. Paris: Payot.

Warhol, Robyn R. 2005. "Neonarration; or, How to Render the Unnarratable in Realist Fiction and Contemporary Film." Phelan and Rabinowitz. 220–31.

Wette, Wolfram, ed. 1992. *Der Krieg des kleinen Mannes: Eine Militärgeschichte von unten*. München: Piper.

White, Hayden. 1987. *The Content of Form: Narrative Discourse and Historical Representation*. Baltimore, MD: Johns Hopkins University Press.

Wieviorka, Annette. 1998. *L'Ere du témoin*. Paris: Plon.

1992. *Déportation et génocide: Entre la mémoire et l'oubli*. Paris: Plon.

Wilkomirski, Benjamin. 1996. *Fragments: Memories of Wartime Childhood*. Trans. Carol Brown Janeway. New York: Schocken.

Yagoda, Ben. 2009. *Memoir: A History*. New York: Riverhead Books.

Yahil, Leni. 1987. *The Holocaust: The Fate of the European Jewry, 1932–1945*. New York: Oxford University Press.

Zehfuss, Maja. 2007. *Wounds of Memory: The Politics of War in Germany*. New York: Cambridge University Press.

Zeitlin, Froma I. 2001. "The Vicarious Witness: Belated Memory and the Authorial Presence in Recent Holocaust Literature." *Shaping Losses: Cultural Memory and the Holocaust*. Ed. Julia Epstein and Lori Hope Lefkovitz. Urbana, IL: University of Illinois Press. 128–60.

Zelizer, Barbie. 1998. *Remembering to Forget: Holocaust Memory Through the Camera's Eye*. Chicago, IL: University of Chicago Press.

Index